Religion and
the Ku Klux Klan

# Religion and the Ku Klux Klan

*Biblical Appropriation in Their Literature and Songs*

Juan O. Sánchez

McFarland & Company, Inc., Publishers
*Jefferson, North Carolina*

LIBRARY OF CONGRESS CATALOGUING-IN-PUBLICATION DATA

Names: Sánchez, Juan O., 1953–
Title: Religion and the Ku Klux Klan : Biblical appropriation in their literature and songs / Juan O. Sánchez.
Description: Jefferson, North Carolina : McFarland & Company, Inc., 2016. | Includes bibliographical references and index.
Identifiers: LCCN 2016012035 | ISBN 9781476664859 (softcover : alkaline paper) ∞
Subjects: LCSH: Ku Klux Klan (1915– )—History. | Ku Klux Klan (1915– )—Language—History. | Rhetoric—Political aspects—United States—History. | Ideology—United States—Religious aspects—History. | Bible and politics—United States—History. | Bible—Criticism, interpretation, etc.—History. | Christianity and politics—United States—History. | Politics and literature—United States—History. | Songs—Political aspects—United States—History.
Classification: LCC HS2330.K63 S26 2016 | DDC 322.4/20973—dc23
LC record available at https://lccn.loc.gov/2016012035

BRITISH LIBRARY CATALOGUING DATA ARE AVAILABLE

**ISBN (print) 978-1-4766-6485-9**
**ISBN (ebook) 978-1-4766-2453-2**

© 2016 Juan O. Sánchez. All rights reserved

*No part of this book may be reproduced or transmitted in any form or by any means, electronic or mechanical, including photocopying or recording, or by any information storage and retrieval system, without permission in writing from the publisher.*

Front cover image of Ku Klux Klan members © 2016 epicurean/iStock

Printed in the United States of America

*McFarland & Company, Inc., Publishers*
  *Box 611, Jefferson, North Carolina 28640*
    *www.mcfarlandpub.com*

# Table of Contents

*Preface* — 1

*Introduction* — 3

## Section I. The Klan, 1920–1930

1. Words and Phrases — 13
2. The Ku Klux Klan and God — 33
3. The Ku Klux Klan and Christ — 51
4. The Ku Klux Klan and the Bible — 67
5. Poetry and Song — 80

## Section II. Beyond 1930

6. Klan Rhetoric — 107
7. God's Divine Providence — 127
8. Christ, Eternal Emperor of the World Wide Invisible Empire — 143
9. Refining the Interpretation of the Bible — 153

*Summary: Thoughts and Connections* — 165

*Appendix A: Doctrinal Statement of Beliefs* — 177

*Appendix B: The Seven Sacred Symbols of the Klan* — 183

*Chapter Notes* — 189

*Bibliography* — 199

*Index* — 203

# *Preface*

God, Christ, and the Bible form the basis of the Ku Klux Klan's dogmatic philosophies and provide the order religious justification of its beliefs and actions. Though recent works have begun to explore the Klan's use of religion, this work directly connects the Klan to religion though the organization's own words. It is unique in that it follows the Klan's religious rhetoric from the heyday of the 1920s to the present, a rhetoric that asserts God's intercession on its behalf.

I have studied the Klan for more than twenty years and what became apparent over time was the lack of analysis of the Klan's use of religion to provide itself validity for its existence. Many works looked upon the Klan's rhetoric and actions as religious intolerance and racism, yet few of the early writers understood how the Klan manipulated religion for its benefit—both for money and political power.

Other works have concentrated on specific periods or groups; this work covers nearly a century of Klan ideology and clearly demonstrates the Klan's use of religion to justify its philosophies—an aspect of Klan historiography as yet not fully researched. Religion, as it does for terrorist and other extremist organizations throughout the world, provides legitimacy to the Klan; religion is the basis for the order's beliefs and existence. Freedom of religion, a fundamental American freedom, and the liberty to interpret the Bible based on one's own views is the basis for the Klan's unwavering philosophies.

The longevity of the Klan can be understood based on its unyielding religious beliefs, beliefs that in fact are reflective of a historically older America. However, whereas America as a society has undergone, and is undergoing, tremendous social and cultural changes, the Klan has kept alive antiquated cultural history predicated on race and religion which maintained a society deeply tinged with a white supremacist ideology.

The Klan thus represents a link to America's cultural past that can be traced to its earliest settlers.

The Klan's vocalizations are a direct reflection of that past, but changes leading to greater equality and inclusion have produced a self-marginalization based on a highly refined and narrow religious interpretation. The social changes that have transformed American society have led the Klan to reject any change that, from its perspective, diminishes the status and position of white America. This work provides an insight into the Klan's tenacious beliefs and an understanding of the critical role and power that religion bestows upon its ardent, dogmatic believers. That these beliefs are not attuned to mainstream denominations is irrelevant; the beliefs provide legitimacy for the Klan's inflexible philosophies because they are *its* beliefs.

This book was begun in 1996; since then it has gone through various transformations and refinements. What must be made clear is that the arguments pursued in the book are based on the Klan's own words. The extensive citation of the organization's written materials will substantiate this.

# Introduction

From the pages of Evangelist C. P. Roney's pamphlet *Is the Ku Klux Klan Scriptural? A Biblical, Sane and Dignified Discussion of the Principles, Ideals and Policies of the Order,* comes the essence of what this work delves into: "The Knights of the Ku Klux Klan is a great patriot, fraternal and benevolent secret order. Its principles, ideals purposes and policies are founded on New Testament Christianity."[1] Roney further stated: "Among the emblematic implements used by the Knights of the Ku Klux Klan, the open Bible holds pre-eminence in rank and in importance. The principles and ideals and policies and practices of the order are founded upon the teachings of the Holy Book."[2] And, concerning the "Christian Faith of the Order," the statement from Hiram Wesley Evans, the Klan Imperial Wizard of the 1920s, should suffice: "The Knights of the Ku Klux Klan ... is cemented with the morale of Protestant Christianity, the organization holds tenaciously to the tenets of Christ."[3] Evans further asserted in the *Imperial Night-Hawk,* the Klan national publication, that the order was "formed, aided, supported, guided, and directed by Almighty God."[4]

Other supporters of the Klan reiterated the above statements by agreeing with or elaborating on such pronouncements. The *Imperial Night-Hawk,* in its October 3, 1923, issue, inserted a small statement in the form of a question which read: "The Klan is founded on the word of God; you're not ashamed of it, are you?"[5] And, Walter C. Wright, a Baptist minister and the Exalted Cyclops of Plainview, Texas, Klan No. 260, said of Christ: "Above all else, Jesus Christ was a Klansman." Wright, like other Klan leaders and supporters, pointed to Christ as the example that Klansmen were to follow. Through emulation of Christ's teachings and activities, Klansmen were to become better individuals for "the living Christ is the Klansman's criterion of character." Klansmen were to "follow His example of Klannishness because ... He was a *real Klansman.*"[6]

But just as the Klan and its supporters used the Bible, God, and Christ to acquire a stamp of approval, so too, were there opponents who decried this type of religious rhetoric by the Klan to obtain legitimacy. In the pamphlet *Confessions of an Imperial Klansman: Hot Tar and Feathers*, Lem A. Dever, a former member of Atlanta Klan 0 ("Self Suspended," as he described himself), pointed out the fallacy of the doctrine. In his arguments against the Klan, Dever stated,

> All blessings come by living in harmony with God's laws. I have warned the Klansmen a thousand times that the success of the Order could be achieved only by practicing the principles of the Sermon on the Mount; that the whole outfit would go to the devil, if God were not really its guide and criterion of character. We now have every evidence that God has repudiated the Klan outfit, because its practices are opposite to its alleged high principles.
> God and one are a majority; can win any cause; but what happens when God is defied? What happened to Satan, according to Milton? Something like this:
> "Him the Almighty hurled headlong, flaming, from the ethereal skies, with hideous ruin and combustion, down to bottomless perdition, there to dwell in penal fire and adamantine chains, who durst defy the Omnipotent arms!"
> Something like that is going to happen everywhere to the Klan. Only an idiot would attempt resistance. (Think on this phenomenon, noble Sir Knights, ye who are always so responsive to the *religious appeal*)[7] [italics mine].

Dever further declared the Klan through "its autocratic system will promote to full development all the varied and foul results of militant ignorance, unreasoning hate, medieval bigotry, and their commercial exploitation by hundreds of 'religious' and 'patriot' shysters." Continuing, he referred to the sales pitch wherein religion was utilized to obtain new adherents as "an irresistible lure to thousands of ignorant fanatical shysters, who engraft themselves upon a movement as lecturers and officials." He also attested to the fact that "many good preachers have been caught in the past, but they quit when they learn the truth."[8]

> The end results of the Klan's program, according to Dever, was the wasting of vast amounts of money throughout the country in promotion of a narrow, belligerent sectarianism and shallow evangelism, making trifles out of essentials, neglecting the fundamental principles which were alleged to motivate them, filling the organization with throngs of persons who were unfit, whose evil influence has been wide and disastrous. Their sole aim is to mobilize members, and their prayer is "God give us Ten."[9] [In reference to the ten dollars paid by initiates upon entering the order.]

Dever then stated the precise reason for the existence of the Klan and its program: "The Klan is a war-time product. It was born of psychopathic hysteria and religious delusion."[10]

Another former member and opponent of the Klan who also addressed the issue of religion in the Klan's ideology was William M.

Likins. In *Patriotism Capitalized or Religion Turned into Gold,* Likins described the Klan as "an organization claiming to be preaching the Gospel of Christ, for we are told 'Christ is the Klansman's criterion.'"[11] Likins asserted that Hiram Wesley Evans, the Klan Imperial Wizard, "has taken the blessed Gospel of the Savior of the world and made the Gospel a financial asset."[12] He reiterated Evans' guilt when he stated of Evans: "Through his exploitation of religion he has turned into gold every principle taught by the lowly Nazarene."[13] Likins' book is an indictment against Evans and the Klan for its exploitation of religion for financial gain, and although he missed the mark, insofar as perceiving that through this maneuver the Klan used religion to obtain legitimacy, he nevertheless pointed out, as did Dever, the Klan's pecuniary manipulation of religion. And like Dever, Likins identified not only World War I as the cause for the rise of the Klan, but he also included other issues which formed part of the Klan's overall philosophy. Cited by Likins were foreign immigration, anti–Catholicism, prohibition, and any other Klan "principles" which would arise "from time to time to suit the occasion and place." The Klan thus began "getting the tens, by capitalizing [on] every sacred principle the average American loves so dearly."[14]

As the above cited sources and the title of this work indicates, the theme pursued by the author is how the Klan used religion to provide itself legitimacy. In essence, the work is an examination of Klan written material that demonstrates religious rationalization to justify its existence. Some may find the connection of religion to the Klan distasteful; that it is a bastardization of a belief held by millions. However, in reality it is no different than what is done by present-day Islamic religious fundamentalist or other groups, both domestic and foreign, who use religion as a means to achieve an end. A religious interpretation would, it is hoped, render a broader understanding of Klan psychology and add to the existing Klan historiography; especially when such an interpretation explores the Klan's own religious ideologies.

The analysis is one that would be inclusive of a large segment of white American society whose views were similar. The key factor in differentiating groups such as the Klan from the general white population as a whole is that the Klan's philosophy is reflected in its rhetoric and practices, including violence. Not participating vocally or actively in racially or religiously motivated activity does not necessarily reflect the true thinking of narrow-minded Americans. For many white Americans, especially in the 1920s, the Klan was the mouthpiece through which their reasoning, hatreds, bigotry, and emotions were vented. Kelly J. Baker in *Gospel*

*According to the Klan: The KKK's Appeal to Protestant America, 1915–1930*, noted as much in her work. According to Baker, as opposed to the post–Civil War Klan, the Klan of the 1920s

> was the most integrated into American society. The membership was composed of white men and women dedicated to the nation, the supremacy of their race, and Protestantism. Most histories briefly note the religious lives of Klansmen and Klanswomen in order to focus on the racism, anti–Catholicism, anti–Semitism, and violence of the order. While it is clear that the 1920s Klan was racist, anti–Catholicism, anti–Semitic, the order's members were indicative of mainstream prejudice of the time.[15]

That the Klan existed, and continues to exist, is indicative of the fact that it still receives support, albeit not in the same quantitative fashion it did in the 1920s. So too, there has always existed a humanistic segment in American society that has maintained moral and conscientious views concerning non–Protestant, non-white minorities; views that eventually supported social, political, and economic equality.

But why delve into the religious foundations of the Klan's and America's religious psyche? Simply put, religion played (and still does) an extremely prominent role in the success of the Klan, as well as other marginal and not so marginal groups in American society, and extremist groups throughout the world. This can easily be determined by examining works on the Klan or other radical groups whether in the U.S. or elsewhere. The fact is that the religious foundations of Klan ideology have been explored only marginally. There have been works that have pointed out this rhetoric and have touched on this aspect of Klan philosophies, but few studies exist that have dissected the Klan's religious foundation. It is only recently that authors have begun to explore this facet of Klan ideology and have partially dissected the organization's use of religion to *authenticate* and *legitimize* its existence. Charles C. Alexander in *The Ku Klux Klan in the Southwest* did detect this characteristic of the Klan: "A fervent religiosity pervaded almost every facet of the Klan movement." He noted the comment by a Klansman who attended the 1924 Klan national convention who remarked on the "revival spirit" at the gathering. Alexander further indicated: "And this revival spirit was evident in practically everything Klansmen did. The crusading zeal most hooded Knights possessed largely accounts for their devotion to the Klan and their fierce loyalty in the face of corruption, ineptness, and cynicism on the part of many of their leaders."[16]

Kenneth T. Jackson, in *The Ku Klux Klan in the City, 1915–1930*, viewed the Klan's religious activity from a different perspective. According to Jackson, "Although there was no formal connection between the Invisible

Empire and any religious denomination, Fundamentalism was the central thread of the Klan program." In pursuit of its fundamentalist objectives, which coincided with that element in American society that decried the loosening of morals and social progress, Jackson further stated, "An almost natural corollary to the Klan's religious orientation was its effort to become a bulwark against 'modernism.'"[17] Of greater importance was Jackson's insight regarding the Klan's place in American society and how an analysis of the Klan is in effect an analysis of Americans themselves:

> Because it is more important here to understand than to condemn, the text does not ring with denunciations of intolerance. The task is to examine the fears, prejudices, and activities of rank and file members. In the final analysis, the Klan was not alien to society or un–American. If it were, the problem would have been much simpler. Rather the Klan was typically American. It prospered and grew to national power by capitalizing on forces already existent in American society: our readiness to ascribe all good or evil to those religions, races, or economic philosophies with which we agree or disagree, and our tendency to profess the highest ideals while actually exhibiting the basest prejudices. To examine the Ku Klux Klan is to examine ourselves.[18]

The work of Bushart, Craig and Barnes, *Soldiers of God: White Supremacists and Their Holy War for America,* notes the religious foundation of the modern Klan and other Christian Identity groups. Such groups operate on a religious belief in which their interpretations and convictions are correct based on *their* religious views. The Christian Identity argument by the Klan and others is also addressed by John Michael Paul in *"God, Race and Nation": The Ideology of the Modern Ku Klux Klan.* The Christian Identity of the Klan and other groups is also explored by Glenn Michael Zuber in *Onward Christian Soldiers! War, Religious Conflict, and the Rise of the Second Ku Klux Klan, 1921–1928.* The one author that directly addresses the use of religion by the Klan as a means to obtain legitimacy is Baker. In her work Baker seeks to strengthen the arguments of more contemporary authors who give greater credence to religion, with respect to the 1920s Klan and other organized groups that propound hate. As noted by Baker:

> The Klan in the American imagination is bound to crosses, robes, violence, and terror, and I am not seeking to rehabilitate that image. The image stands rightly so, but reliance upon this popular interpretation alone overshadows the complicated place of religion, specifically Protestantism, in the Klan's long history. Understanding the central role of religion helps scholars understand better the motivation and appeal of these movements beyond simplistic presentations of frustration and anger, which remain popular excuses for membership in such movements. Moreover, examining movements like the Klan also suggests the ways that religion can inform ideologies of intolerance, violence, and terror, as well as bolster the commitment of members by relying on a more ultimate cause for such insidious agendas.[19]

Although citing Klan printed material in support of their arguments, the exception being Baker, the authors tend to pursue associated tangential augments instead of focusing on actual Klan pronouncements regarding the basis of its beliefs and the religious legitimization of the order. Such legitimization is no different than that of Islamic extremists whose ideology leads them to self-annihilation or mass murder in the process of sustaining their holy war. It is a religious belief, and as such it provides the basis for validation and of a world view, irrespective of what that view may be. Baker again provides an excellent insight into the perspective on religion. She argues that some scholars view religion, as propounded by the Klan, as false religion. Baker's elucidation concerning this assumption and the need to view the Klan's religious beliefs in a more substantive manner follows:

> This desire to set up boundaries between true and false religion does nothing to further the scholarly enterprise. More important, this distinction marks the religion of the hate movement as somehow no religion, which proves problematic for several reasons. First, this allows for the lack of attention to Klansmen and Klanswomen's religious leanings. If they are not authentically religious, then their motivations are not impacted by religion at all. Second and more important, presenting the religion of the Klan as a false religion allows an assumption that religion is somehow not associated with movements and people who might be unsavory, disreputable or dangerous. Religion is at best ambiguous, which means it can be associated with movements we label "good" or "bad," but limiting the place of religion does not mean that religion, specifically Christianity, cannot be associated with the Klan or white supremacists movements more generally. A proper examination would explore how the religion of the Klan impacted its members, practices, and policies without engaging the so-called falsity of the order's religion. This association with false religion means that what Klansmen and Klanswomen wrote and said about their religious backgrounds becomes disingenuous and less credible than other people's writings and declarations.[20]

Zuber's work looks at how the Klan used religion, principally as a means to obtain its sociopolitical objectives by virtue of acceptance of the order by mainstream America. Additionally, as pointed out by more recent works on the Klan, Zuber noted the organization's diversity of social and political aims.

> With its comprehensive nationalist program to reshape religion, politics and education, the revived Klan—fundamentally different from the original men's vigilante group with a racist agenda active in the 1860s—was a religiously inspired nationalist movement. Because it built upon residual wartime euphoria, the political strategies of Prohibitionists, the fraternal bonds of Masonic life, and the religious imagination of evangelical Protestantism, the Klan was popular and instantly credible for many.[21]

Religious propaganda and interpretations have, throughout the ages, provided the strongest incentives for love, hate, and war. Everything becomes crystal clear when the explanation, of whatever the argument or objective may be, is predicated on religion. Religion provides the reason, the rationale, and the sanction for action. Thus, regardless of what is stated or perpetrated it is condoned and defended because religion and biblical interpretations allow it. Justification of actions taken on a religious basis by the Klan is noted by William Vincent Moore in *A Sheet and a Cross: A Symbolic Analysis of the Ku Klux Klan*. Moore noted the pronouncements of the 1920s Klan as being of a "Protestant Organization," a theme reaffirmed by the Klan of the 1950s. Moore also stated, "The Klan was a religious body as well in the eyes of its members." This religious foundation, according to Moore, "effectively divided the world into forces of good and evil and no doubt helped to contribute to the violence in which Klansmen participated. As members of a crusade to save the country and the white race, violence became justified and violence did occur."[22]

Historical examples of activity predicated on religion include the Crusades of the eleventh through thirteenth centuries; the numerous pogroms against Jews; the many religious wars in Europe after the start of the Protestant Reformation; the massacre of millions of Armenians by the Turks in World War I; the continuing religious differences of Northern Ireland; the holocaust of World War II; the "ethnic cleansing" which occurred in Bosnia in the early to mid–1990s; and the current radicalization of Islamic extremists. Indeed, religion has been used the world over as a means to justify whatever action is taken against perceived and actual enemies. This differentiation based on religion is noted by Zuber: "The Klan used religion to define those who were true and false Americans in the same way self-described 'patriotic' circles had defined themselves in opposition to immigrant Catholic culture in the 1920s."[23] However, unlike what Zuber contends, and what is stated by Baker, that Klan religion must be taken for what it is, Zuber sees the religion of the Klan as being different than that of mainstream America and other nationalistic groups: "The centrality of Protestantism in the Klan's version of American patriotism was in stark contrast to the dominant ecumenical nationalism exhibited during the war and the American Legions' nationalism with its sole emphases on respect for the flag, belief in God, and martial values."[24]

With respect to the Klan's perspective, how can one question the Bible if it is the basis for society; if it is, indeed, God's word? Klansmen compared themselves to Christ in their moralistic stand against crime, drinking, dancing, prostitution, and "lewd" movies, just to name a few of the myriad social causes in which they were involved. Religion and the Klan's interpretation of the Bible served as the foundation for the skewed, rationalized, religious reasoning of the organization. However, such interpretations must also be understood to be part of America's cultural history; the Klan simply vocalized what Americans felt and believed. A hard look at the Klan's religious rationalization helps to explain why the Klan said and did what it did and presents another interpretation as yet not fully explored.

If a definition regarding the Klan's zealous religious interpretation of itself and of its philosophies would be attempted, its nearest explanation would be that of an absolute belief system. It is an absolute belief system that allowed the Klan and its supporters to write and believe that it was indeed formed, founded, and directed by God, and that it was because of God's intercession that it would succeed. It is an absolute belief system that, to Klan members, justified their words and actions. Some may view it as an excessive comparison, but it is that same absolute belief system that convinces individuals to fly airplanes into buildings, as was the case on September 11, 2001. It was predicated on a belief, and that belief is predicated on religion.

The sources used for this work are taken from publications produced by the Klan and others who supported the organization, and received the sanction of the Invisible Empire. The argument presented herein is based on their own words as written in support of their dogmatic philosophies. Because this work uses Klan material to make its argument, the decision was made to use as much of their statements as possible, rather than to paraphrase what was stated. In effect, the thesis regarding a religious interpretation of the Klan is substantiated by its own words, not the words of the author.

The works of recent scholars are utilized as a means to bolster the thesis pursued in this work. These scholars have begun the process of dissecting the religious interpretations and beliefs of the Klan and other fringe elements in American society. What the Klan wrote cannot be underestimated and must be accepted as actual representation of its beliefs, whether or not they are actual beliefs, or whether religion is used simply as a means to justify racism, intolerance, and violence. As stated by Baker, "The religious nature of their methods and print material needs much more exploration. Klan print culture is often discarded as propaganda, rather than considered a resource for Klan beliefs, ideologies, and theologies."[25] Moore states this more directly: "The language of the movement was designed to make the position of the Klan more legitimate and to degrade those forces which they opposed. As such, it represented a rational method of responding to a perceived threat."[26] Further, noting the excessive emphasis of recent fundamentalists groups concerning perceived external and internal threats to their status, Moore reiterated that "language is an essential element of symbolic status politics and symbolic acts are forms of rhetoric; functioning to organize the perceptions, attitudes, and feelings of individuals."[27] And although such beliefs may reflect a fringe religious interpretation, it must be taken for what it is—a valid religious belief based on the group's constructs.

The chapters contained herein are arranged so as to strengthen the religious theme of the interpretation. Chapter 1 demonstrates how particular words and phrases were used by the Klan to solicit emotional responses through the imagery and concepts formulated by those words and phrases. Chapter 2 demonstrates how the Klan used God, through its interpretation, to give itself validity and thus rationalize its existence based on "divine" origin, guidance, and intervention. Chapter 3 delves into the Klan's attempt to portray itself as following the teaching of Christ. Here again examples will show that the Klan claimed validity through its emulation, according to its interpretation, of the Son of Man. By portraying itself as being in the service of Christ through their rhetoric and action, it sought acceptance as a religious organization on a reformist crusade. Chapter 4 includes and explains the multitude of biblical passages utilized by the Klan to show it was "doing right" by the Book. In some instances biblical passages are interpreted by the Klan and its supporters to show how the Bible "prophesied" the appearance of its order as it did the coming of Christ. Chapter 5 is similar in nature to Chapter 1 in that it dissects Klan poetry and songs to illustrate how religion played an integral part of the "spirituality" of the organization. It is also reflective of the deeply rooted religious emotions in American society. The material used from chapters 1 to 5 is centered on the apex of Klan activity during the 1920s. Recent scholarly material has also been used as a means of strengthening the thesis.

Because the Klan continued using religious rhetoric throughout the remainder of the twentieth century to give itself legitimacy, chapters 6 through 9 demonstrate the continued use of religion by the Klan beyond the 1920s. The summary chapter attempts to bring together the information and bring to a close the interpretation introduced herein. It also demonstrates how the Klan's usage of God and Christ was modified over time. This modification is much more evident with regards to greatly expanded biblical interpretations providing the Klan, from its perspective, greater legitimacy to its philosophies. The religious interpretation presented herein, it is hoped, will shed new light on a sad chapter in American history, a chapter that continues to this day and which, when discussing the Klan, is replete with hatred, prejudice, and bigotry; attitudes and perceptions which are shrouded in religion. When that chapter will end is unknown; however, what is definite is that the multiplicity of groups, ethnicities, and religions are on this earth to stay.

A final point should be emphasized. There is general agreement in American society of acceptance of the concept of freedom of religion. Everyone has the freedom to their own private interpretation of God and of the Bible (a consistent argument of the Klan). Such is what is being explored and stated in this work. However, when religious interpretations are utilized in such a manner so as to justify demagogic rhetoric, exclusion, bigotry, discrimination, and violence, such interpretations must be questioned whether in this nation or elsewhere in the world.

# Section I
# The Klan, 1920–1930

## 1
## *Words and Phrases*

In their attempt to gain adherents to their organization, the Klan resorted to usage of words and phrases that appealed to the emotions of men. Such speech and written form is not new. Throughout the ages men have used such expression to gain members in pursuit of whatever cause was being pursued. For the Klan there were a variety of causes as suggested in the introduction, and as will become evident throughout the work. Eloquent and grandiose prose were intended to inflate the pride and self-worth of those targeted. It is not difficult to understand how the Klan's writings caused men's heads to swell and to be swept up in the emotions of the time. But rather than continue with explanations, it is best to turn to the written material that the reader may come to understand the spirit of the rhetoric.

Patriotism is a concept that can easily stir and capture the imagination and emotions of men. The Klan used this concept to portray itself as the protector of America. They pledged to stand between the nation and "any agency, anywhere, which seeks to lay its hands upon our Holy American institutions."[1] And when initially inducted into the order, Klansmen were

> bound together as brothers in a common cause by that sacred, solemn and patriotic obligation to which we have voluntarily and gladly subscribed; arrayed in robes of white, like the redeemed host of heaven, emblematic of a pure life and a spotless character; in the light of this fiery cross, the symbol of heaven's richest gift and earth's greatest tragedy; under the fluttering folds of the Stars and Stripes, the symbol of Freedom and Justice, sworn to defend the right, uphold the law and oppose the wrong; we are a part of a Great Invisible Empire, like unto the Church of the Living God during the dark ages of Roman rule.[2]

As may be seen, Klansmen were pledged to protect not just American institutions, but "Holy" American institutions; institutions that had received the blessings of God and were thus beyond normal man-made agencies. How could a "good American" not become involved in the protection of such institutions? Upon initiation into the order, Klansmen were bound by a "sacred" and "solemn" patriotic duty. The duty, being sacred, must be spiritual and godly; and thus had been sanctified. Being solemn, it was grave yet dignified, divine, and hollowed. The types of attire worn were "robes of white" that were equated to the "redeemed host of heaven." They were thus presented as being "of a pure life" and of "spotless character." To complete the illustration that portrayed them to be in the service of the Almighty, they were analogous to the "Church of the Living God." Declaring it more directly and succinctly, the Exalted Cyclops of Monroe Klan No. 4 of Louisiana asserted: "*Patriotism* and *Christianity* are preeminently the moving principles of the Knights of the Ku Klux Klan. The *Flag*, the *Constitution* and the *Holy Bible* are the keystone of Klan Principles."[3]

The concepts illustrated above received greater credence when propounded by Hiram Wesley Evans, the Imperial Wizard of the Klan in the 1920s. At a meeting of various Kansas Klans in Wichita, Kansas, Evans applauded the Kansas organizations on their work for "the Holy cause of Americanism." He also stated he now had the assistance of "a consecrated set of officers" working under him. He went on to state the Kansas Klansmen were "unwavering" in their "allegiance to the holy cause of the Knights of the Ku Klux Klan, I bid you press onward and upward in God's cause, America's cause, and in the Klan's cause."[4] At another meeting, Evans defended the Klan's philosophies against newspapers that attacked the order. He asserted that "as long as our doctrine is a pure and holy one the newspapers won't be able to grasp what it is."[5]

Reinforcement of such ideals was seconded by the Klan's national and state leaders. At the State Fair of Texas in October 1923, Z. E. Marvin, Grand Dragon of the Klan in Texas, stated that in its benevolent undertakings the "great heart of the Klan is sound; that every principle in its structure is wholesome"; that it had "grown in spiritual stature; our moral fiber has been strengthened; we are better Klansmen—which is to say *better Americans*."[6] A month later the Grand Dragon of Oklahoma defined Klankraft (Klan activity in relation to its philosophies) as the "motive power embodying the divine and cardinal principles necessary for the resurrection of that real Americanism" which the founding fathers had when they "drafted the Declaration of Independence and the Constitution.... It is the spirit of pure patriotism ... the exemplification of the noble ideals of chivalry ... the sublime reverence for our Lord and Savior ... the maintenance of the supremacy of that race of men whose blood is not tainted with the colorful pigments of the universe." Klankraft was in essence "the art of inculcating into the heart and soul of man a reverence for Deity ... country ... homes, and each other through inspirational education."[7] The Klan national newspaper, *The Imperial Night-Hawk,* held similar views, but it included another characteristic: "Klankraft is practical Christianity with the milk of human kindness..."[8]

The subject of "human kindness," that is to say love of one another, was the central theme espoused by E. F. Stanton in *"Christ and Other Klansmen" or "Lives of Love": The Cream of the Bible Spread Upon Klanism.* "Love," according to Stanton, "is the theme of Klansmen." In their work on behalf of the white race Klansmen were laboring "day and night." Of importance was that God approved of their labors: "And God is blessing their glad toil. He smiles from Heaven above."[9] In effect, through Klankraft, which Stanton referred to as Klanism, Klansmen were to be involved in acts of kindness and spreading God's compassion and love. However, such compassion and love was usually restricted to whites in racial brotherhood, with minorities by and large excluded. Such exclusion and emphasis on self-love, that is love and pride in being white, was delved into by Paul in *"God, Race and Nation,"* wherein he notes the change in message by the modern day Klan and other extremist groups who profess not to hate others, but rather to espouse love for their white brethren. In effect it is a racial love that advocates for white Americans who see themselves marginalized through intrusion by the federal government and the changing face of American society.[10]

In order to disseminate Klankraft, the Oklahoma Grand Dragon stated there must be a selection of men that "have the true spirit of the Klan at heart, who are worshippers at the shrine and the motto of our order 'Non Silba Sed Anthar' [not for self but for others], ... [men] which will embrace the spiritual, educational, political, vocational and practical phrases of Klankraft." Stating the spiritual phase was the most important, he went on to assert this phase could be accomplished by demonstrating that, irrespective of Protestant creed, all "Klansmen are united in our religious belief" thereby "demonstrating the practical utility of the great doctrine of the fatherhood of God." Accordingly, to further assist with the circulation of Klankraft there should be a supreme effort to "interest all protestant ministers that qualify ... into our order ... by encouraging these ministers to deliver in the pulpit and in the klavern, sermons which deal with the great principles of our order ... by insisting that the Kludd (chaplain) of all Klans, shall at all times be an ordained minister of the gospel." He also stated members themselves "must of necessity affiliate with the church, if they are imbued with the true Klan spirit." In this manner the membership would "awaken interest, not only in the Church itself but in the Klan as well." Not only should the membership work on its own, but it "should work constantly with the ministers of Protestant Churches." They should also work, according to the Grand Dragon, "with but one purpose in view, the worship of our Lord and Savior, Jesus Christ." Also required was the need "to convince the alien world that we are in reality Knights of that great Invisible Empire, founded on the rock of Christianity."[11]

According to the *Klansman's Manual*, Klankraft was an integral part of Klan relationships; it was a fundamental "Kloranic word ... to practice clannishness toward follow Klansmen."[12] Added to the above mandate, the *Manual* also stated, "Spirituality is the ultimate aim of Klankraft."[13] The Klan, according to the manual, was "founded on sterling character ... based upon sacred sentiment ... devoted to the souls of men, and is governed by their consecrated intelligence."[14] The organization was dedicated to "high and holy ideals." Further, to be a member in the Klan, "one must be a believer in the tenets of the Christian Religion." And when initiated, the individual was required to give his pledge: "Before the sacred altar of the Klan, face to face with the Stars and Stripe, and beneath the holy light of the Fiery Cross."[15]

Referring to the fraternal activity of the organization, the Imperial Klonsel (attorney) stated: "we are consecrated to the noble practice of disseminating the gospel we call Klankraft, embracing as it does the reverential acknowledgment of the supremacy of Almighty God, the recognition of His goodness and providence through our Lord Jesus Christ."[16] In justifying the military aspects of the Klan, the Imperial Klonsel referred to the Klan as "a movement; in a sense, it is a Crusade."[17] Further comparisons to a religious crusade were made in the *Night-Hawk* when it stated: "Ours is the noblest lineage; ours is the most sacrificial teaching—therefore, ours must be the noblest and sacrificial lives. See us as we are—as we strive to make ourselves—heroic knights, even as the visored [sic] knights of old times who went about doing good."[18]

Further substantiation of the Klan's religious and patriotic ideals was dealt with in the *Night-Hawk*. Under the title "Christian Citizenship" the Klan's national newspaper commented on various issues. The articles were sub-titled "The Gospel According to the Klan." In the first article dealing with schools, the paper stated, "citizenship in a democracy like ours is essentially Christian." It therefore insisted "on the Bible being placed in the public schools."[19] In the subsequent issue under the same column, it addressed the issue of partisan politics and stated that enslavement to corrupt politicians was at an end. It further stated: "The civic Messiah, the Ku Klux Klan, falsely accused, misrepresented and lied about, is leading the nation into the clear, pure air of liberty."[20] In reference to its benevolent service, which it viewed as a sacrifice, the paper compared its activity to Christ and the founding fathers: "Klansmen believe in that kind of sacrifice which calls for a living body placed on the altar of Service, utilized by man and dedicated to God." And like Christ, Klansmen were "to minister, and not be ministered unto." According to this rationale, it was "the only worthy excuse for existence." The paper further described Klansmen as having been "sired by fearless pioneers, inheriting the aspirations of the undaunted, the ambitions of the idealists, the honor of the chivalrous, the reverence of the faithful," and ended by saying that "the Klansman possesses a position to be coveted by angels."[21]

When the women's Ku Klux Klan was recognized in 1923, women speakers and writers also emphasized the religious aspects of the organization. In its August 8, 1923, issue the *Night-Hawk* included an article that indicated contribution "By a Klanswoman." In reality the contributor was Robbie Gill, the Imperial Commander of the Women of the Ku Klux Klan, who proclaimed the combination of the men's and the women's Klan would be a powerful force due to its divine origin. Gill asserted the "two mighty organizations," had been "bound together by the strongest ties, in bonds not forged by the mind of man, but created by God to bring his people into closer union to Himself."[22]

Gill then interjected the divine origins of rhetoric concerning the United States, an argument very much a part of U.S. cultural history and maintained by the Klan throughout the twentieth and into the twenty-first century: "Who is it doubts that the Declaration of Independence and the Constitution of these United States were God inspired? Who is it doubts that God Himself will prosper and cherish a people who accept Christ as their example, the cross and the living fire as their symbols?" As did other Klan officials and supporters, Gill took the Klan's statement of longevity, "yesterday, today and forever," and assigned it God's sanction by interjecting His infinitude: "Human nature is not immutable; it is only the divine nature which is 'the same yesterday, today and forever.'"[23]

According to Gill, the two orders were forthright concerning their objectives; these were "the highest and holiest that ever actuated a vast body of people." Although remaining vague regarding the country's national enemies, which no doubt included every group from Communists to, Jews to, Catholics, to immigrants; the order's objectives included countering "the malign, secret and deadly influences which have worked consistently, steadily, to undermine the foundations of our government." These forces, asserted Gill, would be countered by the Klan who would meet and overcome them through "active, unified, secret, vital influences for good." And although during the present time it might be impossible to free the country from the "deadly clutches of un–American alien forces," the dream and objective would be kept alive by the Klan.[24]

The threat of "un–American aliens" was also used to stir emotions and gain adherents. Citing certain office holders as "unworthy and conscienceless," a Klan supporter declared, "the powers of darkness in high places have wrestled with the angel of the Lord and the forces of satan [sic] [have] been unleashed in the conflict." And just as American soldiers in World War I had fought to victory, so too, must the Klan fight until triumphant. The writer asserted that "every obstacle spawned in the nether world has been hurled before the marching feet of the shock troops of the Klan." However, the Klan was nearing victory because they had their "eyes ever fastened upon the spiritual purpose and meaning of the conflict." Stating "the armies of the Lord of Hosts are camped round about," the writer affirmed that with such allies "it shall be said of us as of the prophets of old: 'Who through faith, subdued kingdoms, wrought righteousness, obtained promises, stopped the mouth of the lion, squelched the violence of fire, escaped the edge of the sword, out of weakness were made strong, waxed valiant in fight and turned to flight the armies of the aliens.'"[25]

In defense of the order, the Exalted Cyclops of Louisiana's Monroe Klan No. 4, attacked Catholics and Jews and accused them of being in league with criminal elements that opposed the Klan. "Roman Catholics and Jews," he stated, "have sworn to never cease their nefarious propaganda until the Ku Klux Klan are put out of business." All their efforts, however, were to no avail because "the Klan is here, and here it will remain until the last son of a Protestant surrenders his manhood, and is content to see America Catholicized, mongrelized and circumcised."[26] Pointing to immigration coming from "Roman Catholic countries," the Klan official stated the organization's policy was to stop "the Romanizing and mongrelizing of the citizenship of the United States." He also asserted the "Roman Catholic church" and "employers of pauper labor" were "in favor of letting down the [immigration] bars and flooding this country with the very scum of the earth." Yet in the very next paragraph he stated that in order to correct the distorted image of the Klan "made common by a subsidized press," the organization should live "in our daily lives the principles as set forth in the Twelfth chapter of Romans."[27] In another anti-alien/anti-immigration article, the editor of the *Night-Hawk* expounded on the Klan's desire to restrict the franchise. Enveloping the argument with patriotic rhetoric, the editor stated: "In their movement to evangelize American citizenship" the Klan was "proceeding under the flaming Fiery Cross."[28]

The Fiery Cross was but one of the "Seven Symbols of the Klan." (Appendix B includes the Seven Symbols as included in the *Night-Hawk*.) The other six are the Bible, flag, sword, water, robe and the mask. In a lengthy article published in the *Night-Hawk* in December 1923, an "Exalted Cyclops of Texas" explained the meaning of these symbols. The Bible was seen as the foundation of Klan ideology. It was a "constant reminder of the tenets of the Christian religion, and is a Klansman's law of life." The cross represented Christ because of his death upon it and it reminded Klansman "that Christ is our criterion of Character, and His teachings our rule of life-blood-bought, holy, sanctified and sublime." The flag represented, through its colors, the beliefs and ideal of all Americans and the Klan vowed to "forever defend the principles of pure Americanism" it symbolized. The sword when unsheathed depicted the "symbol of law enforcement." To the Klan: "Its presence on our sacred altar signifies that we ... are solidly behind every law enforcement officer in the land."[29] It also signified the Klan's vow to defend flag and country. The water was a purifying agent for those being initiated. According to the Klan, "This God-given, powerful fluid, more precious and far more significant than all the sacred oils of the ancients, is a symbol of purity of life and the unity of purpose. With this divinely distilled fluid we have been dedicated and set apart, in body, in mind, in spirit and in life, to the sacred, sublime and holy principles of Klankraft."[30]

The robe was seen as a leveling and equalizing instrument; it did away with social, economic, or political distinctions. And more importantly: "The white robe is also a symbol of that robe of righteousness to be worn by the saints in the land Yet-to-Come. Klansmen wear this white robe to signify that they desire to put on *that white robe which is the righteousness of Christ.*" But not everyone that wore the "sacred folds of a Klansman's robe" was entitled to do so. For, according to the Klan, there were those who wore it to deceive others, "but *only* a Klansman possesses a Klansman's heart and a Klansman's soul." Wearing the robe, Klansmen sought to hide their imperfections that "through the grace of God and by following His Christ, be able to hide the scars and stains of sin with the righteousness of Christ when we stand before His Great Throne."[31] The mask added to that "symbol of unselfishness" which the robe completed by making everyone equal. It also aided Klansmen in keeping secret their identities thereby preventing criminals from knowing who they were and thus make them more effective in their "aid of the law." With their complete attire, how could it not be possible to "look upon a multitude of white robed Klansmen without thinking of the equality and unselfishness of that throng of white robed saints in the Glory Land?" It was hoped that when "God in Heaven" saw the legions of white robed individuals of the order, He would "find every Klansman worthy of the robe and mask that he wears." And when Klansmen lived according to how they preached, "the title of Klansman will be the *most honorable title among men*."[32] Summarizing the explanations it was stated: "Thus with our symbols we seek to emphasize and impress the sacred, sublime and holy principles of Klankraft. With God as our Father, Christ as our criterion, the Bible as our guide, the cross as our inspiration, and the flag as our protection, we mean to march on to triumphant victory for the principles of right in the Knights of the Ku Klux Klan."[33]

The explanations of the seven symbols changed as time progressed based on the passing of anti-mask laws and the needs of individual Klan organizations. The symbols were explained again in the *Kourier Magazine* in 1933, this time by a New Jersey Klansman. The explanations by the New Jersey Klansman included only six symbols, the Bible, the cross, the flag, the sword, water, and the robe.[34] The mask was not included since by this time anti-mask laws predominated throughout the country, put in place due to the Klan's negative notoriety and the mask serving to hide, not the supporters of law enforcement, but the perpetrators of intimidation and violence.

The Aryan Nations Knights of the Ku Klux Klan revised the explanations, and included fire as one of the principal symbols increasing the number to the original seven. In their explanations the organization interchangeably refers to God as "YAHWEH" and the U.S. flag becomes the Aryan Nations flag to which the order pledges its "undying devotion and our never ending loyalty." Additionally, the organization interjects a racialist explanation asserting, "We believe the Aryan Nations is the true and divine Holy Race of YaHWeH, the lost sheep of the House of Israel." Throughout its revised version of the seven symbols the organization emphasizes its racialist ideology stating it is following the dictates of God regarding separations of the races and asserting they are the chosen followers of God.[35]

The seven symbols have remained constant throughout the Klan's persistent life. Over time it has been the burning cross that has made the most impression, both negatively and positively. Negatively for those against whom it has been used as a symbol of terrorism; a symbol that incites fear, and positively for the Klan as a symbol of their beliefs and as a ceremonial symbol around which it rallies. Moore, in *A Sheet and a Cross*, noted the importance of the burning cross to the Klan and to those against whom it has been directed: "The best-known symbol of the Klan is the burning cross. To the alien world, the burning cross is a symbol of intimidation and indeed it has been put on the property of those individuals and groups which the Klan opposes."[36] The cross is the most important symbol for the Klan as it serves both as a symbol of unity for the organization and a symbol of defiance against its perceived enemies. Moore emphasizes the importance of the various religious symbols for the Klan for in group and out group identification, and the justification for violence: "In effect, the symbolism in the Klan movement provides an environment which is conducive to a holy crusade sanctioned by God and country in the eyes of Klansmen. This sense of mission contains elements of a fight between the forces of good (Klan) and the forces of evil (Klan enemies). In this setting violence is justified."[37]

As a new year's resolution, the *Night-Hawk* exhorted Klan members to work harder to improve American society. It stated that working in unison, the "Millions of Klansmen ... are destined to ... evangelize Protestantism." It further stated aliens were venting their "wrath" upon the order, "but naught can prevail against this organization founded upon Christianity and love of home and country."[38] And just as the early Church had its origins with Christ, so too, according to a writer in the *Imperial Night-Hawk*, did the Klan; just as the early church had been persecuted, so too, was the Klan being persecuted. Through examples that led to the comparison of the early church to the Klan, the writer pressed his argument and declared: "When the Primitive Church is studied from whatever viewpoint, it is seen to be a striking prototype of the Ku Klux Klan movement." The writer also argued that the early church was spiritual, "The same may also be said of those who compose the organization known as the Knights of the Ku Klux Klan." Further, because the spirit was invisible, it was eternal. It was through invisible faith that the Klan, as did Christ with the early church, was working to correct the ills of America. In ending, the writer once again compared the early church and Klan: "Thus we see the Movement coming to life, bearing striking similarity to that movement of the early day called the Primitive Church."[39]

According to a Klan supporter, the order's spirituality and activities made the organization an important element for all townships. The organization, as seen by Reverend Walter C. Wright, was "a vital necessity in every community." He propounded the positive aspects of the order to demonstrate its importance to each community: "The Klan, by its high ideals, noble sentiments and sacred principles, inculcates and cultivates a manly desire to be better, cleaner men, morally, mentally, physically and spiritually." He asserted the Klan was "a great character builder because of its high ideals, noble purposes and sacred sentiments." Demonstrating how the Klan would aid in law enforcement; ensure the "sanctity" of homes through "clean, chaste, moral" living; support education; influence men to attend church; the binding of all Protestants; banding "the white Caucasian race together against overwhelming hordes of colored races," and draw "together native-born Americans against that ever increasing horde of foreigners," Wright stated: "Every community needs this sublime influence of the Klan; therefore the Klan is a universal need."[40] By wrapping itself with Protestantism and enlisting Protestant ministers, the Klan gained legitimacy and adherents.[41] As affirmed by Baker in *Gospel According to the Klan*, "Protestantism ... served as the foundation of the movement, and the protection of its religious faith was a key component of the Klan's mission."[42] Furthermore, Protestantism also came to be understood to refer to white Americans and assisted in defining a white racial identity.[43]

In another article published in the *Night-Hawk*, Wright lectured on the relationship between the "Protestant Church" and "Citizenship." Wright assailed the Catholic Church and foreigners who were seen as "the trouble producers in our country" who "will never become Americanized." Because the Catholic Church and its followers were "directed by a foreign ruler," they could never become good citizens. It was the duty of the Klan then, "to emphasize the essentials of Christian living, defend the common faith, and Protestantism together, 'In the sacred unfailing bond' ... against well organized forces." In order to defeat the "common enemy" it was "the mission of the Klan ... to unite and combine all the forces for good, both religious and political." Paradoxically, the reverend stated: "The Klan is neither a Church nor a political party; yet it is both a religious and a political organization." As to the task the Klan had assigned itself, Wright stated: "It is indeed a holy and sublime mission."[44]

In obtaining further credence the Klan, as an organization, would compare itself to the early church. "What is today, was yesterday, tho' in a modified form or to a smaller degree." Such was stated by the *Night-Hawk* in its comparison of the Klan and the early Church. "History," according to the paper, "seems to be a repetition of human activities on an ascending scale." Jumping quickly into the comparison, it further stated: "The same is true of the present-day movement called the Ku Klux Klan, and that other movement, begun eighteen centuries ago under the leadership of the Nazarene." Continuing, the paper stated the Christian movement begun by Christ had brought "untold blessings to mankind." It stated both movements had similar beginnings, but as to the similarity of the outcome of both movements, this was still "hid in the future." The paper addressed the struggle between "Truth and Error; Light versus Darkness; Intelligence versus Ignorance; Righteousness versus Unrighteousness," and asserted, "The analogy between the primitive Church and the Klan is very evident." The paper presented the Klan as "a movement on the part of native, law-abiding citizens, to organize for the embitterment [sic] of the land." More importantly, the Klan "Commit no greater crime tha[n] to adopt the Bible as their guide, and the Christ as their Criterion." The Klan, according to the paper, sought only to "help, aid, and assi[s]t their Government in their capacity as citizens." Klan members "innocently advertised themselves as Americans one hundred percent." Yet the "misinformed press" printed lies and the order was charged with all types of savagery, and, "Just as in the case of the primitive Church," Klan leaders were "ridiculed, caricatured, imprisoned, or dragged into court." Just as early Christians had courage, spirit, conviction, and faith to persevere, so too, were these qualities "in the hearts of those who call themselves Klansmen." The similarities of the two organizations, according to the paper, must be taken into consideration. The eventual success of the early Church should be noted by those that were hostile to the Klan "lest their opposition come to naught as did that which was launched by those ancient opponents of ... the young Church."[45]

For the Klan, national holidays were a time when they could demonstrate their patriotic fervor. The Klan would, on such occasions, attempt to show just how fundamentally "American" they were. Different types of techniques were used to shroud themselves in patriotic imagery. Reporting on a fourth of July parade in Richmond, California, the *Night-Hawk* stated, "Several floats were entered by the Klan, the best of which was 'Uncle Sam,' called the 'Klansman Unmasked.'"[46] In what was billed as "National Dedication Services" which were held on Stone Mountain in Georgia, the same place where on Thanksgiving Day in 1915 the Klan had been resuscitated, there occurred "a most solemn and impressive occasion" on the same national holiday in 1924. According to the *Night-Hawk*, "Atop the bare Mountain, surrounded by space, one's soul feels liberated and one's aspirations soar to heavenly heights." After "kneeling in the light of a blazing Cross" during which a prayer was said, an address was given in which a Klan speaker said of Stone Mountain: "This place is a shrine for pure and true Americanism." The speaker also stated Stone Mountain was of "that same stratum of which Plymouth Rock is a complementary outcropping." And in a comparison of the Klan to Christ's disciples, the speaker noted the "greatest sermon of Jesus, was the Sermon on the Mount"; also, that when Christ had "paid man's debt of sin," this too was done "on a mountain." Stating Stone Mountain was "a shrine, a holy place," the speaker also said Christ had instructed the three apostles, which had accompanied Him to a mountain top where He was transformed, to serve others. And just as those disciples followed Christ's orders, the speaker said, "Let it be so with us." In ending, the orator asked the attending Klansmen to kneel and pray "as a fitting indication of our desire to re-dedicate ourselves to God and to this Holy Movement..."[47]

The Klan and their brand of religion, especially so in the 1920s, must be seen as an extension of American religious and social/cultural thought of the time. Its legitimacy is no different than that of other movements of that period, and of current right-wing Christian Identity ideology that claims white Christians, not Jews, are God's chosen people.[48] The more radical adherents of this modern ideology argue for a pure race and faith, a white separatist supremacy in which the true chosen people of God are white individuals of northern European ancestry. It is their belief that God made them superior and non-whites inferior; the fundamental difference isn't even intellectual capacity, rather, *spirituality*, which nonwhites are supposedly lacking.[49] In examining the religious theology of the 1920s Klan, its rhetoric and its perspective on race, it becomes apparent their beliefs were very much a part of the American social conscience; the Klan simply vocalized and acted upon what a substantial portion of American society held as social truths.[50] As noted by Baker,

> To assess the Klan as a religious movement shows how the order, like many other movements, struggled with the concepts of nation, race, gender, and even its professed Protestantism. By showcasing the similarity of Klan members to their contemporaries, who perhaps did not possess the white robe or light a fiery cross but found resonance in the order's white supremacy, it becomes clear that the 1920s Klan resonated with the larger American public.[51]

As the year 1925 got underway, Hiram W. Evans, the Imperial Wizard, added his exhortations regarding the Klan's role with respect to Protestantism. In the February issue of the *Kourier Magazine*, which succeeded the *Night-Hawk*, Evans stated the Klan's "manifest destiny lies before us." He called for "active support of Protestant Christianity," and added: "As the Star of Bethlehem guided the wise men to Christ, so it is that the Klan is expected more and more to guide men to the right life under Christ's banner." Evans also called upon Klansmen to "sacrificial service to the Cause of Protestant Christianity..." and to "Christian devotion and high service."[52] In the same issue, the *Kourier Magazine* said of its predecessor (the *Night-Hawk*), "Its ministry was fruitful and far-reaching.... It carried the gospel of the light into the dark places, and made the abuses of power tremble."[53]

The Klan itself had been brought before the "powers" when it was investigated by the United States Congress in 1921. In a lengthy editorial the *Kourier Magazine* touched on the scrutiny it had received and addressed the accusations of the Klan's racial and religious intolerance. Stating the public, juries, and certain political office seekers condemned the order before ever being brought to trial, the paper reminded its readers of the inquiry by Congress and the fact that it had been absolved of any wrongdoing. The paper further asserted it had "been accepted by thousands and tens of thousands of ministers of the Gospel ... and others of equally high repute." The paper further stated the Klan "seeks no favor more that the good will of Jesus Christ." The Klan, according to the magazine, "has no creed but such as is harmonious with the Protestant expression of New Testament Christianity."[54]

Drawing biblical comparisons, the paper equated the Klan to Daniel who, "when his critics were bent upon his defeat, they could find nothing against him but his religion, so it is with the Klan." Drawing another analogy, the paper, as it had done previously, compared the Klan to the church of old: "There exists an exact parallel between the present situation and that of the early Christian church." Much as contemporary society damned the Hooded Order, "The generation in which the church originated condemned the movement, and killed the Christ." Noting that "it took another generation to arise and call Him blessed," the paper stated the need for Klansmen to be patient, "for they have the inward consciousness that their cause is just."[55]

Decrying against what it perceived as "organized forces" composed of "Catholics, Jews," and "Salvationists," a "National Klan Lecturer" entreated on the need for an organization that would unite Protestants. Such an order, according to the speaker, was the Klan which came "like a white robed prophet from the wilderness, crying 'Let all who are on the Lord's side rally to the Fiery Cross and for Christ and country, for home and hope and Heaven.'" The hooded order was "blessed in their benefits to mankind." And if the order was "helping in any degree to 'establish the

Kingdom of God on earth,'" then there was no justification for hostility towards the Klan. The Klan was viewed as an ally to Protestantism; indeed, it was "Protestant's much needed handmaiden."[56]

Expanding on its service as an ally of Protestantism, the speaker declared: "multiplied thousands have been turned to righteousness, won to Christ and enlisted in the churches for service through the efforts and influence of the Klan." Through what was stated were its unselfish works, the Klan was "serving in the sacrificial spirit for the good of others." Reiterating that the Klan was "Protestantism's much needed handmaiden," the orator added: "it helps to save America for Americans and make her an agency of Christ to bless and save the world." Vilifying immigrants who "persist in carrying on all their activities, domestic, social, intellectual, political and religious, in a foreign tongue and holding tenaciously to their racial customs, ideals and laws," the speaker stated, "They often violated the spirit and tried to destroy the soul of America." In fighting against "this mass of alienage in America," the Klan was attempting "to build a great spiritual democracy."[57] Stating that "America was established for a Divine purpose," the speaker ended by expounding on what can best be called a Protestant religious Manifest Destiny:

> Christianity with its transforming power began moving westward when Paul crossed the Hellespont in response to the Macedonian cry and at last it has swept through America to the Pacific slope and now it must roll on across the Pacific like a refreshing flood to bless and save the needy millions of the East or the destructive tides of Paganism and Papalism will overwhelm and destroy us. You and I as interpreters of the Bible and exponents of the Christian religion, as redeemed subjects of Jesus Christ are God's opportunity in the world.... Our mission is to supply the world with a spiritual leadership so enthusiastic and efficient; so consecrated and Christ-like, that we will help to lead the world to the heart of God and the home in Heaven. If the Klan can help in any way, through service to state and church, to make America the first of all the nations to fulfill the will of God, and come with reverent hands to lay upon the brow of Jesus a diadem of glory, it will not have served in vain. To that end we will "serve and sacrifice for the right," with no thought of censure or praise.[58]

As may be seen, the Klan's religious crusade was not exclusive to the United States. Somehow, not explained by the writer, the Christianization of "needy millions of the East," as well as other non-white un–American foreigners would take place without the evident resentment held against colored peoples who were, in the eyes of the Klan, clearly inferior.

Hiram Wesley Evans, the Klan Imperial Wizard, by far the leading exponent of the Klan's Christian spirituality and religious fervor, stated in an address delivered in Ohio: "Joining the Knights of the Ku Klux Klan is like joining the church." In so doing each member was responsible for learning "as far as he can to understand the purposes and doctrines of the Great Cause." According to Evans, "Every Klansman must ... fill himself full of the spirit of the Knights of the Ku Klux Klan and learn to see the vision of our tremendous and holy mission." In Evans' opinion, the charge of the Klan was "beyond comparison the greatest mission that has been entrusted to any body of men today." Not only did this mission involve the "salvation of the world both political and spiritual"; it also involved "the highest vision and purposes, the salvation of Protestantism as a living force in the world and the making stronger the foundation upon which Christianity must go forward."[59]

In another message to Klansmen, the Imperial Wizard asserted Klansmen had "a deeper and finer meaning in the spirit and Divine message of Christmas, than is found even by most Christians." According to Evans, Klansmen had "found a new growth, a new power and a new consecration in Klankraft." The life of the Klansman had become enriched and had a deeper understanding "because he has actually undertaken, more definitely and determinedly than have most other men, to try to bring the Kingdom of God on earth." Klansmen had put their "Christianity to work for others" as well as for themselves. So too, had members of the order obtained "a new and soul-satisfying outlet for all the energies created in him by the power of Christ." Not only had Klansmen been sanctified through Klankraft, but they had also "found a new consecration, and through that a closer union with Divine purpose and the Divine Life."[60]

Consecration occurred when a man became a member of the order, for at that time "he re-dedicated himself to the work of Him who became flesh that we might be saved." A Klansman gave "more freely of his strength for the carrying on of the Gospel"; he became "less selfish; more devoted." It was through his work, work beyond that given by others that a Klansman became "a better Christian." The unselfish work of the Klan was a sacrifice by its members, such sacrifice was required as part of their "salvation." Sacrifice was the key because "there can be no Christianity; there can be no Klankraft, without it!" Sacrifice, when coupled with faith and love, caused Klansmen to be "renewed and strengthened by the Christmas communion with the Divine Soul." Thusly armed, Klansmen could "go forward in His name, doing His work, fighting His battle for righteousness and progress." Evans ended by exhorting his readers to "march on ... till the message of Klankraft has been carried into every white, Protestant home, and the great and Holy mission of the Knights of the Ku Klux Klan has been brought to complete fulfillment!"[61]

To assist in the attainment of the Klan "mission," Protestant ministers were greatly sought by the Klan due to the fact that they could, more often than not, convince their congregations to join or support the cause of the organization. Used extensively, ministers provided a powerful force in promulgating Klan religious ideology. Such was the case of a minister who wrote in defense of the Klan in the December 1925 issue of the *Kourier Magazine*. Defending his decision to become a Klansman, the preacher enumerated a number of negative comments made by a newspaper concerning the order; comments which the minister stated were made by "men and women who are repudiating the Klan because they are without knowledge of the truth." The clergyman cited the twelfth chapter of Romans as "the basic principle which motivates the organization." Citing his own reasons for becoming a member, the preacher said, "As a Protestant minister of the Gospel, I joined the Knights of the Ku Klux Klan because: I believe in Jesus Christ and His Church; I believe in a militant Christianity; I believe in the Cross—a symbol of service and sacrifice for the right." Further defending the Klan, the parson accused the enemies of the order of being "unchristian," especially "when the order attempts to support the Christ and His Church." The clergyman closed by stating he could not be "true to my ministry and renounce an organization which glorifies the Christ and attempts to make the world better and happier by its teachings and program."[62]

Zuber, in *Onward Christian Klansmen*, discussed the large numbers of ministers involved in Klan activity, noting the extensive infiltration by the organization into various mainstream Protestant denominations throughout the nation. Whether ministers joined the Klan believing it provided an avenue to gain religious adherents to their individual churches, for the monetary income provided as Klan lecturers, or because they believed that in so doing they could cooperatively enhance Protestantism, their joining enhanced the Klan as a preeminent Protestant organization. Further, the Klan provided a national, racial and cultural identity that everyday Americans understood and that set them apart from unwanted foreign elements seen as changing American society to the detriment of white native Americans.[63] Alexander, in the *Ku Klux Klan in the Southwest*, also made note of the extensive use of Protestant ministers. He estimated 40,000 ministers had joined the order based on comments by a Klan lecturer who himself was a minister.[64] It is clearly evident that a significant part of the Klan's success was obtained through the use of religion, and religious leaders.

Religion, along with race, were delved into by "A Professor of Philosophy and Religious Education" who expounded on the need for the Ku

Klux Klan. The Klan, according to the "Professor," was an organized movement unified "to put into practice ... the great ideals, principles, and teachings of civilization, of the Church of our Christ, and of Christ Himself." From the perspective of the writer, the Klan was "calling the Christian, democratic white peoples of the earth ... back to their religious duty or the religious or Christian foundations of all true or democratic civilizations." Stating that "Jesus taught the principles of democracy and freedom," the author warned if white people did not heed the call to leadership, that the leadership position would fall on peoples of color. By demonstrating that God and Christ promoted the doctrines of democracy and freedom, and that such beliefs were held by the Klan, the writer could thus place the hooded order in a position of prominence in the stated endeavor. "The Klan," asserted the educator, "is organized to put into the individual life, and into all the practical walks of life, the Christian righteousness which the churches have preached down through the ages." Reiterating that "modern or democratic civilization is built upon the freedom or democratic principles of Jesus," the writer also stated that "a man's patriotism will be measured by his ... devotion to Christ and His teachings."[65]

In another article, the "professor" stated the Klan as "here to save representative government." Again pointing to Christ as the prime mover toward democratic ideals, the lecturer avowed the "Klan stresses Christian principles and laws ... and works with Protestant institutions because it deems them to be nearest to the proper interpretation of Christ." Continuing, the writer also stated, "The Klan would elevate and enthrone only Christian character and Christian principles." The author viewed the Klan as "the only great Christian patriotic organization" capable of "putting the great principles of Christianity and of civilization into all the practical walks of life."[66]

Similar arguments were advanced in an article entitled "Spiritual Re-Birth of the Klan," written by the editor of the *Kourier Magazine*. In the article, the editor compared the Klan to the early Pilgrims. The Pilgrims had "hallowed Thanksgiving by dedicating themselves to the incarnations of that spirit which nationalized itself into America." The Klan had rededicated itself to the same ideals on Thanksgiving night in 1915. However, the Klan's dedication to American ideals "encountered mistreatment and misrepresentation." The Klan was then compared to the early church and the Reformation which had met opposition. But regardless of what the opposition thought, the Klan was "pre-eminently spiritual." Being spiritual, the Klan believed "in the Bible, in the Sabbath, in Jesus Christ." The Klan was seen as the "Soul of America," it was "the Spirit of America seeking to be incarnated in the bodies of Americans" who would live by the "Spirit." Being the soul and spirit of America: "The Klan is invisible, being Spirit." Further, the Klan was to live forever because "that which is seen (visible) is temporal; that which is not seen (invisible) is eternal."[67]

Acceptance of the Klan's perspective of itself as the "soul" of America is important in understanding its place in American society within a religious interpretation. As stated before, the Klan was in fact a reflection of American society complete with all its faults and blemishes. White supremacy, spoken or otherwise, had a long history even before the inception of the Klan. So too, has religion played a long and essential role in American history. And the issue of race mixing has always been intricately interlaced with the two previously cited issues. The Klan, in its religious fundamentalist role, simply vocalized and acted with the alleged acquiescence of God. Baker, in *Gospel According to the Klan*, noted the close connection of the Klan and American society: "To examine the Klan, then, is to examine a group that proclaimed to be the 'soul' of [the] nation without much trepidation. Its vision of nation was not as fringe as it appears. The focus on the hatred, violence, and racism of the 1920s Klan occulted its resonance with American cultural currents."[68] In yet a further insight regarding the Klan's intimate ties to the nation as reflected in its rhetoric and actions, Baker also pointed out: "The order's imaginings of faith and nation point to currents in American religious history, including how nationalism was based on Protestantism, masculinity, anti–Catholicism, and whiteness."[69]

The spirituality and religious flavor of the Klan was demonstrated through revivals. The Imperial Wizard stated that in the process of Americanization, Klansmen "must be evangelists."[70] The *Kourier Magazine* reported on such activity remarking that in New Jersey the "Klans are showing a fine religious spirit." It stated Klan "revivals have a regular average attendance of over fifteen hundred." It further declared that the "religious revival is bringing a deep spiritual feeling into the Klans."[71] And in an article written in appreciation of the Imperial Wizard, the writer, a minister, noted that Evans had said to every Klansman: "The highest note to be sounded in preaching the doctrine of Klankraft is to be the spiritual note."[72]

The religious spirit demonstrated in New Jersey was also noted in Alabama. In this southern state, as reported by the *Kourier Magazine*, "Evangelistic Klankraft" was "a medium of Klan propagation and rebuilding and of public education in Klankraft." The "Tent Evangelistic Meetings" were deemed very successful and were seen as "a most effect expedient in Klan Operations." Such evangelistic campaigns were negotiated through the state Grand Dragon and the local Klan sponsoring the revival. Once a date was agreed upon and advanced publicity was made by the local Klan, a "Klan Evangelist" proceeded with the "Klan Tent Evangelistic Kampaign." Services were held in the afternoon for the Women of the Ku Klux Klan, and occasionally for the Junior Klan. Services began on a Friday and closed on Monday. At the final service only men were allowed, and at that time "the Evangelist delivers a lecture of special confidential interest." Noting that "public evangelism" was used by the churches to spread its beliefs and obtain new members, the paper stated the order's activity was successful and "most adaptable to Klan usage." The "Tent Evangelistic Meetings" were viewed as very effective in countering what the paper called "Mask and Lash" campaigns by the enemies of the hooded order. The paper also listed some of the "Lecture Topics" covered by the "Klan Evangelist." These included: "Jesus," "The Handwriting on the Wall" (which dealt with the Klan's interpretation of how the organization was part of God's plan), "Outline of Prophecy," and "The Message of the Fiery Cross," among others.[73] The Klan, as demonstrated, presented itself as an organization that was deeply committed to "spreading of the Gospel," albeit for the benefit of its own brand of religion, a religion whose major beliefs were not that dissimilar to the beliefs held by the general American public of the time.

And the question was asked: "What is the Klan? Is it a Religion?" The question was posed by H. E. R., a regular contributor to the *Kourier Magazine*. According to the writer, "It is the utmost importance to some and it is nothing to others!" To those who understood the order it was essentially everything, while to those who could not see the righteousness in the order it was "nothing, any more than colors to the blind," or "music to the deaf." Stating the Klan was "neither a *plot*, a *faction*, nor a *party*," the author asserted, "in fact, it is the living voice, saying: 'Do not unto others that which you would not [want] others should do unto you,' on the contrary, 'Do as you would be done by.'"[74] In so doing the writer gave the Klan life, much as life is given to organized religions which are understood to reflect the living word. Greater credence was given to Klan beliefs as a religion when in the succeeding paragraph was written: "It is the clearest, the simplest of all religions—that which has the nearest affinity to the good sense with which God has endowed us, and on this account it is not to be classed with the others. It stands for the *Tenets of the Christian Religion and the Separation of Church and State*."[75]

The above statements were followed by an explanation of what religion does to men once inculcated by its doctrines and made a member. In effect, the dogmatism of religion leads Klansmen to rationalize whatever action they take. As stated by Moore, "In essence, a Klansman dedicates himself to the hooded order and defines his behavior according to that of the group rather than that of the larger society. Again, this characteristic provides an explanation for Klan violence which can be rationalized through the norms and goals of the group which take precedent over those of society."[76]

Taking the issue of religion a step further, the author of a *Kourier Magazine* article stated that all religions have initiation ceremonies which make the individual a constituent part of the church or belief, the writer stated, "The baptism of the Klan is Americanism and virtue."[77] Through these

> the lamp of reason is placed in his own hands. In this he is capable of understanding that which is taught by the organization; he is taught to distinguish good from evil, the true from the false, liberty from license, courage from cowardice, honesty from fraud, generosity from egotism, and above all "real" Americanism in principle and act.... By virtue a member of the KLAN learns to subdue the obstacles arising from ignorance or dishonesty. It is the baptism of honor and knowledge and service; it is initiation into dignity, the grandeur of American humanity, God and patriotism; certainly no religion can lead us near the Deity.[78]

Comparing the Roman Catholic religion to the Klan, the author stated the former was "protected by sovereigns, and sustained by the treasures of the people derived from long years of taxation"; that its "chiefs" were led to "power, opulence, and greatness through its tools." The Klan on the other hand, "depends upon itself, and upon God who created light," and "confers neither greatness, riches or power." It did, however, "emphasize the fact that the proud position that it holds to-day is due to the fact that its real mission is to serve God above all." In closing the writer stated: "Teach and propagate true Klansmanism, and you will have rendered the country a greater service than all its legislatures."[79] Although never answering his question directly, it can be deduced by what the writer stated—from his perspective, the Klan was indeed a religion.

# 2

# *The Ku Klux Klan and God*

Seeking to ascribe divine approval to the existence of the Klan, Hiram Wesley Evans, the Imperial Wizard, speaking at the first annual meeting of the Grand Dragons, referred to the Klan's support of the educational system as "a Holy Cause so far blessed with the support of Almighty God."[1] During the same month in which the above cited meeting took place, there appeared an article in the *Imperial Night-Hawk* in which Evans addressed a large gathering of Klan supporters in Ohio. He asserted the revival of the Klan in the twentieth century was brought about by "men of dependable character and sterling worth who were able to lend some kind of concrete form to the God-given idea destined to again save a white man's civilization." He also referred to the foundation of the order as having been "formed, aided, supported, guided, and directed by Almighty God in the working out of his invisible purposes and his mighty decrees."[2]

At another meeting held in Kansas, Evans again stated his assertion of heavenly assistance to the order saying, "we have through the divine aid of Almighty God a more consecrated set of officers who are serving under me."[3] At still another meeting, Evans expounded on the Klan's need to continue battling against non-white non–Christian elements that threatened "the white man's civilization and white man's religion." He presented the Klan as the organization that defended "the white man's home and children ... whose rights we sponsor—in the name of Almighty God who has lent to this organization His own omnipotence."[4]

Evans again reiterated divine intervention on behalf of the Klan at another meeting. In a lengthy speech given before an assembly of Klan officials and members, the Imperial Wizard first stated the success of the order was not entirely due to his ability, or to that of other Klan officials.

Although he did credit part of the success to Klan officers that assisted him, he also added:

> However, it must be devoutly acknowledged that our achievements are due to Divine Guidance rather than to the Klan's Officiary. I told you last year that Almighty God had not set a Wizard over you to lead you. I tell you today, from the very bottom of my soul, that God has done a greater thing for the Klan than that of giving it human leadership. He has given it His Own Leadership. The Lord has guided us, and shaped the events in which we rejoice. He has held us under His own protection. The fact that we have this Divine Guidance and protection should, and must, increase our faith in the Klan—in its growth in grace and power, in its mission, in its final complete victory. Such guidance and protection demand of every Klansman undivided interest, full strength, dauntless courage, and complete consecration to the cause so blessed.[5]

Part of the mission spoken of in the above passage involved the maintenance of white supremacy and the need to protect American leadership "from inferior blood." Klansmen and Klanswomen, as seen by Evans, "*are of this superior blood,*" they were "*the salt of the earth, upon whom depends the future of civilization.*" Along with maintenance and protection of white supremacy, the Klan also fought against "a camouflaged plea for a universal brotherhood and ... equality of people regardless of race." Those that advocated such ideals were, according to Evans, "seeking the destruction of true democracy." Evans asserted the Klan was pitted against forces that were immoral, unholy, and unethical: "For I solemnly assure you, my fellow Klansmen, that we have just entered into the great battle our God has commissioned us to wage against the hosts of unrighteousness."[6] The Imperial Wizard was confident "that our Cause is right and that Divine approval has advanced it remarkably in this righteous warfare."[7]

God not only assisted the Klan in their divinely imposed movement, He also assisted the order in judicial matters. According to Evans, who addressed various internal legal matters, "the guiding hand of the Almighty enabled us to win every lawsuit." Evans pointed to the attempts by various states to suppress the Klan through judicial procedures; the questioning of the constitutionality and legal status of the order; attacks by various governors; the rise of anti–Klan organizations; the possibility of federal anti–Klan legislation, and the restructuring of the Klan hierarchy. He also noted the challenge to Billie Mayfield, the successful Klan candidate from Texas to the United States Senate, to keep him from being seated. It was "through the guidance of Divine Providence" that "we came through all these perplexing situations."[8]

Turning to religion, Evans stated the Klan supported the belief of religious equality. He attacked the Roman Catholic Church for its "meddling in American politics," and demanded that it "come down from her self-erected pedestal of special privilege." The Roman Catholic Church should simply "take its place alongside Methodist, Baptist and other churches." Evans reiterated the Klan "emphatically declares, on the supremacy of the white race, the genius of the Nordic and Anglo-Saxon peoples, and the free private interpretation of God's Word."[9] To the Klan, their own "private interpretation of God's Word," of Christianity and their place and role within that religion, is what gave them legitimacy. Glen Michael Zuber in *"Onward Christian Soldiers!" War, Religious Conflict and the Rise of the Second Ku Klux Klan, 1912–1928,"* noted the Klan's white supremacist and divine origins beliefs. Wrapped within a social gospel argument, the Klan viewed itself as a powerful assistant to Protestant churches.[10] Zuber also noted the dichotomous assertion's regarding just what the organization was or was not: "Despite claims that the Klan was not a church or a religion, the religious language of leaders strongly suggested that God was primarily using the Klan, and only secondarily the FCC and local Protestant churches, as a vehicle to renew American society."[11]

Evans was not the only Klan official to argue for a "private interpretation" concerning Klan viewpoints on Christianity, nor to submit "evidence" which demonstrated "the stamp of Divine approval on the Organization" that time and again proved "the achievements of the Klan are due to Divine Guidance."[12] Other national and state Klan leaders echoed Evans' assertion of God's assistance to, and protection of, the organization. The Colorado Grand Dragon cited the reason for the emergence of the Klan as the need to "make America safe for Americans!" Striking a patriotic chord, the Grand Dragon asserted the order had been "resurrected in answer to the emergency" and added: "Certainly God must be watching over the destiny of our great order."[13] This was reiterated by the Reverend H. R. Gebhart who, speaking at a revival in Elwood, Indiana, stated, "God is surely with the Knights of the Ku Klux Klan." Referring to the Klan's stated objective of unifying Protestant churches, Gebhart said: "I can see the hand of God more and more in this Klan movement." The churches were, according to the minister, "becoming united in common cause," and he ended by saying, "Thank God for the Knights of the Ku Klux Klan."[14] And the *Night-Hawk* could always be counted on to insert small one- or two-line pronouncements affirming divine assistance. For instance: "The Hand of God can be seen in the rising of the Ku Klux Klan."[15]

Yet another Klan minister, the Reverend Bruce Brown, also pointed to the Klan's rise as originating through divine design. Commenting on "The Conflict of the Ages," the minister named three forces which were contending for supremacy: "Infidelity, Roman Catholicism, and Protestantism." He stated "Protestantism" could "never be reconciled," and that it would battle those forces pitted against it. Stating that Roman Catholicism and Infidelity could never win, he nevertheless indicated that the weakness of Protestantism was "its divisions and discordant teachings." To win, Protestantism had to consolidate and centralize its efforts, to this end: "Providence has furnished the great unifying power through which the ideals of Protestantism, the hope of the world can be realized and the ideals represented by the American flag can be preserved, *The Ku Klux Klan*."[16] Another Klan official said of God's intercession: "under the measureless purpose of the Almighty Who gave us life, and existence to the Klan, we can say with humble hearts and fearless minds, the deeds which we have wrought shall live long after we have passed into the Great Beyond."[17] The Klan leader also implied the order's activities were biblical and again pointed to God's direct influence when he stated:

> In the wide scope of Klan life, moral phenomena appear like those manifestations described in the Book of Kings. The same storm of nature under a different guise; yet in all these, the Lord is not visible to the naked eye. But, like the still, small voice that Elijah heard, there is a divine, invisible power, and, by it the Almighty fashions the destiny of our Order. This agency of God may be termed the Klan conscience.[18]

Other Klan members also upheld the premise of divine origin. This was stated in a letter of support to an evangelist. The communication was received by the Reverend J. L. Bryant after a successful revival in Falfurrias, Texas. The letter stated the Klan's endorsement of the minister and their commitment to "promote the spirit of Christ among men." It ended by adding: "With God and right as our foundation, we have nothing to fear in the erection of our spiritual structure."[19] The belief that God was directly responsible for the inception of the Klan is one that has been held throughout the twentieth century. In the early 1990s, the Louisiana Knights of the White Kamelia asserted "that their existence is directed by God, and their mission of 'white revival' is divinely inspired."[20] Additionally, "The Knights of the White Kamelia continually speak as though God gave them instructions and it was their duty to carry them out."[21] Modern day white supremacists, much as did the Klan of the 1920s, view themselves as upholding the word of God, however, their convictions are much more radical to the point of being anti-government, blaming it for all the ills they see in society. The present-day Klan, thoroughly steeped in their beliefs, as stated by Bushart, Craig and Barnes, have "no doubt in their minds that God is on their side."[22]

In *The Ku Klux Klan Under the Searchlight*, Leroy Curry covered the wide swath of issues espoused by the Klan. Curry intertwined Christian spiritual philosophies with those of the Klan and stated the book was a "production of religious, political, social, economic, patriotic and moral literature thoughtfully arranged and sincerely presented." In presenting the problems facing the nation, Curry stated he was making an "earnest plea for the recognition of this *great American organization* that has done so much to electrify the thoughts of our American citizenship and awaken the American slumbering conscience."[23] One of the first problems addressed by Curry dealt with whether or not American would suffer the same end as early civilizations reaching a zenith and then declining. This was to be avoided through God's will in guise of the Klan who,

> true to the fidelity of a great moral and political awakening, arise under the banner which wears the name of the American Knights of the Ku Klux Klan, and girdled in the armor, bearing the Fiery Cross, that shall stand as a perpetual 'pillar of cloud by day and a pillar of fire by night,' march out under God's great Heavenly Searchlight that is spread out on the crest of this sun-kissed land of ours and shall be visible to the world until Americans have performed their full duty in making America safe for the sons and daughters of men.
>
> Such was the necessity for God's call for the rise of the American Knights of the Ku Klux Klan. It came to revive the spirit of Americanism; to renew our loyalty to God; to increase our devotion and allegiance to the Constitution and the American flag; to recall our duty to our public schools system; to resuscitate and uplift those homely virtues of fraternalism, and last, but not least, to rekindle our love for humanity everywhere.[24]

Alluding to the supposed revelation received by a Native American of the coming of white civilization, Curry once again interjected divine intervention as the "dream was a vision of unimpeachable evidence substantiating the importance of the future rise of the American Knights of the Ku Klux Klan; and the consciousness of our mission was brought out under the powerful rays of God's great Heavenly Searchlight."[25]

Regarding the spiritual aspect of the Klan, this was expounded upon in a lengthy article published in the *Night-Hawk*. It also addressed what it viewed as the negative influence of immigration that permeated American society, and the necessity of the Klan. Entitled "Bramble Bush Government," the editorial demonstrated how Christ had emphasized the "duty of the individual to the government." This was shown through Christ's statement that man should "give to Caesar the things that are Caesar's" and to give to "God the things that are God's." This dual emphasis was indicative that "citizenship and religion go hand in hand," the paper also emphasized the belief that the current government should follow in the footsteps of that which was established by "our forefathers." According to the paper, the government as established was idealistic, and: "It is largely Spiritual, and to be Spiritual means to be invisible."[26]

Turning to those influences in American society that it viewed as detrimental, the paper cited immigration of "non-assimilable" [sic] Europeans, Asians, and Africans which, in its view, would turn America into a polyglot and inharmonious nation. The paper also noted the "growth of machine politics" as bringing about a detachment from the high ideals with which the nation was founded. Coupled with the lowering of the ideals set forth in the Declaration of Independence, the paper expressed its anger against what it viewed as excessive graft and debasing of politics. Turning again to the incoming immigrants, the paper assailed the "philosophies, ideas, suggestions, and the like" which were being brought into the nation, poisoning the "national body," and bringing about national "undoing."[27] The cited threats to America, as noted by the paper "point the necessity for the rise of the Ku Klux Klan."[28]

Along with the *Night-Hawk*, a variety of other Klan publications, and pronouncements by Klan officials, made reference to the intercession of God as a reason for the rise of the Klan. In a small six-page pamphlet claiming to portray the truth behind the establishment of the Women of the Ku Klux Klan, the author noted the creation of the order as a result of work between various women's auxiliary groups and the men's Ku Klux Klan. Once established, women's groups from various states united to form the organization with its headquarters in Little Rock, Arkansas, and claimed the enrollment of over 151,000 members in the first month.[29] The women, "imbued with the high ideals of patriotism and love of home, school and country," were, according to the writer in paraphrasing a hymn: "'Like a mighty army Move the Klans of God,' and nothing can deter their onward march."[30] The writer also claimed the organization would assist the men's order in leading the country on the correct political path. In ending, the writer reiterated the Klan's divine origin and assistance:

> It is our belief that the new order, as was the Klan itself, is born of God, and that it will not perish from the face of the earth until it has accomplished the great mission for which it came into existence.
> In the meantime, Klansmen! Klanswomen! stand firm, do not be deceived, and yield not to the flattering unction of ambitious and false leaders, for God's in His Heaven and the principles of Klankraft are as eternal as His granite hills, and must, and will prevail over all opposition, against all foes without, and enemies within.[31]

In a lengthy article, Hiram Wesley Evans, the Imperial Wizard, made mention of the Klan's divine origin a number of times. First providing a short summary of the Klan's rise and the problems encountered, he then noted its success and preordained rise: "To us who know the Klan today, the fact that it can have grown from such beginnings is nothing less than a miracle, possible only through one of those mysterious interventions in human affairs which are called Providence."[32] Evans then initiated a justification of the Klan's opposition against the various elements comprised of Jews, Catholics and aliens who were usurping the position of "Nordic Americans." Because of the encroachment of un–American elements, Nordic Americans were "now in revolt." The Klan, according to Evans, was taking the lead in the revolt: "This movement to which the Klan, more through Providence than its own wisdom, has begun to give leadership." The Klan was providing "expression, direction and purpose" to "old stock Americans" in "fulfilling their racial destiny." Evans then declared: "This Providential history of the Klan, and the Providential place it has come to hold, give it certain characteristics."[33]

These characteristics were both negative and positive and involved the various elements that made up the Klan. Evans also touched on the religious aspect of the Klan noting the positive and negative consequences of "the evangelistic quality of our crusade. It is 'strong medicine,' highly emotional, and presently brings on a period of reaction and lethargy. All crusaders and evangelists know this: the country saw it after the war." Like others of his time, Evans saw the creation of American as coming about by "the hand of God." So too, did God have a hand in the creation of the "Nordic Race." Invoking race and American traditions extending to the Pilgrims, Evans claimed such traditions were "condensed into the Klan slogan: "Native, white, Protestant supremacy." He then interjected the Klansman's patriotism with respect to Americanism, God, and aliens: "He believes religiously that a betrayal of Americanism or the American race is treason to the most sacred of trusts, a trust from his father and a trust of God. He believes, too, that Americanism can only be achieved if the pioneer stock is kept pure. There is more than race pride in this. Mongrelization has been proven bad."[34] In summing up the Klan's position in American society and its celestial command, Evans affirmed, "The Klan today, because of the position it has come to fill, is by far the strongest movement recorded for the defense and fulfillment of Americanism. It has a membership of millions, the support of millions more. If there be any truth in the statement that the voice of the people is the voice of god, then we hold Divine commission."[35] Further, "the future of the Klan we believe in, though it is still in the hands of God and of our own abilities and consecration as individuals and as a race."[36]

Another Klan supporter also pointed to the divine origin of the order and its mission of protecting America against "foreign elements." According to this individual, "Providence has again raised up great leaders in every community and has caused the Ku Klux Klan to arise among the sleeping ranks of the people to guard America." The writer also stated the "divine" destiny of America would be fulfilled because it was guided by God "and preserved by the greatest movement ever organized since the dawn of time"; preserved, because "the Ku Klux Klan is a divinely inspired organization." Stating also that "Anglo-Saxon people were the Ten Tribes of Israel" which were carrying out God's plan, the author referred to Revelations and asserted the "Scarlet Woman on the Seven Hills" (Catholic Rome) was attempting to gain world domination; that the number of the Beast, 666, was "the number of Roman numerals on the Pope's crown." Continuing, the writer asserted, "This Beast was to almost conquer the world when he should be confronted with a host of white robed figures, who should halt the Beast and destroy its power." Alluding to the election of 1924 in which Al Smith, a Catholic, was defeated in his bid for nomination as Democratic candidate for the presidency, the author stated, "Let any man think for a moment and be honest in his thinking; he will definitely conclude that the Pope all but had this country throttled when the Knights of the Ku Klux Klan came into being." And for men capable of "deep thinking" it was easy to see "the miraculous growth of the Klan is of divine guidance, fulfilling prophecy of centuries ago."[37]

In the vitriolic attack on "Romanism," the author accused the Pope of attempting to "make America Catholic." In the process, Catholic immigrants had been entering the United States "thousands upon thousands of them criminals and unfit." These immigrants had, according to the writer, weakened every aspect of American society. And, God's plan did not include "ignorance, slavery, degradation and despair that inevitably follow the reign of the Pope." To combat the "very excellent Roman Organization" required another group of equal or greater ability. "Such an Organization is the Ku Klux Klan." Because of the quickness of the development of the order, "God's Hand must have been in it." So too, "God's Hand will remain in it to guide its destiny, until His plans have been matured." Thus, the melting pot that is American would be protected from the "mass of human flotsam," the "undesirable, unassimilable off-scourings [sic]" used by Rome to weaken America. This would be so because "thanks to God and to His great plan, conceived thousands of years ago, the Ku Klux Klan came into being."[38]

Another Klan official also raged against the perceived threat of Roman Catholics. Such scathing attacks against Rome were one of the most common and effective forms of gaining new adherents. As part of the Catholic Conspiracy, Rome was constantly pictured as attempting a religious conquest of America through its Catholic minions living in the country. Like other officials, the author presented the Klan as defender of the ideals for which the nation stood, and continuously railed against "allegiance to any foreign power." The Klan, according to the writer, had "legitimate right to say ... that the seat of our government ... is on the Potomac, and not on the Tiber." But America would be kept safe because "the Knights of the Ku Klux Klan is an instrument in the hands of the Almighty God in bringing about the purposes that He desires to accomplish." The Klan, however, had to maintain its obligations otherwise, "if we lose the vision that God Almighty has given us ... if we lose the high and noble purpose that has called us together, then the Almighty God will take the work He has given to us ... and give it to another." But as long as the Klan accomplished its duty "God's purpose will not fail" and "will bless our efforts." Klansmen knew exactly what was required for they were "the masters of the fate of America.... They are the captains of the soul of America."[39]

To protect America, the Klan cloaked itself and the country in religious ideology. The Klan, like many Americans, believed the United States had a "Divine origin" and was being employed by God to carry out His "Divine purposes." They believed that "God dwells in the body of America..." and that "God has clothed Himself with the body of this government for the purposes contained in the Divine will." It was therefore imperative that Americans take their "responsibility and citizenship in this country ... most seriously."[40] According to the *Kourier Magazine*:

> God has a purpose. That purpose may not as yet have been revealed, but He is working to some great end and those in America who believe this country is the national channel through which God is working are offering themselves as a contribution to this national body that the will of God may be more perfectly done. This is carried out in the Klan Chapter, the Twelfth of Romans: "Present your bodies [as] a living sacrifice, holy, acceptable unto God."[41]

The Klan, therefore, viewed itself as an instrument of God in His pursuit to "express His Divine will in government."[42]

Part of this "divine will," as interpreted by the Klan, was their "mission" of "Americanism." Evans, the Imperial Wizard, spoke of this mission as the foremost "ever given to any organization in history."[43] Although the Klan had many detractors regarding its narrow Protestantism, self-proclaimed divine appointment, and its brand of Americanism, author Kelly J. Baker in *The Gospel According to the Klan: The KKK and Its Appeal to Protestant America, 1915–1930*, stated, "The Klan, in its founding, bound Christianity with Americanism, and members professed allegiance to both despite their relentless critics. In the order's white Protestant America, the order envisioned not only that members were the defenders of Protestant Christianity, but also that God had a direct hand in the creation of the order."[44] Additionally, the flaming cross, as a religious symbol, inspired Klansmen in pursuit of strengthening Protestantism and maintaining Americanism in the face of immigration that, to the order, was clearly un–Christian and un–American. To the Klan, this goal was not one pursued for selfish reasons, "instead, was divinely ordained." America, in all its glory, needed to maintain its Protestantism or the future of the nation might be in peril.[45]

It was the Klan's task to defend the nation against those forces that were seen as hostile to America. These were: "cosmopolitanism, socialism, communism, sovietism, anarchism, Judaism and especially Romanism."[46] Evans also stated leadership was needed in America prior to its own assumption of world leadership. This leadership, according to Evans, "has come at last in the Knights of the Ku Klux Klan ... for the Klan is the only leader that has appeared."[47] Evans noted the experiences of the previous two years had demonstrated what the Klan must do. He also said, "It has been one of the signs of the Divine guidance which is holding the Klan in its care, that ... the different leaders and thinkers inside of the Klan have all moved toward the one goal of Americanism."[48] Evans further stated that previous attempts to unify America had failed because prior endeavors lacked a "spiritual vision on which Americans could unite."[49] He then stated,

> It is thus through faith in the instincts and character of our race and through Divine guidance that the Klan has come to leadership in the great task of making America truly American. And since this leadership was not sought, but has come in this Providential way, it now lies upon the Klan as a Divinely imposed duty. There can be no question that God never gives power without responsibility and the Klan—and this means every individual Klansman—now faces the heavy responsibility of becoming the interpretor [sic] of Americanism....
> 
> Another proof of the Divine guidance which has been with the Klan from the beginning is seen in the fact that its organization is peculiarly fitted for this great task....
> 
> ... because of the instincts of the Klan and the vision it has now achieved, we, as the Knights of the Ku Klux Klan have become trustees under God for Protestant American nationalism.... Our mission is a sacred gift.[50]

The mission and sacred gifts was, of course, God-given. An "Imperial Official" asserted this when he stated: "Fallible humans though we are, we have laid hold on Divine resources." Affirming the Klan was "a Christian order," the official stated that the conduct of Klansmen "must find justification in Him." The loyalty of the Klan then, was to God which had given them the tools to become better Christians. This was made clear by the officer when he affirmed, "The character to which we aspire is made possible by the Divine within us." Viewing gravely the mission assigned to the organization, the Klan official cautioned his audience when he stated, "I am sure we all feel the responsibility that is ours not to dishonor the vision, not to betray the trust." Further exhorting his listeners, the lecturer added: "If we are not to dishonor our rich inheritance, if we are not to be disloyal to the vision God has given us we must be willing to ... always do the very best we can."[51] The Klan's obligation to God was reiterated by another Klan supporter, a minister, who stated that the "Ku Klux Klan ... stands for an open Bible, an awakened Protestantism and a personal accountability to God."[52] Still another supporter expounded on the same theme when he addressed the "Sacred Obligation of a Klansman." It was, according to the writer, a "marvelous condition which comes down from the very Throne of our Creator Himself."[53] Yet another minister and author, E. F. Stanton, also emphasized the Klan's divine mission. From Stanton's perspective, "Every order has a special mission. The special mission of the Klan is to remove burdens."[54] The burdens involved the curing of social ills through "Klanisms." And when the "day of restitution" would arrive, it would be the "Klansmen in God's hand" who would implement such action. Part of society's ills included religious and economic freedom. These would be assured through "Klansmen ... whose spirits God has stirred."[55]

In a 1926 new year's message entitled "Onward, Christian Klansmen," the Imperial Wizard again reiterated the claim of the Klan's divine origin. Exhorting the membership to continue in their undertaking Evans stated: "The mission given to the Knights of the Ku Klux Klan, the task we have accepted, presents difficulties and demands sacrifices." Citing attainment of "influence" and "achievements within so short a time," Evans added: "Never has there been clearer proof of the Divine guidance in a mission undertaken and in work being done!" Continuing with his address, Evans affirmed: "Only such Divine guidance could have made it possible, in the first place, for the Klan to achieve the unity of purpose, the strength of organization, the immense membership, the loyalty and consecration which are ours today." Evans also viewed "each new success" and increase of Klan "strength" and "influence" as "merely a new talent given us by the Almighty."[56] In his exhortations, Evans railed against "the undigestible [sic] alien colonies ... political blocs, alien schools, alien churches, alien press ... and other alien influences." But God was on the side of the hooded order, for as Evans proclaimed, "The history of the world, of America and of the Klan, the clear evidence of the Divine Power which has upheld us, all prove that we are in the right. The right with Divine guidance cannot fail." Sounding a clarion call, Evans ended with: "let the watchword be: 'Forward Christian Klansmen! Forward with God to victory.'"[57] In July of the same year Evans reiterate yet again the divine origin of the Klan:

> The strongest proof that the Divine Power inspired the organization of the Knights of the Ku Klux Klan and has been our guide and leader ever since, is found in the fact of the steady and rapid growth in wisdom, in ideals, in principles and in understanding which has marked our history. Nothing less than an All-Seeing guidance could have brought us forth from the fogginess and gropings [sic] of the early years, to the vision and strong purpose which are ours today.[58]

Evans expressed the need to formulate a *"new statement of our purposes,"* which would clarify *"our matured convictions."*[59] According to Evans:

> The pronouncement might take some such form as this:
> The Providential task and the joyful duty of the Ku Klux Klan is to labor unceasingly to defend, perfect, apply, and secure the solidarity, ideals, principles and destiny of native, white, Protestant, patriotic Americanism through study, education, organization and militant action ...
> The Divinely appointed mission of the Ku Klux Klan, its joyful duty and its manifest destiny, are all one and the same—the fulfillment of Americanism....[60]

Following the above introduction, Evans stated the mission of the Klan was to ensure the "fulfillment of God's mighty plan for America," which had been initiated by the English colonists in the New World. Evans stated the America of the 1920s "like our forefathers," was "surrounded by enemies." Evans saw Protestantism as needing strength to fulfill its mission. This "mission" was "one of the most important tasks that has been entrusted to the Ku Klux Klan." The organization, according to Evans, had "been providentially banded together just at this time when the crisis is acute.... God Himself has clearly put our hands to this plow; we cannot turn back."[61] Stating Protestantism was "not only a religion and a salvation," Evans also added it had likewise been the provider for all that was beneficial to American.[62] To ensure the continuation of Protestantism, there was the need to unify it and overcome the splintering effect of the various denominations within this religious belief. To that end, Evans saw "one and only one body of men ... which is fitted and prepared to take the leadership.... That body is the Ku Klux Klan." The Klan, according to Evans, had "come to see this mission of uniting and enforcing Protestantism" as "part of our destiny; part of the task which has been set upon us by Divine Providence."[63]

Coupled with leadership was the need to maintain a vital and clear understanding of citizenship. The *Kourier Magazine* exhorted its readers to become involved in reinforcing their civic duties. The rights of "American freemen and freewomen" had over the course of time been taken for granted. This lack of civic responsibility, however, was not to be allowed, for as the *Kourier Magazine* stated, "But may it be as I believe it will be, that Almighty God speaking to us through the God-ordained agency of this mighty Crusade known as the Knights and Ladies of the Ku Klux Klan will awaken us to a real and assertive and powerful citizenship." The Klan, as an instrument of God, would thus assist in making the Klansman a "professional in American Citizenship."[64]

To that end, the Klan instituted a program to assist its members in becoming better citizens. Addressing the various "rituals" and levels of "Knighthood," a Klan official outlined the many plans and ideas of the organization in implementing the "Kloranic degrees" of the organization. After explication of the rituals and degrees and the various steps to achieve a higher level of "manhood," the official turned to the matter of a "Book of the Klan." The intention of this work was to assist Klansmen in better understanding the true meaning of "Klankraft." In order to prepare new recruits for their divinely appointed mission they would be trained in Klankraft. This training was compared to military training wherein individuals from a variety of backgrounds are molded into a unified force. Employing part of a nursery rhyme, the official stated the above cited analogy thus: "So it is with the Klan. The Klan has recruited the high, the low, the rich, the poor, the butcher, the baker, the candle-stick maker." The book noted above would not only serve as "an official, authoritative, comprehensive, understandable exposition of Klankraft" for Klansmen to follow, "but shall give to the alien world, possibly for the first time, an insight into the true meaning, the motivating power, and the Divinely-directed destiny of Klankraft."[65] Stated in a slightly different manner, A Klan official from Illinois said of Klankraft: "Every principle of Klankraft demands that every man who loves his country must labor under the cross of Christ and recognize the fact of a ruling providence in the affairs of the Klan."[66]

Being "Divinely-directed," as noted previously, meant the Klan was spiritual. In a "devotional service" prior to the opening of a Klan meeting, a Klansman stated his desire to address the organization concerning "spiritualizing the Klan." The official asserted, "We who are Klansmen believe in our hearts that the Klan was spiritual in its inception. We believe that it was raised up of God to meet a great need in America.... Born of God it is spiritual," and the work required of the order "must be spiritual."

Reiterating the divine origin of the order, the official stated: "The purpose of our Organization is bright, noble, Heaven-born and Heaven approved." Continuing with the espousal of the "spiritual" aspects of the order, the speaker again returned to the God-ordained theme: "The tenets of the Christian faith have become the foundation of this great God-born, God-inspired, God-directed, God-protected Organization." Presenting the Klan as the organization which would conquer the enemies of God and spread Christianity throughout American society, the official intimated the power of the Hooded Order: "The Klan is of God, and the gates of Hell shall not prevail against it. All the powers of night shall not hide, all the forces of the enemy shall not penetrate its line; for if God be with us, who can be against us?"[67]

The Klan, as viewed by its devotees, had been brought to existence by God to fight the enemies of America. This was the theme struck by J. Thomas Heflin, a United States Senator and Klan official from Alabama. Heflin also pointed to the divine origin of the Klan and noted that various types of fraternal orders had, over the years, come into existence "to combat evil alien influences." Heflin asserted that whenever forces or individuals were needed to combat such conditions as then existed, "God will produce him." He affirmed that many organizations were at that time serving for the benefit of America, "but one came into existence with keen vision, with lofty purpose, with superb courage, one that knows no fear; that has battled and is still battling." Heflin declared the organization "is the Ku Klux Klan of the United States of America."[68] Heflin also equated the Klan to Christ, for just as Christ stated, "Know the truth and the truth shall make you free," so too, was the Klan "trying to get the truth and to get the truth disseminated."[69]

Truths, as proposed by the Klan, were addressed in a lengthy speech before a Klan gathering by Hiram Evans, the Imperial Wizard. Attacking Alfred Smith, the democratic political leader of New York, Roman Catholicism, alienism, and advocating Americanism, the Imperial Wizard compared the Klan with the secret orders of the Dark Ages. Calling it the "Age of Chivalry," the time period was asserted to be the era in which "orders of knighthood" developed. These knights, according to Evans, "bound themselves to unselfish service by holy vows." These orders defied the Pope and other "autocratic" leaders and preserved "the light of spiritual and human independence." Evans asserted the Klan, a secret order, was still opposing "would be autocrats" despite "slander and prosecution, because we are the heirs of those who bore the torch through the Dark Ages."[70] The Invisible Empire, as seen by Evans, has "drunk from the wells

## 2. The Ku Klux Klan and God

of philosophic truth preserved through the Dark Ages by the secret orders." The Klan has "drawn light from the knights of Chivalry." According to Evans, the Klan "inherited (under God's Providence) the mighty spirit of the pioneers." Finally, Evans declared: "Ours the destiny, God-given, to keep America free; secure from all the rotting evils that are destroying Europe.... Ours the destiny, God-given, to maintain ... the high ideals and principles of our forefathers." The Ku Klux Klan, the benefactor of America, "must always labor with consecrated self-sacrifice and with growing understanding for the common welfare."[71]

Obtaining adherents to the order for the "self-sacrifice" and "common welfare" was not that difficult. A Klan supporter wrote an article which defended the mask and secret aspects of the Klan in such a manner that it could not but lure new members to the order. The writer used concepts, images, and metaphors that made the organization appear mythical, romantic, and quixotic in nature. Beginning by portraying America as a "land of tantalizing beauties and entrancing mysteries," the author asserted that "of all is entrancing mysteries ... the Knights of the Ku Klux Klan" is "the most mysterious and strange."[72] After this assertion the author continued with a long description demonstrating the hidden, mysterious, and enthralling aspects of the order.

> Its genius is peculiarly American; beautiful, difficult, paradoxical; a charming puzzle, restless as the eternal seas, but steadfast as the promises of God to man. Elusive as the spirit of the rainbow treasure; distant too, and cold as some dead planet twirling in the cosmic drift as if lost in the infinitude of space; with all burning light; yet nearer than my shadow made by the descending sun down the western slope. Ancient and honorable, old in principle as time itself, yet the embodiment of youth. A laughing spirit, weeping in her laughter. Apparently, as fickle as the autumnal zephyrs but as true to you as the stars are to the skies. As placid as the calm that follows the war of the elements; as quiet as the silent dominions of the dead; as noisy betimes as the shock of contending armies; as clear as day but impenetrable as the empyrean night. A beautiful heart revealed for all to see, woo and conquer as they may—and yet a fortressed heart mystically enshrined, as impgernable [sic] as the rock of Gibraltar that will not yield! A giant of Atlantean proportions; yet a beauteous maid, a mere wisp of a girl, even a Joan of Arc, whose destiny is God's raising the siege impressed by the cohorts of evil. Hercules cleaning the Augean stables of national filth, rebuking the roaring cataracts of crime, silencing the hissing geysers of shame. An angel of mercy drying the widow's tears, scarce begun—not leaving that beautiful mission to time and physical exhaustion....
>
> Verily, its greatness rests in its difficulty; is due to its impenetrability; its impenetrability to its mask. By the mask you will see the [K]lan's glory, but you shall know it not! Christ the Messiah, masked in human form, made sentiment the glory of God, but men knew him not. Behind that mask there moved the God, unseen, unknown.
>
> Wise and luminous is the reason for the mask. Sanctified in history by its martyrs ... rejuvenated into greater glory by contemporaneous events. It is that

knightly visor which graces well any imperial son of this classic republic. It is that glorious raiment that gives the perspective which leads unto invisibility—an invisibility as potent, justifiable and glorious as that of God and the hosts of Heaven....

The mask is the bulwark of secrecy; secrecy is the Alpha and Omega of strength.[73]

Utilizing figurative expressions, metaphors, mysticism, kaleidoscopic, and mythological and supernatural inferences, the writer intimated a number of times the divine aspects of the Klan. It is a "Joan of Arc whose destiny is God's raising the siege impressed by the cohorts of evil." It is "an angel of mercy drying the widow's tears." Like God who, in human form, was unknown to man, so too, do men not know the "Klan's glory." And of course the mask is "sanctified" and leads to "invisibility as potent, justifiable and glorious as that of God and the hosts of Heaven." Finally, the mask allows for "secrecy" which is the "Alpha and Omega of strength." Indeed, as will be demonstrated in Chapter 5, the Klan was "another form of God."[74]

Another Klan supporter, a minister, E. F. Stanton, also defended the secrecy under which the Klan operated. Stanton first stated, "God is Klanish and Works Secretly." He then asserted that the reason for opposition to "being Klanish and working secretly" was that, unlike the Klan, its opponents did "not rightly divine the word of truth." In effect, Stanton argued that although Christ did nothing secretly, God, however, "worked secretly." He further asserted, "Every organization that has ever blessed the world has been compelled to work secretly. The world always crucifies its saviors." According to Stanton, early Christians were compelled to operate secretly and early Jewish military leaders operated in secrecy in order to protect their people. So too, "Prompted by the same motive, Klansmen meet, secretly, at night, to inspect American walls that are being torn down and the gates thereof are being burned with fire." Opponents of the Klan and the mask were motivated by ignorance, "because they misunderstand their motives."[75]

Not only did the Klan's opponents not understand the organization's use of the mask and secrecy, they also misunderstood being "Klanish," nor did they understand the Klanishness of God, or his direct intersection in creation of the hooded order: "Fact is, God is the author of Klanism. I do not mean the KU KLUX KLAN. He is the author of that, also. But I mean Klanism in its broadest and deepest sense, which is older, broader and deeper than the 'Invisible Empire.'" Seeking to explain his reasoning, Stanton stated God was the originator of Klanism upon his selection of the Jews as his "peculiar people." Further justification of Klanism was advocated when Stanton, as did Wright, stated, "Christ practiced Klanism" in his relationship with Israel. Finally, Stanton provided the ultimate justification,

## 2. The Ku Klux Klan and God

Jewish Klanism and—God's law: "In a word Gentile Klanism means the restoration of Jewish Klanism to the Jews. That is God's decree. All true Klansmen are such lovers of law—God's law, like the Klansman Christ, they say, 'Thy will be done.'"[76]

The "American Knights of the Ku Klux Klan" included women who also assigned "divine" intervention to the creation of the order. A Klanswoman, in an article published in the *Night-Hawk*, asserted the success of both the men's and women's Klan orders stating: "there is no righteous thing that may not be accomplished by the combined efforts of these two mighty organizations, already bound together by the strongest ties, in bonds not forged by the mind of man to bind the mind of man, but created by God to bring his people into closer union with Himself."[77] In another article, the *Night-Hawk* printed the creed which was adopted by the women of the Klan. Much like the men's organization, the women's creed advocated Protestantism, anti-foreign principles, white supremacy, patriotism, education, and equality for women. It also stated: "We believe that under God, the Women of the Ku Klux Klan is a militant body of American free-women."[78]

Another woman and Klan supporter addressed yet other issues of concern for the Klan. Alma Bridwell White, editor of *The Good Citizen* of Zarephath, New Jersey, and bishop of a Protestant sect known as the Pillar of Fire, was the author of three pro–Klan books that were exceedingly anti–Catholic and attacked anti-prohibition politicians as well. White, a champion of Klan ideology, argued that women as "newly enfranchised citizens," should hold those seats in Congress then in control of "wets." Asserting that women are those that suffer the most due to violation of laws, White stated, "The Ku Klux Klan, in the providence of God, has declared for law-enforcement and the punishment of bootleggers and all other law-breakers who engage in the illicit traffic."[79] Equating the Klan to the biblical David who "took the head off the Philistine," White declared, "God will use this organization to set up the standard of Americanism that has broken down."[80] Viewing the Klan as the organization which would protect women's rights, White stated the order would receive the support of women as long as they "insist on American ideals and American fair play." Finally, supporting the idea of white supremacy White asserted: "The Klan stands for the supremacy of the white race, which is perfectly legitimate and in accordance with the teachings of Holy Writ, and anything that has been decreed by the all-wise God should not work a hardship on the colored race."[81] White reiterated the issue of white supremacy through her explanatory interpretation of the Klansman's Kreed:

> The Klan believes that America is a white man's country and should be governed by white men. Yet the Klan is not anti-negro and is the negro's friend. The Klan is eternally opposed to the mixing of the white and colored races. Their creed is: Let the white man remain white, the black man black, the yellow man yellow, the brown man brown, and the red man red. God drew the color line and man should so let it remain.[82]

In the last book of her trilogy in defense and support of the Klan, White asserted, "In all ages God has raised up men and movements for special purposes."[83] White's literature was exceedingly anti–Catholic and portrayed the "indissoluble groups" that were entering America as detrimental to the nation's social, cultural and business communities.[84] She noted Martin Luther and the Reformation as examples of God's intercession on behalf of man. She also stated individuals and organizations that "enlist in a righteous cause" were never "without opposition." In their fight against "Romanism," the "Heroes of the Fiery Cross" were "lighting up the dark ravines of papal iniquity ... ignorance," and "superstition."[85] White first quoted Christ who said, "Every plant, which my heavenly Father hath not planted, shall be uprooted." She then asserted the divine origin of the Klan when she declared: "The Klan is a tree of God's own planting and will never be rooted up until it has accomplished its work." She further affirmed: "Nothing can undo what has been brought about by the Knights and Women of the Ku Klux Klan. Divine illumination has come to the multitudes through their accomplishments, and a great harvest is yet to be reaped."[86] Noting that the "Gospel is being preached in" the "klaverns" of the Hooded Empire, she stated those critical of the order "will fall into the ditch they have dug for others."[87]

Turning her attention to another "indissoluble group," White portrayed Jewish movie makers and theater operators as morally degrading white females who, "once as pure as the morning dew," have lost their innocence and "purity." White classified Jewish immigrants and employers as "human vultures" and "moral lepers and seducers, who hate the Christ of Calvary and the purchase of His blood!" She called upon the "Heroes of the Fiery Cross" to battle "under the banner of American Protestantism." White assured the Klan of success because the Hooded Order had received divine blessing. She asserted God "has made you the standard-bearers, do not betray your trust or be intimidated by the foes of liberty and the vampires of society." Not only had the Klan received God's blessing, but assurances could also be obtained from the Bible. White asserted, "You will find in the pages of Holy Writ every encouragement to inspire you in pressing the battle."[88]

# 3
# *The Ku Klux Klan and Christ*

There were numerous ways in which the Klan compared itself to Christ. In a November 1923 article, the *Imperial Night-Hawk* addressed the idea from a political perspective. The paper asserted: "The shackles of thirty years of bondage to corrupt politicians are ended. The civic Messiah, the Ku Klux Klan, falsely accused, misrepresented and lied about, is leading the nation into the clear, pure air of liberty."[1] The following month the paper again addressed the political activity of the organization. The editor of the *Night-Hawk* stated the influence of the Klan on national issues was being studied by politicians and newspapers. According to the editor, "It is generally agreed that a new civic Messiah will be born in the Bethlehem Manger of the American ballot box in the year of 1924."[2]

From a religious standpoint, Alma Bridwell White cited the Bible to validate the existence of the Klan. In her book *The Ku Klux Klan in Prophecy*, White compared the Klan to Christ. She bitterly assailed the Roman Catholic Church and stated it "has failed to grasp the magnitude of the Knights of the Ku Klux Klan, the star of Hope, that has recently arisen in behalf of human progress"[3] The *Kourier Magazine* also drew the comparison, quoting various Klan statements concerning the beliefs and ideals of the order, it stated, "The Klan is being made to go through the fire, and though the furnace be heated seven times its wonton degree, the Klan will emerge triumphant without even the smell of smoke upon its garments, for it is One like unto the Son Of Man."[4] And in a pamphlet entitled *The Ku Klux Klan: Yesterday, Today, and Forever*, William Joseph Simmons, the first Imperial Wizard in the twentieth century, stated the Klan "adheres strictly to the tenets of the Christian religion," and that "the entire teachings of the Order is that our present civilization rests on the teachings of Jesus Christ." He further stated that at every lodge meeting of the Klan "Jesus Christ is lauded and his teachings expounded and the constitution and regulations of the Order set forth that the living Christ is the Klansman's criterion of character."[5]

In yet more comparisons, a Klan minister cited the opposition to Christ and His eventual crucifixion. He also noted the persecution of Saul of Tarsus after his conversion when he preached on behalf of Christianity, and just as Christ and his followers were oppressed, so too, was the Klan. According to the Klan official: "History repeats itself: To-day an Organization, whose high aim is to advance and practice the principles taught by our Savior, Jesus ... is the most maligned and misrepresented."[6] Citing an address given by Hiram Wesley Evans, the clergyman restated the Imperial Wizard's rhetoric when he compared the Klan to the "great multitudes" noted in Revelations 7:9 who were dressed in "white robes." Taking this cue, the churchman rhetorically stated, "White robes! Who is worthy to wear the white robe—emblematic of the spotless purity Jesus came to establish throughout the earth? They who daily strive to comprehend and emulate the life of their Criterion of Character." In a direct comparison the minister followed with the exact quote from Revelations: "These are they which came out of great tribulation, and have washed their robes, and made them white in the blood of the Lamb."[7]

Another Klansman, a "prominent Texan," drew a more direct comparison through the persecution of the Klan and Christ's crucifixion. The Klansman noted the federal government had investigated the Hooded Order with the intent of "stopping its 'illegal activities' and dispersing its membership." According to the Texan, "Three times the Federal Government has said as Pilate said of Christ, 'We find no fault in them.' But still the angry, blood-thirsty, lawless, un–American mob cries, outside the Halls of Justice, 'Crucify them. Crucify them.'"[8] E. F. Stanton also provided the same comparison while indicating the Klan's opponents would be excluded: "Klansmen, Like Christ, the Great Klansman, are being laughed to 'scorn,' 'despised,' and accused of being rebels. But they answer, 'God will prosper us, We, His servants, will arise and build, but ye have no portion, nor right, nor memorial in America.'"[9] The persecution paranoia of the Klan is one that members of the order reiterated throughout the twentieth century. Called to testify before the un–American Activities Committee in 1965, Calvin Graig, the Grand Dragon of Georgia's United Klans of America, vocalized the same obsessive distrust and Christ-like persecution: "Graig saw this act as an attempt to punish a true Christian and true American. In October 1965, he told a Klan rally in Grant Park in

## 3. The Ku Klux Klan and Christ 53

Atlanta that it's your Holy Bible, the Constitution of the United States, the American flag, and your liberty on trial.... I'll feel like Christ as he toted the cross for being persecuted for what I believe."[10]

The use and meaning of the cross to Klansmen was explained by Leroy A. Curry in a book published in 1924. Curry stated, "Americanism and the Christ" were "symbolized and commenorated [sic] by the Fiery Cross." It meant, according to Curry, "an unfaltering recognition of Christ as the Klansman's or the American's criterion of character."[11] Not only did it serve "as the criterion for American life," it also stood "for social purity and holds the life of the Son of God."[12] Curry also addressed the second coming of Christ and stated America was included in this final judgment. From Curry's perspective, deliverance was to be received because "The Christian Klansman today ... looks upon the gift of the Son of God as the great Corner Stone of Salvation."[13] But the mission of the Klan was as yet incomplete; it was the responsibility of "this great American organization" to free "America from the possibilities of despotism and the anti–Christ." It was still working to make America "safe for clean democracy, social purity, and the Voice of Christ."[14]

Further explanations concerning the cross were made by a Texas Klan official. Prior to delving into the significance of the cross the official called the "language of symbolism ... the most beautiful." The Exalted Cyclops then explained the "Seven Symbols of the Klan" and how they were part of the "sublime ceremonies of Klankraft." He went on to list the symbols "in order of their importance: The Bible, the Cross, the Flag, the Sword, the Water, the Robe, and the Mask." He stated the "symbolic meanings ... make a wonderful impression on Klansmen" and also gives a "surprising emphasis to the sacred and sublime principles of Klankraft." The purpose for the symbolic explanation of these symbols was to make the individual members "a better Klansman, and have a higher, nobler and holier regard for, and opinion of, the Empire of Chivalry, Honor, Industry, Patriotism and Love."[15]

The official also referenced Christ through the cross which had been "sanctified and made holy ... by ... Christ." He further asserted that the cross "stands in every Klavern of the Knights of the Ku Klux Klan as a constant reminder that Christ is our criterion of character, and His teachings our rule of life-blood-bought, holy, sanctified and sublime." He further stated: "We have added the fire to signify that 'Christ is the light of the world....' As fire purifies gold, silver, and precious stones ... so by the fire of Calvary's cross we mean to purify our virtues."[16] The editor of the *Kourier Magazine* also delved into the use of fire by God and the Klan. He cited God in the burning bush, Ezekiel and the rings of fire, the pillars of fire that assisted the Jews in their escape from Egypt, as well as other instances in which God was represented by fire. Such incidents were "enough to set forth the idea that God uses light or fire, for the purpose of revealing Heavenly visitations. It is with this thought in mind," asserted the editor, "that the Klansmen adopted the figure of a fiery illuminated cross." For the Klan the burning cross held a deeper meaning than it did for others: "An illuminated cross on a hill-side at night may appear foolish, and will so appear, to those who do not understand the Spiritual significance behind the act." The editor introduced an analogy when he alluded to non-supporters and opponents of the Klan and stated that some "may wonder at the foolishness of the act—others may scoff or sneer, just as people did 2,000 years ago when the followers of Jesus Christ were regarded as a laughing stock of the earth." But Klansmen knew better because "they believe in the Christ and they believe in the lofty teachings of His cross."[17]

In reference to the robe, it was "a symbol of that robe of righteousness to be worn by the saints in the land Yet-to-Come." Interjecting the vision of the apostle Paul when a prisoner on the isle of Patmos, the Klan official stated, "the saints robed in white" represented "the righteousness of Christ." Klansmen, who took Christ as their "criterion of character" endeavored "to follow His teachings." In so doing, "Klansmen wear this white robe to signify *that they desire to put on that white robe which is the righteousness of Christ*, in the Empire Invisible, that lies beyond the vale of death where there will be no more parting and no more tears."[18]

The spiritual attitude of the Klan; Christ as God and as Church, was addressed in a lengthy article entitled "The Re-incarnation of God." The *Kourier Magazine* addressed the subject of God's manifestation to man, and man's search for God. The paper noted the various ways in which God has shown Himself to man, including the re-incarnation in the form of Christ. Turning to the Bible, the paper stated: "In the language of Revelation, the candle-stick typified the Church, as a lamp-stand—a giver of light." Stating also that the Church was beginning to fail, and was in danger of losing its spirituality to "a jealous Christ, Who is unwilling to see His Church fall into disrepute by failing to perform its high Spiritual duty."[19] The paper asserted:

> Amid this process of withdrawal of the candle-stick, arose the Klan.... On every hand there went out the challenge to a militant host to assemble in the name of Christ, superior to sect or selfish creed, and rally to the Person of Christ.... America was again being called to the colors, but this time it was to enlist under the

banner of our Invisible Commander, the Prince of Glory. The Protestants were protesting; they were protesting against the removal of the candle-stick, the extinguishing of the Church, "which is the body of Christ."[20]

The paper also stated the Klan was supporting the Church to reestablish its spirituality. And as to the Klan's birth, the paper asserted, "It was for the purpose of restoring His Living Body, the Spirit-filled Church that the Klan movement arose."[21] Upon further elaboration of Christ, the cross, and the Klan, the paper stated in metaphoric rhetoric:

> The risen Christ can not be correctly typified by a lifeless cross, but a Cross A-Flame. It requires an illumined Cross to typify the glorified Christ, standing on the Easter side of the grave. This Cross the Klan has illumined. It blazes forth in the sky as the signal for all spiritually-minded Protestants to rally to its call. It dispels the night. It radiates with life. It challenges the militant soul. The Cross! The burning Cross! The Fiery Cross! Just as Moses cried: "Who is on the Lord's side? Let him come unto me," (Ex. 32:26), so does the Klan cry: "Who is on the side of Christ? Let him rally to the Cross A-Flame."[22]

Manifestations of Klan activity, which demonstrated how the Klan rallied to the cross and thus emulated Christ, were printed in the *Kourier Magazine*. In one such anecdote the Grand Dragon of Virginia spoke of the visions that many had received throughout the ages. He spoke of the vision of Christ and of his unselfishness. In so doing, the Grand Dragon stated that had Christ had a slogan to vocalize his vision it would have been "NOT FOR SELF BUT FOR OTHERS." Superimposing the Klan slogan onto the proselytizing of Christ was an attempt to emphasis the similarities between the Invisible Empire and the Savior. Citing the problems and uncertainty that America was then experiencing as a form of tribulation, the Grand Dragon brought the comparison to its conclusion: "Out of this came another vision—as Unselfish as that of Christ Himself—and the Klan was born."[23] Another Grand Dragon cited Christ, and the cross, and purifying fire as a means of demonstrating the Klan's uplifting efforts to serve others:

> The cross, once the symbol of darkness and ignomy, [sic] is changed on Calvary to the symbol of light and honor. Fire, the symbol of purification, through sacrifice attracts good and loyal men; the Fiery Cross our sacred emblem is the lifting up of a personality who said, 'And I if I be lifted up will draw men unto me.' Klansmen acknowledge this drawing power and dedicating themselves to our Cause are consecrated in the light of the Holy Fire, ever devoted and bound by indissoluble bonds.[24]

With the end of 1923 upon them, the *Night-Hawk* urged Klansmen to rededicate themselves in the coming year to the betterment of American social, governmental, educational, and economic conditions. The paper pointed to "the Pilot Imperial, Christ Jesus, whose teachings all Klansmen follow" as the example of an individual who brought about great changes, and it exhorted all Klansmen to "catch the Master's spirit!"[25] A similar exhortation was included in the December 1924 issue of the paper. In a printed speech delivered by an "Imperial Official," the Klan leader spoke of the need to ensure the order "must ever proceed from, or be the expression of, an unimpeachable motive."[26] Because humans were fallible, the official emphasized

> we have laid hold on Divine resources. Please remember this if you forget all else that I say. We are *a Christian order*. Our conduct must find its justification in Him. Our choices and decisions must be in accord with His will. Jesus the Savior is also Jesus the Master. When He calls us unto Himself he calls us to share His view of life, to take His attitude toward God, to have His faith in men. We must follow Him not alone for what He is but also for what He would have us do. For we cannot be Christians and reject the program of Jesus Christ. He does not want anybody's "moral support"; He demands absolute allegiance. When He died for His principles He implanted them forever in the consciousness of the race. Perfect love, honor, righteousness, and services are found in Him alone. To go out upon the great adventure which we as Klansmen say is ours, without Him, the trustworthy Leader of all time, would be to court certain defeat.
>
> Everything, I repeat, in the last analysis depends upon the spirit of motive that dominates us. Our attitude toward Jesus Christ, therefore, is the supreme test of our loyalty to the principles of the Knights of the Ku Klux Klan.[27]

Further comparisons of the Klan to Christ and his benevolence were made by the *Night-Hawk* when it addressed the issues of service and sacrifice. The paper stated: "The new, or Christian, order of worship calls for something alive." According to the periodical: "Klansmen believe in that kind of sacrifice which calls for a living body placed at the altar of Service, utilized by man and dedicated to God." In lecturing on what was required of Klansmen, the paper listed the qualities ascribed to Christ. Essentially, a Klansman "In his service to men, his method is to overcome Evil with Good." The paper reiterated the duty of a Klansman to ministration when it stated, "By becoming an active benefactor he presents his body a living sacrifice, believing it to be acceptable to God because it is his reasonable service to his fellow man." The paper then reminded its readers of Christ's service to humanity. Christ "came not to be ministered unto, but to minister." Klansmen were to follow this example for, as the paper pointed out: "To minister, and not to be ministered unto, is the only excuse for existence."[28]

Yet another comparison of the Klan to Christ was in the pledge taken by the membership to be the "salvation of Americanism and of Protestantism." In so doing the Klan was prepared "to tread the pathway to

Gethsemane or Calvary in order to make good our pledge." The Klan was thus prepared to "sacrifice" itself for the benefit of America.[29] Regarding the monetary gifts given by the Klan to various charities, the Reverend James Hardin Smith said, "Jesus would look on these men and commend their work." Klansmen, according to the minister, were not "a bad group of men" as depicted by contemporary newspapers. The robes and masks worn by the Klan were seen as the reason the Klan was "bad." But the clergyman asserted this was not so and implied Christ would approve of the robe. "Men may disguise themselves and go on missions of mercy and kindness. I think Jesus would have worn a robe such as they use, but because he did not wear a robe the mob ... crucified Him. I am not sure that Jesus would bid these men to take off their robes."[30]

Constantly being attacked by those opposed to the philosophies of the organization, supporters fired back by comparing themselves to Christ and his hardships. A Klan supporter writing in the *Dawn*, said of those attacking the Invisible Empire: "Klansmen: We are being fought from all sides, we are being persecuted by our enemies, just as Jesus Christ was when He taught the principles that we are trying to preserve." The writer asserted that Klan "principles are taken from the teachings of Christ.... We are working for God and our fellowman."[31] Writing in the same vein, Alma Bridwell White pointed to the "persecution, falsehood, and misrepresentation" with which reform movements throughout history have been denounced. Christ was attacked in much the same manner as He was viewed "as an offender and law-breaker and was finally taken out and crucified as a common criminal." When needed "reform and benefactors of society have arisen," but as usual there exist elements in society "with whom the hammer and nails could be found, ready to spike them to the cross." The Klan, according to White, "have arisen at this time to correct social and political evils, and they have been misrepresented and persecuted in a similar manner as other great reformers."[32]

The reforming activity referred to was an impetus in the work being undertaken by the Invisible Empire. Pointing to the revival in 1915 of the organization on Stone Mountain in Georgia, Evans stated, "The ceremony on Stone Mountain was the visible and audible manifestation of a reincarnation." As such the resurgence of the Klan was equated with the Protestant Reformation of the sixteenth century. But the Reformation, as seen by Evans, was one which was continuous, although through time its effectiveness waxed and waned. The Reformation, or those ideals embodied by the Reformation, because it was continuous, was in constant search "for an organization or movement (body) which comprises much idealism and the possibilities of extended and diversified application." Such an organization was the Ku Klux Klan, for as Evans asserted: "The angels that have anxiously watched the Reformation from its beginning must have hovered about Stone Mountain, Thanksgiving night, 1915, and shouted Hosannas to the highest heaven." The reason for such angelic exaltation, according to Evans, was the appearance "on that rock [of] a body ready for immediate and tremendous service." The Knights of the Ku Klux Klan, according to Evans, "is, beyond the peradventure of doubt, the most comprehensive, adaptable and powerful body with which the Reformation has thus clothed itself."[33]

Evans then asked whether the Klan had a soul, to which he answered, "Yes." Asking next what the soul of the Klan was, Evans first asked if the Reformation "which has taken residence in the Klan" had a soul. The reply was: "It has never perished." Elaborating on the continued existence of the Reformation and what soul meant, Evans concluded that the Reformation continued to exist because "God is the soul—the life—of the Reformation." Through Evans's explanation of the continued existence of the Reformation, the Reformation's existence in the Klan; that the Klan had a soul; that the Reformation too had a soul and that God was the soul of the Reformation, the end result was that the soul that existed in the Klan through the Reformation was in essence God. Evans, however, did not stop here; he continued to elaborate by stating, "God was manifest in the Flesh." This was done through his son Jesus. And since "God is in Christ," this meant that "Jesus, therefore, became the soul of the Reformation, and He will be its soul until it shall have accomplished its age-long task." Having made the extension, Evans added: "Hence, the Knights of the Ku Klux Klan, an embodiment of the Reformation, has for its soul the Living Presence—Jesus the Christ."[34]

An integral part of the reforming activity was the maintenance of white supremacy. In a 1924 pamphlet published by the Klan entitled, *Why You Should Become a Klansman*, a series of reasons were cited and directed at white males in support of such a decision. First and foremost was "preserving the integrity, the blood-purity, the traditions, the ideals, and the heritage of the White Race." This was seen as "the Racial Mission of the Klan." Adding that if an individual believes in "Practical Christianity," the person should belong to "an organized movement that believes, not only in an open Bible ... in the personality and power of Jesus Christ but also in the full Christ program of unselfishness." The "sacrificing and helpfulness" should not be carried on with the "blare of trumpet or noise of clanging cymbals, but 'in secret' as commanded by the one Master of men,

Jesus Christ." The Klan in its "secret" rituals and support of "American Protestantism," and "Law and Order" not only followed Christ's commandment, but was like Christ in His mystical ministrations.[35]

To fully appreciate the influence and importance of Christ to each Klansman, the Baptist Minister Walter Carl Wright of Plainview, Texas, expounded on how Christ was the example to follow. In an article entitled "A Klansman's Criterion of Character," Wright began by stating the prime purpose of the Klan was to develop character in men. Wright stated character was "of the inner-man, while reputation was of the outer-man." "Character," according to Wright, was "the soul," while reputation was "the body." When man was judged by God he was judged on his character; when judged by man, he was judged by his reputation. It therefore became imperative, from the minister's perspective, that a Klansman fully understands what was meant when he took "Christ as His Criterion of Character."[36]

Wright thus undertook to point out prominent features of Christ's life "as they pertain to the fundamental principles of Klankraft and the development of *real*, dependable character." By showing how Christ demonstrated character throughout His life, Klansmen would thus "be better prepared to build such character as he exemplified when he walked with men." Wright came to the point quickly when he stated, "Above all else Jesus Christ was a Klansman." Elaborating on this statement, Wright asserted Christ "was a member of the oldest Klan in existence—the Jewish Theocracy." Continuing, Wright stated Jews believed in Jewish supremacy just and "we believe in white supremacy"; that throughout forty centuries Jews had "maintained the purity of their racial blood." Jews had thus "been Klannish since the days of Abraham; and Christ was a Jewish Klansman, not only by birth, religion and association; but by teaching and practice as well."[37] Clearly, Wright was manipulating the life of Christ and the circumstances in which He lived to show how He had been "Klannish." This "Klannishness" was what members of the Invisible Empire were to keep in mind when dealing with society. "Klankraft" and "Klannishness" went hand in hand and essentially meant working for one's own group. In the case of the Klan this meant whites, especially fellow Klansmen.

The in-group concept was clearly demonstrated by Wright when he continued with the life and ministry of Christ. Jesus "first selected twelve of His fellow Klansmen to assist Him in his work." Noting that Christ told his disciples to go "not by way of the Gentiles, nor into any city of the Samaritans," but instead "to the lost sheep of the house of Israel," Wright stated: "This was not selfishness, but His Klannishness." Wright also observed that Christ later sent His disciples "two by two into the cities of

His own people." Emphasizing again the in-group ministrations of Christ, Wright stated, "He was truly Klannish in all things honorable." Yet another example of Christ's "Klannishness" was demonstrated by Wright. The occasion was when Christ refused to answer the woman of Canaan and stated, "I am not sent but to the lost sheep of house of Israel." Christ's "Klannishness" was life-long for, according to Wright, "His whole life was unselfishly devoted to his Klan—the Jews."[38]

But Christ expanded his ministry beyond the Jews, something Wright clearly knew and which he also manipulated to show how this pertained to the Klan. It was not until after Christ's resurrection that He authorized "any one to carry the gospel and the plan of salvation to others outside of His Klan." When such activity began, Christ "founded a Klan of his own, based not on blood, family relationship, social standing, influence or wealth; but on man's *real*, sterling worth and dependable moral character." Wright further elaborated by stating Klansmen were distinguished by their inner aspects; their spirituality, "chivalric head … compassionate heart … prudent tongue and … courageous will … dedicated and devoted to the sacred and sublime principles for which He had paid the supreme sacrifice." Since Christ's Klan, as interpreted by Wright, was based on character, the preacher could now tie the two organizations together: "The prime purpose of His Order was to develop character, and Christian manhood. That is why we have chosen Him as our Criterion of Character." And in an even more direct comparison the minister stated: "So let us, as Klansmen, strive to follow His example of Klannishness, because He is our criterion. He was a *real Klansman*."[39]

Having explained why and how Christ was the Klansman's criterion of character, and urging Klansmen to emulate the Klannishness of Christ, Wright then began a lengthy illustration of the characteristics of Christ that Klansmen were to incorporate. Christ was of course unselfish and Klansmen were urged be true to their motto of "Not for self but for others." Klansmen were told to follow Christ's example of sacrifice. "Klankraft," according to Wright, "demands a living sacrifice; one that is holy, morally clean." And as Christ was charitable and had forgiven his enemies, Klansmen "should cultivate that spirit of charitableness which He manifested toward his persecutors." The meekness and humility of Christ built virtue and character, the traits needed by Klansmen to keep a proper perspective. "Then let us," declared the minister, "follow our Criterion of Character and be 'meek and lowly of heart.'"[40] And so it continued, each characteristic of Christ elaborated on by Wright should be emulated and embodied by Klansmen.

Kelly J. Baker in *Gospel According to the Klan: The KKK's Appeal to Protestant America, 1915–1930,* also cited Wright and noted how the Klan utilized Christ to emphasis Klannishness. The Jewishness of Christ was deemphasized while his Klannishness is made more prominent, it is His humanity, His moral characteristics that are highlighted, this is what Klansmen are to develop as part of the process of uplifting themselves. In effect, the Klan simply viewed itself as the new clan employing the Klannishness of the Jews in the guise of a Christian organization. As noted by Baker: "Wright attempted to re-narrate early Christian history so that it reflected the structure of the order. To say Jesus was a Klansman provided the order with religious legitimacy for its cause, and thus the order claimed Jesus as the role model for Klansmen's behavior."[41]

Wright's emphasis on Christ and the Klan's usage of Him as a spiritual and organizational leader was echoed by another member of the hooded order. Seeking to stress the spiritual aspect of the order, and to answer the reason for the Klan's rapid rise, the writer noted that "all who sought membership within the order must believe in the teachings of Christ and must commit himself to such beliefs." According to the author, "here rests the final secret of the fast growth and of the gripping appeal the Klan was to make." The Klan was an order whose members were true Christian believers who through Christ's teachings aided America and offered "their program as a great order." "This," asserted the writer, "is the why of the Ku Klux Klan." The work of the order needed to permeate all of society including the government itself. As stated by the author: "Ours must be a program that will re-emphasize Jesus Christ and things spiritual as the basis for all government." The survival of the Klan itself was predicated on its Christian program: "If we want the Klan to continue to live and thrive we must dedicate her every program to purposes that will bear the light of the Founder of our religion, even Jesus Christ."[42]

Another minister and contemporary of Wright also wrote in support of the Klan. E. F. Stanton's book, *"Christ and Other Klansmen" or "Lives of Love": The Cream of the Bible Spread Upon Klanism,* was an attempt to portray the Klan as an organization that would bring the faithful back to the church. In the bibliographic notes on Klan sources, Kenneth Jackson in *The Ku Klux Klan in the City* stated that Stanton's work was "a strange mixture of biblical tales and stories about Klansmen."[43] Stanton, like Wright, stated that "Christ is a Klansman." For Stanton, Christ's admonition of the Scribes and Pharisees was akin to what was taking place during the 1920s. Stanton saw "Christ the Klansman's guide" blaming government officials for their lack of public support thereby causing "millions" to falter in their religious needs. The Klan, however, was taking it upon itself to correct official misconduct: "Therefore Klansmen cry: 'Return to the Constitution.'" Taking up the pronouncements of the Klan, Stanton declared, "We need 'faithful' men in office. Men whose slogan is 'Love and Loyalty to God and America.'"[44]

In another biblical comparison, Stanton saw the Klan as the bulwark against American's enemies. He stated, "Christ and Klansmen are Builders,"[45] and then proceeded to the biblical story of Nehemiah who seeks to rebuild the wall of Jerusalem after the Israeli defeat and their captivity. Nehemiah, as did Christ, wept for his people, so too, according to Stanton, do Klansmen weep "over and [are] working for their race." And just as Nehemiah defeated his enemies, "Klansmen will surely defeat their foes. The foes of God."[46] Stanton then provided a brief explanation of the condition in which America found itself, thus justifying the need for the Klan in re-instilling religion and addressing the ills of American society:

> Like Nehemiah, Klansmen are sad because of present conditions. Owing to almost unbearable and rapidly increasing burdens placed upon the people by "hypocrites" who sit in "Moses' seat," the gospel of Christ is no longer obeyed. Fifty years ago, practically every adult and most children were Christians. Now, the reverse is true. The old fashioned shouting camp meetings and other spiritual feasts have passed away. The masses do not attend church at all unless some evangelist excites them. Sinners no longer cry for mercy. A few stick up the finger that is slick with unforgiven sin. There are but few active churches in rural districts and almost all others are active with formality only. Our church wall lieth waste and their gates are burned. Our National wall, the Constitution, is crumbling beneath the fingers of foreign foes. Our flag, whose stars and stripes represent the sores and stripes of the Klansman Christ, by aliens and aliens at heart, is being dragged in the dust. "America," the sweet song that has helped men of love to live lives of love, is being hissed by rotten Romans. Politics are polluted pools of polished ticks. Commercialism is cannibalism. Society is no longer sobriety. Men who once borrowed money from neighbors without giving security can hardly get money now with security. Women who once dressed decently, now wear clothes high and low. High at the bottom and low at the top. Girls have lost their timidity, and are more brazen than boys. Children rule the roost. Men do not love their wives as Christ loves the church, and women blaspheme God by disobeying their husbands.[47]

Stating that American society was "starving for soul food ... like Nehemiah Klansmen have heard the word of Hanani, they have 'wept' and 'mourned' and 'fasted' and 'prayed' and now they are rebuilding America." The Klan, like Nehemiah, would "turn a great assembly against their oppressors." By inference, Stanton then implied the divine connection of the Klan to God: "Seldom, if ever, in the history of civilization has an order grown so rapidly as has the 'Invisible Empire.' It is the most visible invisible thing in existence."[48]

The editor of the *Kourier Magazine* followed a different logic in seeking validity for the Klan's religious zeal. Noting the excessive influence of foreigners and non–Protestants in American society, the editor emphasized Protestantism as the avenue that would lead to religious equality. According to the editor, this is what the Klan was undertaking, "and in doing so ... it is being consistent with the Constitution, as well as with the doctrine of Jesus Christ, Himself."[49] Christ and the Christian emphasis of the Klan were echoed by the Imperial Wizard in a message printed in June 1925. Noting the Roman Catholic Church had proclaimed 1925 a "Holy Year" and that Catholics would visit Rome, it thus became true that "all roads lead to Rome." Turning the above statement to the advantage of the Klan, Evans exhorted his followers: "For the Klansmen of America, let all roads lead to Christ. Be militant knights of the religion of our Lord and Savior, Jesus Christ."[50]

Being religiously militant was not the only prominent aspect of the Klan. Another characteristic much condemned was the order's propensity to secrecy. This issue was defended by the editor of the *Kourier Magazine* by demonstrating how Christ himself had employed this methodology. The editor noted that on Palm Sunday Christ had "terminated a period of seclusion." In order to enter Jerusalem "Jesus had held secret converse" with an individual whose animal Christ was to use. Sending two of his disciples ahead to obtain transportation, they found the tied ass whose owner asked "a certain question" when the disciples were in the process of untying the animal. When the disciples gave the appropriate answer the owner allowed them to take the ass. "Had they given the wrong answer," the owner, according to the editor, "would not have allowed them to untie the animal." Such arrangement "clearly shows the willingness of Jesus to resort to secrecy." The editor then asserted: "No one thinks of accusing Jesus of duplicity, because of resorting to methods of secrecy. He was simply employing the best means available under the circumstances."[51]

Citing other instances in which Christ employed guarded designs in the last week of His life, the editor asserted they were "an illustration of the numbers of times Jesus resorted to secrecy and the wisdom displayed by Him in so doing has already been intimated." The author again emphasized, "No one is inclined to condemn Jesus in His use of such methods." That Christ employed such procedures was "perfectly proper." As viewed by the editor: "They were the most natural way under the then existing circumstances." Further, "instead of blaming Jesus, we would rather blame the situation brought about by His enemies which caused Him to be compelled to resort to such secrecy." Having established that Christ employed secrecy and that such usage was brought about by His enemies and circumstances, the editor could now justify through analogy the Klan's own practice of such methods. From the editor's perspective: "In America, we have a Christian organization called the Knights of the Ku Klux Klan. Their methods may be mysterious and secretive. Shall we blame them, or shall we blame the conditions which force them to adopt such methods?"[52]

Somewhat opposite of the secrecy used by Jesus and favored by the Klan, was the love demonstrated by Christ. Just as Christ represented love, so too did the Klan claim that its doctrine represented the same caring as Christ. In an eight-page pamphlet published by the Klan was stated: "the mission of the Klan is harmony, and the message of the Klan is love."[53] Delving into the various types of love exhibited by man, the pamphlet noted the type of love the Klan claimed it stood for. This was: "Love in its beneficent aspect" which "not only desires the good of others, but the desire shapes itself in earnest endeavors to promote the well-being of others."[54] Love being reciprocal, God not only loves man, but man must also love God. Coupled with love of/for God, man also must love other men. Thus love of God was shown through "worship and service ... and true Klansmen must respond to His claims."[55] This love was given through Klankraft. This was a fraternal love, it meant "every Klansman will do his own work, unselfishly, devotedly, and in full-hearted co-operation with all other Klansmen." The work of Klankraft and love was to be followed at all times, seeking divine guidance the writer stated, "May the unseen Head of the Klan enable us to learn it." The philosophy was important because the Klan must love "those who are not of us, and those who are against us." There could be no other course of action because "this is the mandate of the Master and the doctrine of the Klan."[56] The *Night-Hawk* also expounded on the issue of love and Klankraft. Noting it to be "The True Spirit of American Klansmen," the newspaper stated, "Love of one's fellow-man, respect for the rights of others, the spirit of the Golden Rule—this is Klankraft, as it is taught in every klavern." Also: "The purpose of the Klan is to capitalize love—to promote goodwill and the spirit of kindness."[57] And, "The Fiery Cross of the Ku Klux Klan is the symbol of love and self-sacrifice."[58] E. F. Stanton proclaimed the same argument, included God's approval, compared the Klan to Christ due to their "persecution," and noted the heavenly rewards the Klan was to receive:

> Love is the theme of true Klansmen. They worship God aright. To lift the burden from the race, they labor day and night. And God is blessing their glad toil, He smiles in Heaven above. And to the Klansmen there, proclaims: "Earth's Klansmen work in love."

## 3. The Ku Klux Klan and Christ

They clothe and feed the sick and poor, and visit those in jail. Their lives proclaim the Lamb of God whose love shall never fail. Tho' persecuted, like their Lord, they ne'er return a word. In Heaven above where all is joy, they'll reap a rich reward.

They will restore the good old paths, repair the widening breach, with joyful hearts they will obey their Lord's command, "Go Teach." Their growth is rapid, light of love is shining far and wide. And that's because the Son of God is walking by each side. Some happy day their Lord will "shout," "Descend from Heaven above." Then true Klansmen will know the depths of God's forgiving love. They will rise and sweetly sing, "The Victory is won." Their Elder Brother shall proclaim, "My Brethren, Come, Well Done."[59]

A more extreme comparison to Christ was that which the editor of the *Kourier Magazine* undertook. The metaphoric resemblance in this case, was that of Hiram W. Evans to Christ. Playing off the book of Bruce Barton, *The Man Nobody Knows*, in which Barton delves into the life and qualities of Christ, the editor points out the similarity of qualities in the personality of the Imperial Wizard. The editor noted that Evans was a "publicly confessed" disciple of Jesus. Delving into Evans' background, the editor stated the Klan leader was a descendent of "pioneer stock." Further, Evans continued in the footsteps of his ancestors and is a man "saturated with the spirit of the Anglo-Saxon pioneer." Just as Christ was a pioneer in His ministry, so too, was Evans a "moral pioneer." The comparison becomes more pronounced when the editor, speaking for Evans, would have him, "like the Christ," say: "Many good works have I shown you—for which of these do you wish to kill me?" A further comparison is accomplished when again, playing off of Barton's work, he noted the author listed the "three elements of a successful leader," these being "Personal Magnetism.... The gift of Seeing Powers in Men of Which They Are Unconscious," and an "Un-ending Patience." Noting that Barton draws a parallel between Christ and Abraham Lincoln, the editor states that "with the same propriety the mind of the reader could be called to the similarity existing between Jesus and Hiram Wesley Evans." Stating that both Christ and Lincoln were "magnetic," the editor also states that "Hiram Wesley Evans is magnetic, and the reason is, the disciple not only should but can be like unto his Master."[60]

The editor further stated that neither Christ, Lincoln, or Evans argued. The Imperial Wizard was seen as having no need of "flights of oratory," or use of "intricate rhetoric." Instead, what Evans used were "simple words, in plain speech, expressing simple ideas from the heart of a Christ-like man." As to the ability of seeing in others what they themselves could not, "the head of the Klan possesses that gift." It was the same ability that Christ possessed, although Christ possessed it "in a superior degree."

In patience, Evans had no equal because he "demonstrates the central calm of the destructive cyclone." And just as Christ held no fear of public opinion, "This can, also, be said of Hiram Wesley Evans." Finally, Evans also had the power to see into the future, for, as the editor asked: "What is a seer, if it is not one who sees? Hiram Wesley Evans sees. He knows God, and he knows what God has in store for those who dare to trust Him."[61]

Commitment and perseverance of both Christ and the Klan was another area in which similarities were perceived. Many Klan writers and supporters, when referring to the existence of the Klan in the nineteenth and twentieth centuries, would end their assessment of Klan's durability by stating: "here yesterday, here today and forever,"[62] or the shorter version which stated: "yesterday, today, and forever."[63] In either case, the statement referred to their continued presence and commitment to their philosophies. Pointing to the commitment of Christ and His pursuit of a better world for man, the *Kourier Magazine* applied its own rhetoric concerning the Klan's persistence to the teachings of the Savior: "Jesus Christ, the same yesterday, *today* and forever."[64] Here again is the equation of the Klan to Christ, albeit instead of portraying the Klan as Christ, the reverse has been done. In this case Christ was fitted into the image the Klan created for itself—one in which longevity was a central characteristic.

# 4

# *The Ku Klux Klan and the Bible*

"Klansmen stand on the Bible," So stated Hiram Wesley Evans in an interview with Edward Price Bell, a writer for the *Chicago Daily News*. The pronouncement by Evans placed the Bible as the foundation "of Klan principles and Klan doctrine." He further stated, "Klan quality is Christian quality."[1] In another interview given by Evans, the *Night-Hawk* quoted the often stated principles that the Invisible Empire held and defended. In the interview, Evans repeated the order's pro-law enforcement, pro-education, and pro-health stand. Concerning the organization's emphasis on Christianity, Evans stated, "Klansmen stand on the Holy Bible.... Klansmen are whole-heartedly Christian.... In the whole structure of its thought and policy Klan quality is Christian quality."[2] And the *Night-Hawk,* in reporting the funeral of a Klansman, cited the statement of a minister who, dressed in full Klan regalia, extolled the worthiness of the Klan because "the Ku Klux Klan—its tenets from Genesis to Revelations. Romans, twelfth chapter" was based on "the good—the Bible."[3]

A biblically based interpretation was the basis of Klan religious beliefs in the 1920s, and continues with the twenty-first century Ku Klux Klan. Modern-day Klan members point to the Bible as the source of their beliefs and as support for Christian Identity doctrines. So too, do they argue against the perceived downfall of American society because of Jewish influence.[4] Klansmen argue that without the Bible they would have no basis for their beliefs, including white supremacy. Such beliefs are deeply held because, from their perspective, they are part of God's laws.[5]

Constantly seeking to give themselves legitimacy through biblical interpretation, Klan leaders and supporters of the 1920s cited and construed the meaning of the scriptures to extract from the Bible their reason for existence, or to give validity to actions and beliefs. Such an attempt was undertaken by the *Night-Hawk* in a series of articles in 1923. Entitled "The Gospel According to the Klan," the November 21 article made reference to Acts 16:25–26 in which, through an earthquake, Paul and Silas obtain their release from prison. According to scripture, Paul and Silas were jailed for driving out a demon from a woman who was being utilized as a fortune-teller. The writer of the article interjects dialogue when Paul and Silas were brought before the magistrates to show, as the Bible does, that the earthquake occurred through divine intervention. After the dialogue and dismissal of the case against Paul and Silas, the writer asserts: "There is a modern parallel to this Biblical story—Paul represents the Protestant Church, Silas the K. K. K. The one betrayed, misrepresented, the other falsely accused, hated, imprisoned, shackled in the dungeon of boss rule." The writer affirmed that American men and women (Klansmen and Klanswomen) were becoming aware that they could "break the shackles of boss rule politics and be free."[6]

Defense of Protestantism and the Protestant Church was a critical aspect of the Klan's religious philosophy. However, it was more important and of greater significance to portray Christ himself as a Protestant. This was done in an article in the *Kourier Magazine* wherein the biblical life and obstacles encountered by Christ were included. His opposition to the Scribes and Pharisees, who were referred to as "priests," as a means to identify the Klan's opposition to the Catholic Church was also included. The opposition of Christ is referred to as "but another way of saying the life of Christ was one unending protest." The opposition to the Jewish "priests" was viewed as Christ desirous of freedom of religion; his disputing of tradition was, according to the writer, to counter placing "tradition above the word of God." This was also a challenge by Christ against the "priests." To emphasize Christ's opposition, the writer stated, "The young Protestant boldly declared His opposition to the 'traditions of the elders,' and dared to assail their stronghold of religious monopoly." When challenged by the elders regarding the lack of tradition by the disciples, the writer affirms, "Squarely the young Protestant stood His ground, and hurled back at them a counter accusation of more importance: 'Why do *you* transgress the commandment of God by your traditions?'" A more clear protest by Christ was the "manly protest recorded in the twenty-first chapter of Matthew." This is in reference to Christ clearing out the money changers from the temple, this in opposition to the "priests" who "were clearly in favor of financial income, rather than spiritual fruits." Thus it was that "Jesus approached this motley throng with his soul full

## 4. The Ku Klux Klan and the Bible  69

of surging protest." When threatened by religious leaders, "the young Protestant stood his ground, declaring Himself in behalf of soulful services, and protesting against the usurpation of the priesthood." Alluding to the battle being led by the Klan in support of Protestantism against other religions, the writer asserts that Christ "was fighting the battle of Protestantism alone, but He had Truth and Right on His side, and was, therefore, able to withstand his attacks."[7]

By far the most cited biblical passage was the twelfth chapter of Romans which asked the faithful to present their bodies as living sacrifices. In another article of the series, the *Night-Hawk* exhorted its readers: "Present your bodies, a living sacrifice.... The cross of Jesus stands for a crucified body, and that is enough reason why you and I should offer our bodies."[8] A Klan official, an Exalted Cyclops, declared: "In a Klavern you will always find this wonderful Book opened at the twelfth chapter of Romans.... It is a constant reminder of the tenets of Christian religion, and is a Klansman's law of life."[9]

Another Klan official and Baptist minister, Carl W. Wright from Plainview, Texas, used biblical interpretation to show how Christ's life was like that of a Klansman. Wright asserted that Christ "was a member of the oldest Klan in existence—the Jewish theocracy." He also stated the "klannishness" of the Jews extended far into the Jewish past and that "Christ was a Jewish Klansman ... by birth, blood, religion and association," and "by teaching and practice as well." Wright cited Matthew 10:5–6, in which Christ commanded his disciples to seek "the lost sheep of the house of Israel," and His later sending of disciples "two by two, into the cities of His own people," to show that Christ "was truly Klannish in all things honorable."[10] The above biblical citation and interpretation by Wright was simply an attempt to explain why Klan members should be "Klannish" and assist their own (meaning other members of the Klan), and certainly exclude anyone who did not fit within their definition of "Americanism." Jews, due to their "code of ethics" regarding business did "not always harmonize with Christian ideas or Christian principles." However, as noted by the Exalted Cyclops of Monroe Klan No. 4 of Louisiana, "Klansmen commend the Klannishness of the Jew, knowing that it is one of the main reasons for his universal success." Based on the Jewish example, "Klansmen are sworn to practice klannishness toward Klansmen, not only in their commercial, material and social relations, but in their moral and spiritual relations as well."[11]

In his article on the Klansman's Criterion of Character, Wright also cited Matthew 15:21–28 and continued to show "further proof of "Christ's

"Klannishness." Wright stated that Christ's refusal to minister to the gentiles prior to his resurrection was indicative that "His whole life was unselfishly devoted to his Klan—the Jews."[12] Here too, is a reinforcement of the Klan's views to assist "their own." It is Christ's "Klannishness" that the members of the hooded order are to emulate. Throughout his rhetoric, Wright continued to cite the Bible to buttress his argument. He quotes Romans 12:4–5 which refers to all Klansmen as being "one in the body of Christ," to press the justification for "Klannishness." And still again Romans 12:10 and 12:15 which advocates affection, brotherly love and the assistance to each other. Going to the heart of the Klan's philosophy of "sacrifice and service," Wright cites Romans 12:1 which asks for presentation of the body as a living sacrifice for service to God. This passage is viewed as the most important to the Klan for just as Christ sacrificed and served, so too must a Klansman "follow His example and sacrifice and serve." Wright asserted that "the greater the sacrifice the more noble the service." Further, "Klankraft demands a living sacrifice; one that is holy, morally clean." Citing Romans 12:14 and 12:17, Wright stated a Klansman should be forgiving to their enemies, respectful of the law, and honorable in their dealings. Following Christ as his example, and the biblical guidelines promoted in the above mentioned passages, "a Klansman," according to Wright, "should be the very *soul* of honor."[13]

Returning to re-emphasize the importance of Romans chapter 12 to Klansmen, Wright wrote a complete outline of this chapter which was printed in the *Night-Hawk*. Now titled "The Twelfth Chapter of Romans as a Klansman's Law of Life," the editor inserted a note that indicated the significance of the chapter "on the principles of Klankraft as set forth in this wonderful scripture." Outlining the entire chapter, Wright stated it contained the "practical rules for Christian living," that "Klansmen have adopted it as their Law of Life because it presents so many of the sacred principles which the Klan seeks to inculcate."[14] After demonstrating verse by verse how this chapter formed the basis for a Klansmen's life and activities, Wright then stated, "As applied to Klankraft this wonderful chapter teaches us the following practical lessons and principles":

1. Sacrifice and service.
2. A transformed life to meet God's will.
3. Humility and modesty.
4. The necessity of many members in one body.
5. Unity of the body and relation of its members.
6. Definite work of each individual member.

## 4. The Ku Klux Klan and the Bible

7. Service of ministering and teaching.
8. Simplicity, wisdom and cheerfulness.
9. Abhorrence of evil and love of the good.
10. Unselfish fraternal fellowship.
11. Industry, activity and spiritual service.
12. Joyous hope, patience and prayer.
13. Benevolence and hospitality.
14. Returning good for evil.
15. Sympathy in both joy and sorrow.
16. Unity of thought, harmony and equality.
17. Avoid evil and be honorable.
18. Service to live in peace with all men.
19. Seek no vengeance. Leave that to god.
20. Treat your enemies with kindness.
21. Overcome evil by doing good.[15]

Wright concluded by asking God and Christ for daily guidance for Klansmen and stated, "The unselfish aim of Klankraft is to make America safe for Americans."[16]

Another Klan minister also interpreted the Bible to show that the organization was alluded to in the scriptures. Quoting Revelations 7:9–11, this clergyman took the passages which referred to the multitudes in white robes from different lands and with different languages as being those that had immigrated to North America and established the United States. Then quoting Rev. 7:13–15, in which the Bible speaks of the innumerable white robed multitude that sits before God, the cleric wondered "if God did not notice the plight of His children and their helplessness before a common foe." In so doing, "He raised up a new order wherein all Protestantism could join hands in a common purpose to promulgate the teachings of the Man of Galilee." To make the deduction and interpretation complete, the minister stated: "Those who have donned the white robes of the Knights of the Ku Klux Klan have become a multitude which no man can number." Adding a spiritual enticement he ended: "I can hear the strains of that great swelling chorus, 'Onward, Christian Soldiers,' as the members of the empire over whom Christ is King takes up the glad refrain."[17]

The Grand Dragon of Mississippi also referred to this passage in Revelations. Pointing to divisions and problems created for "Protestant Christianity" as a result of World War I, the Klan official made note of the rise of the Klan. He noted that a light had appeared in the form "of a Fiery

Cross," the Klan official stated the rays from the cross illuminated "the figures of men in spotless raiment typical of the Cause they serve." These individuals had come "out of the great tribulation and have washed their robes and made them white in the blood of the Lamb." God was praised "and hymns of thanksgiving ascend to Him Whose seal is set upon them." Klansmen—the white robed figures were, according to the Grand Dragon, God's "instruments of salvation." To confront the ills that had been thrust "into the midst of a sin-racked, despairing world, have come with marching feet, and uplifted banners, The Knights of the Ku Klux Klan."[18] The Imperial Wizard, in a speech delivered before a Klan gathering, also cited Revelations. Evans stated that Paul at Patmos "beheld Christian soldiers, from his day to the end" who were "clothed with white robes." According to the Imperial Wizard, it was Klansmen who were worthy of wearing the robe for it was "they who daily strive to comprehend and emulate the life of their Criterion of Character. 'These are they which came out of the great tribulation, and have washed their robes, and made them white in the blood of the Lamb.'"[19]

Although Romans and Revelations were the most cited chapters in the Bible, other passages were also referred to as a means to legitimize the Klan. Beginning with a citation of Daniel 2:31–35, yet another minister, the Reverend J. P. K., addressed the interpretation of King Nebuchadnezzar's dream by Daniel. He refers to these passages, particularly to the cutting of a stone image from a mountain wherein the Bible states "the stone that smote the image BECAME A GREAT MOUNTAIN and filled the whole earth!" From this point onward the clergyman begins an extensive explanation of various biblical kingdoms and empires until, according to his interpretation, the United States is founded through the leadership of George Washington, the "Joshua of America." Referring back to the mountain from which the stone was cut, the interpretation is as follows: "At the very spot called Stone Mountain, God caused to be cut out a stone without hands that is a spiritual organization, called the Invisible Empire of the Knights of the Ku Klux Klan." According to the reverend, "This organization, this stone cut from the mountain" was ensuring the separation of church and state. Railing against the League of Nations and the Pope, the minister stated the "stone cut from Stone Mountain" had been successful against its enemies.[20] Adding a prophetic ending to his work, the minister stated:

> And the stone that smote the image shall conquer the earth—that is the stone cut without hands, from the mountain, will itself become a great mountain and fill the whole earth. The Invisible Empire of the Knights of the Ku Klux Klan, is

## 4. The Ku Klux Klan and the Bible

therefore, according to this prophecy, the organizing and establishing of the kingdom of God in the whole earth. The details of the prophecy harmonize perfectly with what has already occurred.[21]

In another reference to Revelations, a Klan minister cited chapter three, verse eight, which refers to the door opened for mankind. The Klan minister stated that "the door symbolizing opportunity for service has been flung wide open, not by us but by God!" Further, the clergyman ascertained "there has been thrown open by Providence the door of the Klan as an avenue by which he can go to the rescue of our beloved land." Citing five reasons why the door had been opened and that the Klan must fight against the evils with which the United States was threatened, the reverend asserted, "If the Knights of the Ku Klux Klan refuse to go forward God will set them aside and raise up some other agency." Paraphrasing the Declaration of Independence, he then stated, "To this end, the Knights have come forward to pledge their lives, their fortunes, and their sacred honor."[22] Becoming bolder, the minister put words into God's mouth when he stated,

> God is speaking: "Oh Klansmen, what have I left undone to fit you for this hour of America's need? I have called you out of darkness. I have entrusted you with My most secret wish. I have created you with the instinctive love of liberty. I have thrust upon you the blessings of both earth and heaven. Now I turn to you. Behold, I have set before you a door open, which none can shut. I will go with you. Prove Me now, and see if I will not do a strange and marvelous work in all the States that shall perpetuate forever the glory of the Land of the Free and the Home of the Brave."[23]

Using various forms of imagery and even national monuments, Klan supporters demonstrated the biblical foundations of the hooded order. In the second of three books written in support of the Invisible Empire, Alma Bridwell White included on page nine a depiction of what the hooded order represented. A drawing of the Statue of Liberty shows her upholding, instead of a torch, a Klan hood. In her left hand, instead of the Declaration of Independence, she is clutching the Bible. The caption beneath the drawing reads: "The Face beneath the Mask."[24] The drawing portrays the Klan as the upholders of liberty represented by Lady Liberty as she removes the hood; the Bible represents the Klan's profession of their Christian foundation. The mask, or at least what the *Night-Hawk* interpreted and stated was a mask, was first worn by Moses. Citing Exodus, chapter 35 (this is a mistake by the writer or the printer, reference to the veil—which the paper calls a mask—is found in Chapter 34), the periodical stated Moses "was the first man to put on a mask while doing good."[25]

The Klan's assertion of their Christian and biblical foundation was also professed by an official of the Invisible Empire during the opening ceremonies at one of their meetings. According to the officer, Klan activity was seen as beneficial to American society in order to counter "the ravings of ignorance, the rottenness of political demagogues and the threats and thunders of the Vatican or its subjects." Expounding on the need for continued Klankraft, the official affirmed the need to conduct the order's teachings "according to the genius of true Protestant Christianity." It was the "educated Klan mind" that should "govern America." Because of this it was "important then that the chief cornerstone of Klankraft is founded upon the Bible, that great library in Heaven." As viewed by the official, "Klan education" was important in order to develop men's "physical, intellectual and moral constitution." Indeed, "Klan religion is his moral and spiritual obligation to his God."[26]

In the first of her three books in support of the Klan, Alma Bridwell White utilized the Bible to validate her interpretations concerning the Invisible Empire. Support was given to White's renditions by the fact that the Imperial Representative of New Jersey, Arthur H. Bell, wrote the introduction to her book. Bishop White, according to Bell, "has long been considered one of the foremost warriors in the battle between darkness and light and is well able to bring forth in an understandable manner the true status of the Roman Catholic hierarchy and the Ku Klux Klan as pointed out by the greatest book of the ages, the Holy Bible." And although readers might become fearful due to what they would read, fear would be replaced "by hope and confidence as the prophecies are pointed out placing the victory in the hands of the righteous."[27] White also inserted a note to the reader in which she stated that each chapter "shows the nature of the Roman Catholic hierarchy and the Ku Klux Klan from some incident in the Bible."[28]

Turning first to Revelations, White identified Rome and the Catholic Church as the city "built on seven mountains" which is "spoken of in Revelations 17:9 as the seven heads 'on which the woman sitteth.'" Rome is the "Scarlet Mother" because in Revelations 18:16 the Bible refers to a city "that was clothed in fine linen, and purple, and scarlet." And since the Cardinals wore "scarlet, also fine linen" along with jewels and other finery, the woman spoken of that sits on the seven hills is in fact Rome.[29] Painting a vivid picture of Roman Catholicism as power hungry and desirous of world domination, White interprets anything associated with Catholicism as evil and malevolent, and states the Pope "is none other than the Antichrist."[30]

White also asserted Rome was attempting to keep people in the dark concerning biblical teachings. The "Scarlet Mother" has used all its powers to "combat spiritual enlightenment" and "is terrified at the sight of the white-robed army which has arisen." White affirmed that "God has raised up this great patriot organization to unmask popery." It is the forces of evil, "the enemies of truth" which has brought about the unsettling conditions and are the reason "the white-robed army has appeared" and has "offset" the objectives of Rome. Just as the Klan has derailed the evil intentions of Rome, so too, has it defended the concepts under which the United States was founded.[31]

Citing Revelations 12:13–16, White interpreted the passages to indicate the discovery of the New World and the inception of the United States by Protestants. White declared that "Rome came across the great sea with her un–American hordes" in an attempt to destroy Protestantism. "But now come the Knights of the Ku Klux Klan in this crucial hour, to contend for the faith of our fathers who suffered and died in behalf of freedom." These "rescuers of the Constitution" are "heroes of a new Reformation ... robed in white, emblematic of the purity of the principles for which they stand." Once again White asserted the Klan's origin is divine in nature: "The Knights of the Ku Klux Klan, who have sensed the danger, have been raised up by the Almighty at this critical time."[32] E. F. Stanton, a minister, was more direct regarding biblical prophecy and the Klan. According to Stanton, "By reading Micah 7:2 and the first chapter of Habakkuk, (the three K's in the word 'Habakkuk' mean KU KLUX KLAN) you will see the truth."[33] Truth, according to Thomas Heflin, senator from Alabama, in a speech at the Fourth Imperial Klonvokation, was what the Klan was providing regarding keeping "un–American" men out of political offices. "The Bible says," declared Heflin, "Know the truth and the truth shall make you free. The Master himself said that. And the Klan is trying to get the truth and to get the truth disseminated."[34]

During the 1920s when the Klan reached its zenith, and in which White was writing, were viewed as "days of scriptural fulfillment." White compared the Klan to the "Lutheran Reformation" and viewed the former as being involved in a "desperate battle" in which the "powers of darkness" were opposing the Klan's efforts to "make the world a better and safer place in which to live."[35] White alluded to the Jewish Conspiracy of world domination through wealth. Not only were the Jews attempting such an unsavory maneuver, but they are aligned with the Catholic Church. This alliance, dominated by the "Scarlet Mother," is seen as "the last resort of Diabolus to destroy democracy and wrench the world from the grasp of Protestants."[36] However, all is not lost because "the Klansmen with their undying principles, with the tenets of Christian religion will uphold the Constitution" against the forces opposed to American society. Providing divine origin, White then stated, "Judging by the rapid growth of this great organization, we dare to say that it is the instrument in God's hand to preserve our American ideals and institutions."[37]

White compared the Klan to another biblical army—that of Gideon whose army saved the Jews from "Baal worship." Addressing contemporaneous events, White stated, "At this time, the Lord has raised up the Invisible Empire to wage bloodless warfare against Rome's religio-political system." And just as Gideon worked during the night to tear down Baal's altars; just as Moses did not worship God in the presence of Egyptians, so too does the Klan wear its mask. It was, according to White, only by studying the "pages of Holy Writ" that an understanding of the need for such secrecy was obtained. White also stated that seven signified perfection and that the number represented the "white-robed army that has now multiplied until it numbers millions." In an inversion, as Gideon and his army were now the Klansmen, White cited Judges 7:12 in which Gideon and his army defeated the Midianites and Amalekites. According to White, "Those brave Klansmen blew their trumpets, broke their pitchers, and, holding their lamps in their hands, cried, 'The sword of the Lord, and of Gideon.'"[38]

Turning next to Luke, Chapter 10, White addressed the deeds of the Good Samaritan. Rome and the Catholic Church, according to White, instead of preaching the gospel of Christ "has wounded, robbed and penalizes the human race down through the ages." Thus the Catholic Church represented the thieves and mankind the victim, but "at the psychological moment the Knights of the Ku Klux Klan appeared on the stage of humanity with a creed ... which is perfectly in accord with the principles of the New Testament." White again noted God's intercession on behalf of humanity through the Klan: "The Almighty in His wisdom has chosen both men and women of dependable character and is enlisting them under the Stars and Stripes and the Fiery Cross." Coming to the point, White then plainly stated the analogy: "The members of this great organization are the Good Samaritans of this age, breaking the bread of life to those who have been victims of ecclesiastical and political tyranny."[39]

Returning to Revelations, White addressed the eventual battle of Armageddon. She again asserted that Satan, through "the papacy, the most effectual weapon of satanic power the world has ever known," is contending for world supremacy. But, according to "Holy Writ," the result of the battle will be the defeat of these evil forces. Just as the biblical battle will result in defeat of the evil forces, so too, has a "white-robed army ... been raised up to save the cause of humanity, and their program will be carried out preparatory to God's program." White also stated that "political Romanism" was weakened during World War I due to the fact that it failed to defeat England "with the sword of the Kaiser." At the end of the war "God raised up the white-robed army in the United States ... to continue to enlighten the people."[40] And just as John the Baptist laid the "gospel axe" at the "root of the tree," so would the Klan "lay the axe at the root of the tree of papal power."[41]

White then cited Revelation 11:15, which speaks of the kingdoms of the world becoming the kingdoms of God. Here, White makes another comparison: "If God sees fit to work in behalf of His own cause and kingdom through an 'Invisible Empire,' it is useless for man to make a protest." The Klan is thus seen as but another of God's "kingdoms." Attacking the Catholic dogma of transubstantiation, deification, absolution, and convents, White praises the Klan "as the army divinely appointed to set the forces in operation to rescue Americanization and save our Protestant institutions from the designs of the 'Scarlet Mother.'"[42] Turning to I Kings 18, White equated the Klan to the prophets of old: "The Klansmen are the prophets of a new and better age ... they have seen the cloud arising out of the sea, destined to fill the heavens and pour out its contents."[43] But the cloud was not a mere cloud, it was "the white cloud of Klansmen with the fiery cross ... destined to bring about a mighty revolution in politics and religion."[44]

Another individual which attempted to portray the revival of the Klan as being prophetic in nature was Leroy A. Curry. According to Curry, the coming of the Klan was revealed to an Indian in a dream. The dream, asserts Curry, "was a vision of impeachable evidence substantiating the importance of the future rise of the American Knights of the Ku Klux Klan; and the consciousness of our mission was brought out under the powerful rays of God's great Heavenly Searchlight." It is while the Indian slept that "the messenger of God told his story in a dream to the redman [sic] of the wilderness." In the dream there appear on the shores of America "thousands of honest, hard-working, liberty-seeking and God-fearing men and women." The dream is the story of "four hundred years of human history" revealed to the Indian "through the unimpeachable witness of an infinite searchlight that shone partly on the physical shores of America." As the Indian stands "frightened and trembling" there appears to him a mysterious figure who "was clothed in a garment of white, a symbol of the justice and purity of his message; and he carried a burning Cross, emblematic of Christ's life that must some day be made the foundation of all society and all governments." But the messenger was exceptional, for he was "robed in a color as white as the snow, might be described in the likeness of an angel sent down from heaven to ... disclose the infinite secrets of God through the rays of a great searchlight."[45]

Alluding to Stone Mountain, Curry continued with the revelation and stated the messenger from the mountain top "preached the message that revealed the story of the oppressed races of mankind and told of a land where God's adopted children might come to live and carry out the divine purpose of Almighty God." And the messenger, "scaling the mountain-side and bearing the Fiery Cross ... lifted his head toward the heavens, he prayed to the only True and Living God." In the dream the messenger tells of the story of a place "where Christianity and law were unknown, where the core of civilization had decayed and fallen from the hearts of governments." It is a place that is separated by the hand of God; on the right are "the spirit and goodness of God ... on the left were the direful influence and hatred of Satan." The messenger asked the Indian, "Which do you want, Americanism and the Christ, or despotism and the anti–Christ?" The messenger stated God "had planned their society." He not only chose "their color, religion and ideals, but he did not overlook the vital importance of excluding all other races, religions, philosophies and ideas of government ... that would hinder the ... progress of the people chosen for fulfillment of the redman's dream."[46]

In his dialogue with the Indian, the messenger addressed the concerns of the Klan which were being neglected by American society. Addressing the Indian prophetically, the messenger stated he may return "some day to warn these people's children" of their failure to fulfill their responsibilities. And return he does, for "on one cold bleak night, just approaching the nation's Thanksgiving Day, in the year 1915, the Great Searchlight of God was turned upon the silent story of the redman's dream." Thus, according to Curry, the messenger returned to America and awakened "to activity the greatest army of men and women that ever unsheathed a sword in defense of a righteous cause." The prophetic dream of the Indian is fulfilled—from pre–Columbian times which predicts the coming of Europeans to the New World, to the revival of the Klan in 1915 to answer "America's greatest question: Which to you want 'Americanism and the Christ, or despotism and the anti–Christ?'"[47]

In support of white supremacy and "racial purity," a Montana Klansman cited Deuteronomy 7:1–3, in which God led the Jews into new lands where they would conquer their enemies. In these verses God also forbids the marriage of the conquering Jews and their adversaries. Such admonitions are also pointed out by the writer in Joshua 23:12–13 where the successor of Moses again orders the Jews not to intermarry with those they have conquered. To strengthen the biblical contention of racial purity, the writer also quoted Nehemiah 13:25 and 13:27 where intermarriage is again forbidden and points to the sin of King Solomon for his transgressions with "foreign women." The Klansman in his supporting arguments stated, "If God commands racial purity among the Jews, why is it not good for all races?" Utilizing the eugenic beliefs of the time, the writer asserted that "inter-racial marriages breed criminality," and that "pure races are the races most receptive to moral teachings." The above stated reasons were, according to the writer, "why God demanded a pure race." The explanations also added to the justification for "klannishness."[48] Klanishness was part and parcel of the overall training and implementation of Klankraft. Jess F. Story, a Klan representative from Illinois in a speech before the Klan's Fourth Imperial Klonvokation, noted the importance of the Bible to Klankraft. According to Story, Klankraft was to be "conducted according to the genius of true Protestant Christianity and by a people who are devoted and true to humanity." He then emphasized, "How important then that the chief cornerstone of Klankraft is founded upon the Bible, that great library of Heaven."[49]

In an essay contest held by the *Kourier Magazine* in which its readers participated by writing on the topic of the "Twelve Commandments of Patriotism," the journal published essays deemed worthy of recognition. In effect each essay was simply a list of "commandments" Americans were to follow as part of their patriotism. The essays demonstrated how the Bible continued to be central to Klan philosophy. In "Laws of Patriotism" written by Lois Carlson, commandment number 12 stated, "Thou shalt recognize Christ as thy Criterion and the Bible as thy guide. There is no commandment greater than this." In another essay, "My Creed of Patriotism," composer John W. Holt in commandment number two wrote, "Neglect not the Scriptures for they are God's message to the world."[50]

The continued reference to the Bible as foundation of the Klan's beliefs and basis of its order continued beyond the 1920s. As will be seen in Chapter 9, the Bible would become the crucial instrument in the Klan's religious ideology. Through their interpretations it became an essential tool used to justify every aspect of their religious philosophies. The Bible provided justifiable interpretations granting the Klan validation as God's chosen, or rather, God's lost tribes composed of White Aryan Christians and the Jews, through biblical interpretation became the spawn of the devil—the anti–Christ.

# 5

## *Poetry and Song*

As demonstrated in the previous chapters, the Klan used various religious and biblical interpretations to substantiate their existence. Zuber, in *"Onward Christian Klansmen,"* makes note of how the religious ambiance created by the Klan produced an appeal to join the organization for a higher purpose:

> A number of factors helped create this religious atmosphere: frequent invocations of God, Christ, and Christian ideals; the use of Christian symbols like the cross; the singing of hymns; sermons by ministers. In the early years, Klan spokesmen likened the movement to another Reformation or altruistic Crusade destined to save the nation.[1]

One of the factors noted by Zuber is included herein—songs. Another factor influenced by religion is poetry. In the composition of poetry, the two prominent themes used by Klan members and their adherents are religion and patriotism. These two themes, as may be realized, can evoke emotional responses which are then set to words. Songs, by virtue of their structure, and the fact that they are also products of emotions originating from deep feelings associated with strongly held beliefs, are included in the chapter. As done numerous times before by others, Klan songs were composed whose lyrics addressed their concerns and were sung to the tunes of established songs. Perhaps the most famous example of this is *Yankee Doodle* which (according to some historians), was sung to the tune of an English alehouse ditty. Some of the songs and poems composed by and for the Klan underwent the same process. It is to these poems and songs, and their interpretative meaning that we now turn. The chapter is divided into two parts; part one addresses poetry and part two addresses songs. Where indicated, the tune of the song is included.

# Part One: Poetry

The first piece interweaves three themes: identification, patriotism, and religion. It portrays the Klan as mysterious, youthful, strong; a protector of the nation, and religious in nature. It is one of the most well-known compositions in support of the Klan. The Klan is, according to the author (who led the Women's Ku Klux Klan in Indiana), the essence and "The Soul of America."

**The Soul of America**
by Daisy Douglas Barr

I am clothed with wisdom's mantle;
Age and experience are mine,
Yet I am still in the swaddling clothes
    Of my existence.
I am strong beyond my years;
My hand typifies strength,
And although untrained in cunning,
Its movements mark the quaking
    Of the enemies of my country.
My eye, though covered, is all seeing;
It penetrates the dark recesses of law violation,
Treason, political corruption and injustice,
Causing these cowardly culprits to bare their unholy faces
    In the light of my all-seeing revelations.
My vision is so broad
That my daily meditations force upon me new problems,
New situations and new obligations.
My feet are swift to carry the strength of my hand
    And the penetrations of my all-seeing eye.
My nature is serious, righteous and just,
    And tempered with the love of Christ.
My purpose is noble, far-reaching and age-lasting.
My heart is heavy, but not relenting.
Sorrowful but not hopeless;
Pure but ever able to master the unclean;
Humble but not cowardly;
Strong but not arrogant;
Simple but not foolish;
    Ready, without fear.
I am the spirit of Righteousness.
They call me the Ku Klux Klan.
I am more than the uncouth robe and hood
    With which I am clothed.
YEA, I AM THE SOUL OF AMERICA.[2]

The next piece was written by a minister, it also deals with the three themes dealt in the previous poem, but its concentration on religion is through the symbol most representative of the Klan, the "Fiery Cross."

**The Fiery Cross**
by Reverent W. H. Stephens

Higher, ever higher, mounts the Fiery Cross;
Farther, ever farther, o'er the land it goes;
Spreading holy principles of righteousness and truth,
Liberty and justice, for aged and for youth
Deeper, ever deeper, in the hearts of men;
Firmer, ever firmer, its truths are sinking in;
Teaching them that Purity's the only thing worthwhile-
That Equality, morality, must overcome what's vile.
Sweeter, ever sweeter, is the story that it tells;
Greater, ever greater, the respect it compels;
For it overcomes corruption, and everything that is bad;
To the weak gives inspiration, cheers the lonely and the sad.
So higher, ever higher, may the Fiery Cross arise,
Till its scintillating glory fills the Nation's longing eyes,
Heralding the victory that for us all awaits,
Through the ruling "by the people" of these great United States.[3]

Because the Klan saw itself as fighting for a righteous cause, their actions would inevitably result in a just reward. That reward was heavenly recognition, recognition that would include Klansmen among the "heavenly host."

**Untitled**
unknown author

When the last great task is finished,
And the workers are silent and dead;
When the censure and reward of nations,
From the Ledgers of Heaven are read;
The Klansman will join that assembly,
And shout with the redeemed as they sing;
"All honor to Christ our Redeemer,
All praise to Christ our King."[4]

The patriotic theme is seen in the next piece, included is the Klan's perspective of their good works. Klankraft is extolled, Klan teachings are presented as pure, and membership in the Klan is done for unselfish reasons. Included is a symbolism of the Klan as Christ, for it (the Klan) is the "bright star of hope."

**Untitled**
unknown author

Then, what will you do with the Ku Klux Klan?
March to the front as a red-blooded man,
Or skulk in the rear as a craven untrue,
And sow tares in the wheat, as our enemies do?
You receive the blessings our Kraft came to bring,
You drink the pure water from the Empire's spring,

From the Fiery Cross you receive the same light.
Did you join the Klan from unholy wishes?
And follow the Camp for the loaves and the fishes;
No! You are MEN, and you know you are,
You are going to follow the lead of the Star,
The bright star of Hope is the Ku Klux Klan,
And do, and dare, to the very last man
As our fathers did our Country to save,
And Keep it "The Land of the Free and
The Home of the Brave."[5]

Jesus Christ, the central figure in the religious dogma of the Klan, is the central theme in the next poem. Included in this piece, as the Klan did in much of their literature, was a solicitation for Christ's assistance and protection in their endeavors.

**A Klansman's Prayer**
by W. F. R.

Jesus, Son of the morning,
    Another day begins,
Grant us fresh light and wisdom,
    Release us from our sins;
Now, with thy wakening Klansmen
    Facing the rising day,
Give us thy strength and blessing,
    Ere we turn to our work away.
Jesus, Lord of the noon-tide,
    The sun stands high in the sky,
Temper and guide thy Klansmen,
    Faithful to do or die;
Teacher of Truth eternal
    Our very souls arouse,
Here, 'midst the marts of Mammon,
    Keep us true to our vows.
Jesus, Master at even,
    Thy Fiery Cross doth call,
Give us to do our duty
    Whatever my befall;
Now as our legions gather,
    And the stars come above,
Light in each Klansman's secret heart,
    Thy fiery flame of Love.
Jesus, Shepherd at midnight,
    Watch O'er Thy sleeping flock,
Protect 'gainst snares and dangers
    The powers of evil concoct;
Criterion of Klannish manhood,
    Exemplars pure and bright'
Keep us unsullied and steadfast,
    Teach us to live aright.[6]

In many instances Klan members and their supporters used the works of others and changed the wording to fit Klan ideology or themes. One such work is the following in which a Klan member entirely rewords the poem of William Herbert Carruth entitled *Each in His Own Tongue*. The essence of the Carruth poem centers on the beauty of the handiwork of God. The reworded Klan poem addresses the much believed idea of the United States having its origin as part of God's plan. It addresses the American Revolution, independence, and the ideals and concepts which America represents. It also states the hooded order to be "Another form of God," working to correct what it sees are the wrongs and evils in American society. Note also that the revived Klan is viewed as a "Savior"; a theme explored in the previous chapters.

**God in the Klan**
by a member of Kanyon Klan No. 9
Grand Canyon, Arizona

An age of sorrow and darkness,
The fall of ancient Rome.
A new world then discovered,
And many a happy home.
A struggle for independence,
And justice won the sod.
Some call in Evolution,
And others call it God.
A land of free religion,
Where each may have their belief.
The voice of all the people,
Elect their leader and chief.
A land of free education,
Without a tyrant's rod,
Some people call it Freedom
And others call it God
And now a regular "Melting Pot,"
With foreigners galore;
Catholicism raging wild,
For power—ever more.
But then there came a Savior,
With face turned from the clod,
The noble Knights of the Ku Klux Klan,
Another form of God.[7]

Joining the Klan was interpreted as bringing about a transformation in men. Through Klan teaching and doctrine (Klankraft) men became purer, cleaner. Their vision became clearer, focused, and centralized; they thus fully understood the task before them. Indeed, with a new vision, a clearer mind, purer thinking, a new MAN was created—such was the power of the Klan, through God. In the following piece the words in parenthesis are intended to demonstrate how the negative aspects of man have been surmounted by Klan doctrine. God's power, in conjunction with Klan principles, has brought about a metamorphosis and has created a "higher, nobler" individual.

**Transformation**
by H. E. R.
It has made him a Man * * * not a mere machine:
Flesh that responds, senses new and clean,
He has hated (how keenly!) and loved (how meanly!);
He has thought (how tamely!) and worked (how lamely);
He has called *this* worthless; he has thought *that* fine;
He has turned * * * vain pride! * * * Life's water to wine.
But now he has learned the Creator's Plan * * *
It has made him a Klansman! It has made him a Man!
It has taken him away from the years that hasted;
Washed him anew from these sins that wasted;
The joys swift speeding; the fashions receding;
Loving words unspoken; rash promises broken * * *
Away from the over-known, over-heard, over-seen * * *
Out of the rabble, the tumult, the spleen * * *
Through Time unrecked [sic] forever leading,
Onward and forward, the faster speeding,
Into the Free and the True * * * God's Own Plan * * *
Having made him a Klansman * * * it made him a Man![8]

The following poem interweaves the teachings of Christ and patriotism. The symbolism used to demonstrate the influence of Christ and the concept of patriotism is the burning (fiery) cross—the Klan standard.

**The Fiery Cross**
by E. C.
It stands for the light that Jesus spread
In teaching and through sacrifice
That light which streams from overhead
Dispelling darkness, greed and vice
It stands for faith, which like a fire
Burns steady in the patriot soul
In time of crisis flaming higher
To light us toward the sacred goal.
It speaks its message from the hill
Though Midnight blackness wraps the earth
And proves that men are watchful still
O'er principles their sires gave birth.[9]

From a religious perspective, the Klan preached the idea of brotherhood; of the need to overcome the dark side of human nature. In this sense it preached the essence of the "good book" and the teachings of Christ. The problem is that through its dogmatic racial/religious thinking, the hooded order saw only darkness in non-white, non–Protestant groups. These groups could not be redeemed because of their inability to understand patriotism; adherence to the wrong religion; devotion to un–American ideals, or their inferior racial makeup. But Protestant whites could be saved thus the Klan, in its religious crusade, worked towards uplifting this chosen group. In the next poem may be seen the battle between good and evil in man as represented by Dr. Jekyll and Mr. Hyde. Ultimately, the good in the white race can succeed if it suppresses Mr. Hyde and allows Dr. Jekyll to shine through and overcome the dark side of human nature.

**Our Dr. Jekyll and Mr. Hyde**
by a Prominent Vermont Klansman

Yes, Dr. Jekyll and Mr. Hyde
In Spirit still with abide,
As double man who look two ways,
And lives two lives mid scorn and praise!
He lives in me and lives in you
As Dr. bright [sic] and cheerful, true;
But when he shows his other side,
His other self in Mr. Hyde.
The Pharisee as moral man
Is surely built upon that plan;
We deem him good, but fail to see
His other side of low degree.
The politician with a smile
Is built that way, who for a while
So loyal seems; his other side
For selfish ends is Mr. Hyde.
The hypocrite whom we deride,
Do more or less in all abide;
The truth we do not always speak,
Because our moral sense is weak.
By Dr. Jekyll if we would
We all could be a brotherhood,
But other self-that's Mr. Hyde
Too oft defeats the other side.
Then Dr. Jekyll is not free,
With Mr. Hyde in you and me,
Nor lesser grow; in all the race
Can clearly see his ugly face.
The answer is: it cannot be
Till Jekyll in us all is free
To hold his own with faith and might
Then live the good, enjoy the right.[10]

The symbol of the cross again appears in the following poem. The prominent theme in this particular piece is rejuvenation through religion. However, attention should be paid to the fifth stanza. This part of the poem alludes to the "divine" origin of the Klan. Not only is there a call to man, but there is a call to the Klan. The succeeding stanza also refers to the Klan's motto "Non Silba Sed Anthar" (not for self but for others) which alludes to their "unselfish" works.

**The Fiery Cross**
by B. W. B., Klan Giant,
  San Diego, California

From out the dark a wraith,
  Weird, looming 'gainst the night!
Device of ancient faith,
  A Cross! A flame! A light!
And lo, the pagan flame
  Consumes the badge of trust,
Until gray ash doth claim
  A Cross returned to dust!
Thus will this human cross,
  The fire of spirit fled,
Return to earth its dross;
  Gray ash, all cold and dead.
But as the flame doth burn
  The oaken cross away;
So shall the spirit earn
  Release from earthly clay.
A message unto man,
  A precept now retold,
A call to man and Klan
  Comes thus by symbol old:
To burn away the dross
  Of self, that clogs the Soul;
For selfish gain is loss
  In climbing toward the Goal.
For self 'tis shame to serve;
  But honor high to give
Our best without reserve
  That chivalry may live.[11]

As religion was central to Klan legitimacy, the organization saw itself as proselytizers in God's work. As such they were involved in attempting to turn individuals from their errant ways and thus gain new or renewed converts to the teachings of Christ. This was, with the support of God, a primary reason for their existence. The next poem addresses the need for God's assistance in the proselytizing activity which the Klan claimed was the essence of their existence.

**Soul Winning**
by Kligrapp of Beaumont 7, Texas

Give me a passion the lost to win,
    To save lost Souls from Hell and sin;
Let me, Oh Lord, as I pass this way,
    A kind helpful word say each day.
Create in me a clean heart Oh God,
    As the paths of life I trod;
Give me the tact that I might need,
    Give me courage to sow thy seed.
Give me the message that I should bring,
    As I tell of Christ my King;
Make me an Ambassador for the lost,
    Winning their Souls what ere the cost.
Give Souls for my hire,
    Of thy work I shall not tire;
Give me a passion the lost to win,
    And thy praises I shall ever sing.[12]

May times Klansmen, when giving speeches at meetings, would interject some poetry as part of their presentation. Such poetry was tied to the topic material included in the speech. This is the case with the next piece. The writer addressed the need of the Klan to continue in their work and bring "the real light of freedom from the horde of un–American aliens" to America. The light was "in the form of the fiery cross, the symbol of Christ, and the Ku Klux Klan."[13] And, if not done by others, then certainly, America can depend on the Ku Klux Klan.

**Awake! Awake!**
by the Grand Klokard of Kentucky

My country wanted a man one day
    To speak a message of cheer
To hearts that were weary, tired, and sad,
    And weighted with mighty fear.
She asked for yours, but it was busy quite,
    With your own affairs from morn to night.
Your country wanted a hand one day
    To do a loving deed;
She wanted two feet, on an errand for her
    To run with mighty speed.
But you with pleasure were busy that day;
    To her gentle call you answered "nay!"
And my dear country—was her work undone,
    For lack of willing hearts?
Only through manly men does she speak to men
    And then, through the Ku Klux Klan.[14]

By far the most commonly used title and symbol was the cross. Nothing need be said concerning the next poem; it follows the same theme as others—religion and patriotism.

**The Fiery Cross**
by the Klaliff of "Old Glory" Klan
  No. 385, PA.

Upon a lofty hill side
  A blazing cross of fire.
Sends forth its glorious radiance
  While flaming ever higher.
It stands for pure devotion
  For service for the right
For sacrifice and noble deeds
  For truth and love and light.
And as we gaze with reverence,
  Upon the Fiery Cross
May flames of love go through our hearts
  And burn up all the dross.
May we be fired with love sublime
  For our own country dear
And stand for all her principles
  Without a doubt or fear.
And as the cross its radiance sheds
  Upon the landscape wide
May every faithful Klansman's heart
  Be filled with solemn pride.
And as the sparks still upward fly
  And vanish in the night
Breathe silently a prayer to God
  Who leadeth us aright.[15]

As may be easily seen in the next poem, the main theme is anti–Catholicism. The piece harks to the founding fathers who are calling for the protection of liberty and freedom. These are being threatened by Rome which, according to Klan rhetoric, is planning to overthrow American institutions and subordinate the nation to the Pope and Catholicism. Klan rhetoric constantly warned of Roman Catholic influence which originated in Italy. Catholics in America, who owed their allegiance to Rome, simply were incapable of understanding the concept of patriotism and thus could not become Americans.

**Awake! Klansmen**
by a Klansman of Uptown Klan No. 213,
  Realm of Illinois

Awake, you sleeping Klansmen!
Awake and hear your call,
For all the world is asking–
Will you rise, or will you fall?
Shall we sleep? Not forever.
We shall heed our fathers' call,
With them, surrender never
Our Liberty, Freedom for all.

> Go forth, I say, to battle
> And fight with all your might
> The Papal plot and curse
> And spread the Gospel Light.
> For Christ alone is our Savior;
> He died to set us free.
> He is our mediator
> Twixt God and you and me.
> We need not Priest, Confessor,
> No masses, high or low,
> But Christ, our Intercessor,
> Who rose from the grave, you know.
> Oh, Klansmen! Klansmen, hear me!
> Go get your brothers in
> And you will share the Glory.
> A Soul, a Heart to win.[16]

A consistent argument found in Klan rhetoric is the idea of right and wrong. This argument was used both from a religious and patriotic perspective. The Klan steadfastly portrayed itself as being "in the right" as Protestants and "One Hundred Percent American." All those outside or beyond the influence of the Klan (especially those who opposed the order) were seen as being erroneous in their actions and thinking and thus "in the wrong." The next poem is suggestive of this type of conviction.

> **No Title**
> by J. N. M., E. C., (Exalted Cyclops)
>   Klan No. 76, Illinois
>
> Who is on the Klan's side
>   Always true?
> There's a right and wrong side
>   Where stand you?
> Thousands on the wrong side
>   Choose to stand
> Still 'tis not the strong side
>   True and grand.
> Come and join the Klan's side
>   Ask you why?
> 'Tis the only safe side
>   My Man.[17]

Dealt with in previous chapters is the Klan's symbolic representation of themselves as modern day Crusaders. Just as the Crusaders of the eleventh to the thirteenth centuries fought for Christianity in their attempt to regain the Holy Land, so too, does the Klan see itself at war against forces which it claims to be anti–Christian. These forces included a wide spectrum of individuals and groups who were non–Protestant, non–Anglo-Saxon/Aryan, or whose philosophies were deemed to be counter to American ideals. The four main groups primarily identified by the Klan as enemies of American principles were Roman Catholics, Jews, Blacks, and any incoming immigrants who were considered incapable of becoming Americanized. The following poem implies the similarities of the Klan with the "Krusaders" of old.

### A Krusader
Grand Chamberlain of the Realm of New York

I've heard of Krusaders in days long ago
Who traveled o'er land and o'er sea.
Their love for the Savior to eagerly show
And like them I now wish to be,
Their hopes and desires were in earnest accord
They searched for a Savior King's grave,
And they traveled with hearts true and brave
as their way to save,
I'd be a Krusader for my country's sake to protect
the great U.S. A. at its best,
Like the Krusaders of old, I have a duty to perform
to Keep all enemy's [sic] from our shore,
For my Savior and my Home, and my country's sake
I hereby pledge, never to forsake, my country and my Kamp,
As the Krusaders of old, I will not have to be told,
to keep Old Glory in its place,
Will you dear friend put your armor on,
as all Krusaders of old—fall in line with your armor on—now.
For God, Home and Country, I will always be true as Krusaders of old,
don't have to be told, to be true.[18]

The next composition revolves around the Klan Klaverns—the meeting places of the organization. Portrayed with a "home sweet home" type of image, it is seen as a "haven" for Klansmen. The piece also includes reference to the Klan of the eighteenth century and their assistance in securing "White Supremacy." Reference is also made to Stone Mountain, the "shrine" and "holy place" of Klan birth. Additionally, reference is made to the Klan's propensity to "investigate" those elements in American society which, from their perspective, threatened the nation.

### Klan Haven
Night-Hawk–Roosevelt Klan No. 11

Tonight the latest song should be
Ku Klux Anniversary,
So I will sing if you'll agree,
A verse, or two, or three;
The first that I will sing is this,
Lets [sic] do our little bit,
And go to Klaverns when they meet
And not stay at home and sit.
The next that we should recall

> Is a scene we'd like to fix,
> When first the Klan was organized
> In Eighteen Sixty-Six:
> A mountain top was their meeting place,
> A hundred men pledged faithfully,
> And now today we live to see
> Their gift for "White Supremacy."
> The third verse, lets investigate,
> Then I know you will agree,
> You should protect your dearest ones
> And so insure their liberty.
> And now to end let's not forget,
> Tho o'er this World we roam;
> We'll never see a finer sight
> Than our Klan Haven Home.[19]

Patriotism and religion are again the main theme of the following poem. However, along with reference to the cross, mention is also made of the robes "without a spot" which have been equated with the multitudes in Revelations.

> **A Klansman**
> by C. A. B., Chicago, ILL.,
>  Uptown No. 213
>
> 'Twas in a Klavern long ago
> They initiated me.
> There and then I took my oath
> A Klansman I should be.
> Up and down my back there went
> A wholesome honored thrill
> For every little word I meant
> With freedom of my will.
> I did not say a single word
> For fear or cause of hate
> But truths that everyone has heard
> In these United States.
> I heard a whistle soft and low
> The marching then did stop,
> And in the Fiery Cross's glow
> Saw robes without a spot.
> I knew right then as I looked on
> These men were strong and bold
> Then I with them did join in their song
> God help, Our Oath, to hold.
> Fear not to enter you who can,
> You'll find us strong and true.
> Our name you know, The Ku Klux Klan.
> Our Flag, Red, White and Blue.[20]

In the midst of the Great Depression, and two years before the *Kourier Magazine* ceased publication, the Klan was having difficulty maintaining its membership and remaining a viable organization. Times were such that eking out a living was more important than retaining membership in the Hooded Order. This was clearly understood by Klan leadership who saw the empire they had founded crumble before the economic onslaught. Those individuals who tenaciously clung to their dogmatic interpretations tried to keep the order afloat by recruiting new members or by coaxing prior affiliates back into the organization. The struggle to continue amidst the insurmountable economic and changing social atmosphere is the theme of the following poem.

**Shall We Quit or Shall We Fight?**
by J. E. M., Great Kludd,
    Province No. 4, Realm of Ohio

I want to let go, but I won't.
    I'm sick, it's true,
    Worried and blue,
    Worn through and through—
But I won't let go.
I want to let go, but I won't.
    There are battles to fight
    By day and by night,
    For God, Home, and Right.
I'll never let go.
I want to let go, but I won't.
    'Midst legions of wrong
    Let this be my song:
    "Oh God, Keep me strong
That I may never let go."[21]

As may have been noted, in some of the previous Klan poetry there appear requests for God's assistance. Throughout the Klan's written material there appear short two or four line pieces seeking God's aid and guidance to remain strong and faithful to Klan ideology. The next four line poem is an example of such supplication.

**Loyalty Prayer**
author unknown

To Thee, oh, God I call to Thee—
True to my oath, oh, help me be
I've pledged my love, my blood, my all;
Oh, give me grace that I not fall.[22]

The following is a pirated poem that represented the "manly" and "high ideals" claimed by the Klan. Included in the prayer which precedes the poem, are the Klan's claim of divine origin of the organization; its philosophy of Klannish, fraternal unity amongst "men of kindred thought," and it's ideology of white supremacy. First published in 1879, it was initially written and entitled *Wanted* by J. G. Holland. The same wording was kept except for the last four lines which were added by William Joseph Simmons. Simmons also retitled the work *God Give Us Men*. The poem is best read in the manner found in the October 1936 edition of the *Kourier Magazine* where it follows *The Klan Kreed*. The combination of the Kreed and poem pointedly demonstrate the spiritual aspect of the organization as professed by the Klan.

### The Klan Kreed
[author unknown]

I believe in God; Ineffable; Infinite; Eternal; Creator and Sole Ruler of the universe; and in Jesus Christ His Son our Savior, who is the Divine Word made manifest in flesh and demonstrated in life.

I believe that all men are free moral agents, each responsible for his every **act, free from subservience to potentate, prelate or priest**; each entitled to direct communion with God and accountable to Him.

I believe that God created races and nations, committing to each a special destiny and service; that the United States through its White, Protestant citizens holds a Divine commission for the furtherance of free government, the maintenance of white supremacy and the protection of religious freedom; that the Constitution and laws are expressive of this Divine purpose.

I believe that it is the duty of men of kindred thought, in fulfillment of these Divine purposes, to unite fraternally; that by so doing they increase the fellowship of men and more effectively carry out the will of God; that the Knights of the Ku Klux Klan is an Order in all ways conforming to these great principles.

### God Give Us Men

God give us men! The times like these demand
Strong minds, great hearts, true faith and ready hands.
Men who the lust of office does not kill;
Men whom the spoils of office cannot buy;
Men who possess opinions and a will;
Men who have HONOR; men who will not lie;
Men who can stand before a demagogue,
And damn his treacherous flatteries without winking!
Tall men, sun-crowned, who live above the fog
In public duty and private thinking;
For a while the rabble, with thumb-worn creeds,
Their LARGE professions and their LITTLE deeds,
Mingle in selfish strife, Lo! freedom weeps;
Wrong rules the land, and waiting justice sleeps.
God give us men!
Men who serve not for selfish booty.
But real men, courageous, who flinch not at duty;
Men of dependable character; men of sterling worth:
Then wrongs will be redressed, and right will rule the earth
God give us men![23]

The theme of the next poem is anti–Catholicism, similar to the adage that was to arise during the cold war of "better dead than red." This piece essentially states "better Protestant than Catholic." Implicit in the piece is that non–Protestants do not have the right to be Americans.

**Priest or Kluxer?**
unknown author

I'd rather be a Ku Klux in robes of snowy white
Than to be a Catholic priest in robes as black as night,
For a Ku Klux is an American,
And America is his home,
And the priest owes allegiance to the Pope of Rome,
And really hasn't got the right,
To claim America as his home.[24]

Different from the type of poetry included so far, the next poem shows how the hooded order attempted to make light of the innumerable accusations brought against the organization. Although not covering the typical themes that other pieces have dealt with, it is included to show how poetry was utilized to make the Klan appear less insidious.

**"The Goat"**
by Mrs. S. E. Bauchle

At last I've found
A reason for
The million things
That make one sore.
I never thought of it before,
Just blame it on the Klan.
Your furnace smokes,
Your tires are flat,
Your brakes won't hold,
You've lost your hat,
Don't rave and roar and kick the cat
Just blame it on the Klan.
"Fifty for speeding,"
Pretty steep,
Your rent past due,
You'd like to weep,
You see I. O. U's in your sleep,
Just blame it on the Klan.
Are you to blame if you're broke?
You are not,
You know why you lost the last jack-pot,
If heaven is too high,
And hell is too hot,
Just blame it on the Klan.[25]

Using a similar technique, there appeared another poem which ridiculed Louisiana Governor John Parker's attempt at curbing the Klan.

Like the previous piece, it did not include any of the Klan's favorite themes, it was simply a barb aimed at the governor.

**"Hearsay"**
anonymous

Absolute knowledge I have none,
But my wife's sister's washerwoman's sons
Heard a policeman on his beat
Say to a laborer on the street
That he had a letter just last week,
Written in the finest Greek,
From a Chinese coolie in Timbuktu,
Who said the negros [sic] in Cuba knew
Of a colored man in a Texas town;
Who got it straight from a circus clown,
That a gang of South American Jews,
Who knew of a swell society rake,
Whose mother-in-law would undertake,
To prove by her seventh husband's sister's man
That Governor Parker of Louisiana can't handle
The Ku Klux Klan.[26]

## *Part Two: Songs*

The following is a song which, like previous works of poetry, interweaves themes important to the Klan. Along with the Klan's anti–Catholic spirit (which included a nativist strain), it includes pro-school ideology (although not directly addressed but which advocated greater competition against parochial schools and reducing or eliminating teaching in public schools by Catholic teachers).

**Song of the Klan**
by the Great Klaliff, Prov. 2, N.Y.
(Tune of the Stein Song)

Hail all Hail the Ku Klux Klan,
Guardians of our Nation,
Fearing neither threat nor ban,
True to every obligation
Native born and tried and true:
Christians marching onward,
The Cross of Christ our only Banner.
The emblem of the Ku Klux Klan.
We will fight all our might to keep every school in our National [Nation?] Free
Let the Laws of our Land from Roman diction untainted be
In the sight of our God we are marching to certain Victory
That our Flag with its stars and stripes may wave on high Free!
Onward with the Ku Klux Klan.

Wake for there's work before us.
Heed the summons every man
Show the foe they can't ignore us.
Though we far outnumbered be
Right is our mighty armor!
AMERICA we hear you calling
The soldiers of the Ku Klux Klan.[27]

The next piece interweaves the two themes that until now have predominated—religion in the form of the cross, and patriotism.

### Onward Klansmen!
by Klan Giant, San Diego, California
(Tune unknown)

Onward, Klansmen, Onward!
With the Cross of Fire;
Onward for our Country,
Klansmen never tire;
Ku Klux Klan forever
Marching in the van;
All for God and Country,
Homes and fellow man.

*Chorus:*
Onward, Klansmen, Onward!
With the Cross of Fire;
Onward for our Country,
Klansmen never tire,
We're a mighty legion,
Battling for the Right;
We will never falter,
Marching toward the Light!
On for Home and Country,
'Til 'tis right that rules;
Onward with our Cross and Flag,
Onward for our Schools.
Protestants Awaken!
Guard against the foe!
Host of evil threaten,
Now as long ago.
Klansmen ever faithful;
Falter nor lag,
Forward to the battle
Neath the Cross and Flag.[28]

Anti-Catholic sentiments and patriotism are the overriding themes of the next composition. Rome is pictured as attacking and undermining American freedoms and government in an attempt at "foreign" control. The popular belief of secret "popish" plots and Catholic heretical and superstitious beliefs is very much evident.

**Patriot's Battle Hymn**
unknown author
(Tune unknown)

Freeborn Americans, behold!
Within our starry banner's fold
    The Romish viper lurks
Even now in Home and School and State,
With secret intrigue born of hate,
    Her deadly virus works.
Scourged from the land beyond the sea,
Her Jesuit minions forced to flee,
    Find refuge on our shore;
They come to sow the seeds of strife,
To make our land with treason rife,
    And Rome our conqueror.
In cloistered hall beyond the ken
Or watchful eye of fellow men,
    Their cursed plots they brood;
By pope absolved, their greed for gold
And lust for power have made them bold
    Against the common good.
Rome never sleeps, she changes not,
Her creed has ever been a plot
    'Gaisnt human liberty.
She dulls the conscience, dwarfs the mind,
Her superstitious fetters bind
    All souls that own her sway.
And shall we, craven, stand and see
Our native country bow the knee
    To foreign potentate?
Nay, deem not this but idle fear,
Rome's scheming vassals bide the hour
    When she shall rule the state.
Rouse then, ye patriots! front this wrong,
The hour has struck, the battle's on!
    Against this pirate crew.
Be not deceived by false pretense,
The freeman's ballot, your defense,
    Let every vote ring true![29]

As with other compositions, the following interweaves patriotism and religion through the "Fiery Cross." However, in this piece the third verse also refers to the Klan philosophy of "Klannishness" pertaining to a Klansman's duty of being bound to each other; to stand together fraternally and racially because it is a "sacred" duty.

**A Klan Hymn**
by J. W. T., Klan No. 44, Oregon
(Tune unknown)

Stand up, stand up, Ye Klansmen,
    Ye Soldiers of the Cross.

Be true and loyal ever,
   It must not suffer loss.
Fight on and on to victory,
   Our country we must save.
We'll press the battle onward,
   Be men both stout and brave.
Fight on, fight on, Ye Klansmen,
   Follow the Drum and Fife.
Lift high the Royal Banner,
   Fight on, it means our life.
Beneath the Fiery Cross,
   We pledged our life to Thee.
That we'd be true and loyal,
   And ever ready be.
Klansmen be true and loyal,
   Your Oath do not forget.
Stand by a Klansman always,
   Your duty do not neglect.
We are bound together,
   With loves most sacred tie.
We all must stand together,
   Never part until we die.
Lift up, lift up, Ye Klansmen,
   Hold high the Fiery Cross.
To it be true and loyal,
   It must not suffer loss.
We've pledged our life our all,
   That we would defend.
Till every Foe is vanquished,
   And Righteousness can stand.[30]

The next song, like other pieces, includes the Fiery Cross as part of the title. Religious in nature, the composition addresses the Klan's duty to Christ and country. It also alludes to the Klan as Crusaders.

**Let the Fiery Cross Be Burning**
(Tune—"Let the Lower Lights Be Burning")

On the hill tops, on the mountain,
   Brightly gleams our mystic sign,
Calling Klansmen to the fountain -
   Filled with drops of love divine.
*Chorus:* Let the Fiery Cross be burning,
   Spread its beam o'er land and sea;
Satan's wiles forever spurning,
   Bringing Christ to you and me.
Serried ranks in stainless armor.
   Kneel before the flaming tree,
Pledging life and wealth and honor,
   All for Christ and Calvary.
*Chorus:* Let the Fiery Cross be burning, etc.
Side by side, always Non Silba,

> Songs of praise and promise sing,
> Hand in Hand, always Sed Anthar,
> All for Christ, the Klansman's King.
> *Chorus:* Let the Fiery Cross be burning, etc.
> Clasp the Cross, Oh, Klansmen peerless,
> Pledge to God thy strength anew,
> Stand ye forth erect and fearless,
> Strike for home and kindred true.
> *Chorus:* Let the Fiery Cross be burning, etc.
> Rally 'round the sacred Altar,
> Purged of sin and baseless fear,
> Ne'er shall Knight in armor falter,
> Nor shall craven enter here.
> *Chorus:* Let the Fiery Cross be burning, etc.[31]

The following song, as have other Klan material, interweaves religion and patriotism. In their patriotic fervor the Klan included references to their philosophy concerning school and Americanism by using the images of the Little Red School House and Uncle Sam.

**The Klansman Ranger**
author unknown
(Tune—Texas Ranger)

> Come all you Ku Klux Klansmen and listen unto me;
> I'll tell you all a story of nineteen twenty-three.
> My name is nothing extra, so it I will not tell;
> Here's to you Ku Klux Klansmen, I'm sure to wish you well.
> When I was almost sixty I joined the Ku Klux Klan;
> We marched out to East Hammond and there we took our stand.
> Our leader there informed us, perhaps he thought it right,—
> If you ever reach the Truth, you'll have to get more light.
> The Fiery Cross was lighted, it brightened up the sky;
> The Truth dispels the darkness, the day is drawing high.
> The Ku Klux Klan is growing, their ranks are filling fast;
> They've volunteered forever, the die's forever cast.
> I heard the thousands cheering, our leader gave the command;
> To arms, to arms, he shouted, and by your banner stand.
> We took the obligation upon our bended knee;
> We volunteered forever all through eternity.
> I thought of my great nation, likewise my Bible too;
> I thought of Old Glory—the Red, White and Blue;
> Of the Little, Old Red School House and dear old Uncle Sam;
> And the thousands all around me, they said were Ku Klux Klan.
> Perhaps this is your nation, likewise your Bible too;
> Perhaps it's your Old Glory—the Red, White and Blue;
> But if it's not your nation and you are bound to Rome;
> I'll give your some advice, sir—You had better go back home.
> I am a Ku Klux Klansman as oft I've said before;
> My nation and my Bible I'll stand by forever more.
> May they be ever right as you can plainly see;
> I've cast my lot with both of them all through eternity.

The Ku Klux Klan are coming to clean things up to stay;
The enemy must retreat—he sure has had his way.
So rally all you Klansmen many a million strong;
The enemy is a foaming—he can't last very long.
We'll fight them to a frazzle with all that's just and right;
We'll meet them on the battle field where Jehovah gives light
We'll drive away the darkness from this, Old Glory's land;
The Ku Klux Klan are determined to rout them every man.[32]

Religion and patriotism are again the two themes of the following song. Of prominence is the anti–Catholic strain. Note should be taken of the allusion to the Klan's longevity. This is alluded to not only in the title, but also in the fact (according to the song) that it will still present at the time of Christ's return.

**When Time Shall Be No More**
author unknown
(Tune—Battle Hymn of the Republic)

When the papal forces gather as they always have of yore;
When they fight that last great battle all along the Limbo shore.
When they cuss and dam and rattle and they all rip, tear and swear;
You may rest assured forever that the Ku Klux Klan Will be there.
*Chorus*
The Ku Klux Klan are coming and they are coming now to stay;
And when they get to working they will clean things up, I say.
For they'll lit the Fiery Cross and it's brighter every day;
For the Truth is marching on.
When the greatest war's upon us and destroyers plough the sea;
When the papal castle crumbles and the human race is free;
When they cuss and dam and rattle and they all rip, tear and swear;
You may rest assured forever that the Ku Klux Klan Will be there.
*Chorus*
When the papal kingdom topples and its ruins rise in smoke;
When the poor deluded sinners cast away the faker's yoke.
When Christ gives light and freedom and he cleans the Limbo lair;
You may rest assured forever that the Ku Klux Klan Will be there.
*Chorus*
When the time of hell is over and Limbo's had its day;
When the faker's purgatory has forever passed away.
When the Dove of Peace is monarch and the Sword becomes a share;
You may rest assured forever that the Ku Klux Klan Will be there.
*Chorus*[33]

Religion and anti–Catholicism are major themes (in this case anti–Irish as indicated by the usage of the term "Caseys." The song also interjects the symbol of the Klan—the "Fiery Cross." As with other Klan material, non–Protestant "foreign" elements are pictured negatively (seen as cowards and mentally defective) while Klansmen are courageous, religious, and, in following the "Fiery Cross," are "fighting for the right,—truth against the wrong."

## I. The Klan, 1920–1930

**Hold the Fort**
author unknown
(Tune unknown)

See the papal force advancing, the old pope driving on;
Yellow backs and weak knees falling, -half-baked ones gone.
All the Caseys, all the bishops, all the little ones;
They are coming with much cunning but they'll soon be done.
*Chorus*
Hold the fort for I am coming, Jesus signals still;
Wave the answer back to Heaven by thy grace we will.
Ho my Klansmen see the signal blazing in the sky;
Fiery Cross by the millions, victory is nigh.
All the Ku Klux Klan are coming many millions strong;
They are fighting for the right—truth against the wrong.
*Chorus*
See the glorious banner waving, hear the bishops blow;
The Ku Klux Klan are sure to triumph over every foe.
The Fiery Crosses bring the dawning of a brighter day;
The darkness is disappearing, it must pass away,
*Chorus*
Fierce and long the battle rages but our help is near;
Onward comes the Ku Klux Klansmen, cheer my comrades cheer.
The Ku Klux Klan have come to conquer and they'll do or die;
There's no yellow backs among them, —that's the reason why.
*Chorus*[34]

A number of historical interpretations and comparisons are included in the following piece. First is the equation of the Klan to the Pilgrims who were in search of religious freedom; a freedom which, according to the Klan, it was protecting. Second is the encounter of civilization with "savages" wherein God assists his chosen people and the Indians are defeated. Just as the Pilgrims of old were successful in overcoming their adversities, so too will the "modern Pilgrims" succeed in their quest "for life, liberty and light." The piece includes references to the Bible which, as demonstrated in Chapter 4, was the bedrock of Klan existence and philosophy. Also mentioned is the Klan's desire to place and use the Bible in the public schools. Another item, previously touched upon and viewed from a religious interpretation is of America being the "promised land." And of course no Klan work would be viable without inclusion of patriotism.

**Freedom's Home**
unknown author
(Tune—Wearin' 'O the Green (or) The Soldier of the Legion)

Our fathers crossed the sea to build a Freedom Home;
They sacrificed for you and me to get away from Rome;
There were men with hoary hair amidst that Pilgrim band;
And now you see gray haired men who join the Ku Klux Klan.
*Chorus*

The Ku Klux Klan are coming all along the line;
They are all dressed up in uniform and they are looking fine.
Yes they are looking fine, yes they are looking fine;
They are all dressed up in uniform and they are looking fine.
The savage was on this side but the other side was hell;
The Pilgrims they did not fear—for here their God did dwell.
He led them o'er the rough old sea into the Promised Land;
And now the modern Pilgrims are the good old Ku Klux Klan.
*Chorus*
The Ku Klux Klan are marching with that old banner bright;
They've crossed the Rubicon for sure, for life, liberty and light.
That grand old starry banner must ever wave on high;
The Klansmen will defend it,—they'll defend it till they die.
*Chorus*
Do you see the Red School over on the hill?
It was built by our fathers and they put it in their will.
It's the symbol of the Public Schools that must forever stand;
There are millions to defend it now—they are the Ku Klux Klan.
*Chorus*
There is the open Bible,—the symbol of the free;
Surround it now with gattling [sic] guns to insure our liberty.
Put it in the Public Schools and put it there to stay;
If you have to use your gattling guns use them right away.
*Chorus*
If you take the Bible for your guide on the ship of life;
You'll never need to fear the breakers of bitterness and strife;
The Bible is the only guide for all true loyal men;
It will guide you to the star of Love that shone 'round Bethlehem.[35]

The following composition addresses the "divine" origin of the Klan. Upon its "birth" heaven was filled with joy and "Gabriel blowed his horn." The Klan is the "manna" that is to be given to humanity (or at least America); it will "spread the light of Truth everywhere." The song also alludes to the Klan's "law and order" philosophy and includes the ever reliable inspiration of patriotism.

### When the Ku Klux Klan Was Born
author unknown
(Tune—When the Roll Is Called Up Yonder)

On that bright and cloudless morning when the Ku Klux Klan were born;
And the glory of their birthday we did share;
There was joy all over Heaven, for Gabriel blowed his horn;
When he saw the pure white robes they did wear.
*Chorus*
When the roll is called up yonder,
When the roll is called up yonder,
We'll be there.
Yes the trumpet of the Lord did sound but the time shall be some more;
For that birthday broke eternal bright and fair;

When the Ku Klux Klan were born over the Dixie shore;
Then like manna they sprang up everywhere.
*Chorus*
Let's labor for the glory and improvement of mankind;
Let us spread the light of Truth everywhere;
Then when our march is over down the long slopes of time;
And the roll is called up yonder, we'll be there.
*Chorus*
The time is surely coming and the day is drawing near;
When corruption must go down with the past;
Stand by the Constitution and you'll never need to fear,
For Old Glory will be waving till the last.
*Chorus*[36]

As with previous compositions, the following is anti–Catholic in nature. The piece also includes allusions to the "divine" origin of the Klan. This can be interpreted through the fact that God's "hand is writing on the wall." It is also seen in the Klan's acquisition of "faith, zeal and courage" through which it "dares to do the right." This is possible because "God gives it [faith, zeal and courage] to the Klansmen." As in previous works Catholics are portrayed negatively, in this case as "wine-soaked sons of sin" and murderers who adhere to the wrong brand of Christianity; they are part of "the faking gang."

### When the Ku Klux Klan Came In
unknown author
(Tune unknown)

At the feast of the bishops and that old faker man;
They were seized with consternation when they saw the Ku Klux Klan.
They were all corn-fed cattle and wine-soaked sons of sin;
And their bones began to rattle when the Ku Klux Klan came in.
*Chorus*
It's the hand of God on the wall; it's the hand of God on the wall;
Their records were found wanting, they never could be trusted;
But that had is writing on the wall.
Their chains were being forced on our good old Uncle Sam;
The greates[t] feast of all was before the faking gang.
But old Uncle sure did kick, he said it was a sin;
Then the Fiery Cross was lit and the Ku Klux Klan came in
*Chorus*
Their knees began to knock and their bones began to rattle;
For all their gold and silver could not save those corn-fed cattle.
Their kingdom was weighed down with the basest sorts of sin;
No wonder they got rattled when the Ku Klux Klan came in.
*Chorus*
Their deeds were recorded, their awful deeds of gore;
They've murdered many millions and would like to murder more.
This blood cries from the ground against the Man of Sin;
Their days are surely numbered, for the Ku Klux Klan came in.
*Chorus*

Yes, their deeds are recorded there's a hand that's writing now;
Truth and Justice shall triumph, and you'll all have to bow.
For they have built on corruption and every sort of sin;
They sure did get excited when the Ku Klux Klan came in.
*Chorus*
See the brave Ku Klux Klan as they stand before the throng;
And rebuke those wine-soaked sinners for their dirty deeds of wrong.
As they read out the writing, it's the doom of one and all;
For their kingdom now is finished, says the hand upon the wall.
*Chorus*
It takes faith, zeal and courage that dares to do the right;
This God gives to the Klansmen, it's the secret of their might;
In their homes on mount or valley, in shack or palace hall;
They understand the writing of the hand upon the wall.
*Chorus*
Their evil empire's ending they sure have had their day;
And with them sin and sorrow shall forever pass away.
So good by [sic] you old boozers, farewell you faker gang;
You've wrecked your ship in Hades and there is where you land.
*Chorus*[37]

# SECTION II
# BEYOND 1930

## 6

## *Klan Rhetoric*

With the exception of Chapter 5, which contains printed material after the 1920s, all previous chapters dealt with the Klan of that decade. The exception is the inclusion of material from more current authors whose studies delved into the religious characteristic of the 1920s Klan. In such instances, the material was utilized as a means to substantiate the religious interpretation of this work. This chapter is inclusive of material from the 1930s to the present. The data will demonstrate the continued emphasis on religion by the Klan to maintain their legitimacy, keep their organization alive, and garner new members.

The Klan never ceased to espouse its philosophies and enshroud them in religious rhetoric. The Klan Creed, as written and published in the January 1932 issue of the *Kourier Magazine*, began with the words "I believe in God." The creed also included the Klan's belief in Christ and "that God created races and nations, committing to each a special destiny and service"; that within the United States the "white Protestant citizens hold a Divine commission for the furtherance of free government, the maintenance of White supremacy and protection of religious freedom." It was the duty of Klansmen "to unite fraternally for the fulfillment of these Divine purposes." By following their creed of fraternal unity the Invisible Empire would "more effectively carry out the will of God," and, it was clearly understood "that the Knights of the Ku Klux Klan is an Order in all ways conforming to these great principles."[1]

As noted in previous chapters, the Klan solicited God's assistance in defense of the nation. The organization asked God for "the necessary intelligence to meet these problems through the principles of the Klan." It asked God to "keep ablaze in each Klansman's heart the sacred fire of devoted patriotism to our country and its government." And, through Christ, the Klan beseeched God for assistance: "Oh God! For Thy glory and our good we humbly ask these things in the name of Him who taught us to serve and sacrifice for the right. Amen."²

Addressing the myriad of problems confronting the nation, an Exalted Cyclops of Wisconsin asserted that Americans had "apparently lost some of the Idealism of other days, I have referred to the ideals which our forefathers brought to these shores. The ideals of genuine democracy, a free religious life, the building of a righteous ministering nation."³ Viewing the world as "a neighborhood and the human family as a brotherhood," the Klan leader asserted:

> I believe it's time for each Klansman to live up to the sacred oath taken in regard to his duty to God, that this country is near a revival of religion, religion that places its emphasis upon right relations with God and our fellow men; that will bring back prayer, honest dealings, faithfulness to the duties of life; that will teach us never to engage in any laudable undertaking without invoking the aid of God.
>
> To help its realization, the swords of the K. K. K. Ks. are consecrated, and of His Kingdom there shall be no end.⁴

As demonstrated, it was through Christ that Klansmen represented the best of humanity. Symbolic of the service provided by Klansmen was the order's "Klan Kard" whose significance embodied unselfish Christian and patriotic objectives. The "Kard" signified citizenship in

> the Invisible Empire and carrying the title of Klansman, a most honorable title among men, that he is a follower of Jesus Christ a Klansman's Criterion of Character, that he is a citizen in a land where democracy rules and brotherhood prevails, that he is a member of an organization that is serving the Nation patriotically, without reward, but with a determined meaning for preservation of American ideals and institutions, that he is an American citizen.⁵

Furthermore, the Klan's focus and utilization of Klankraft would assist in disseminating the good works of the organization. Klankraft, when coupled with religion, was the key to correct and proper living. According to a Kligrapp of Georgia, "Klankraft is a system of living. It is something, as we are reminded in our oath that binds us, as Klansmen together, not only to ourselves, but to God as well." If a Klansman "has fellowship with God, he will find some practical way to show his real relation to Klankraft and its ideals." The Klan official also asserted: "Klankraft is not a luxury.... We need Klankraft and religion to go forward in our movements." To demonstrate how religion and Klankraft would go hand in hand, the writer then stated three reasons for such beliefs:

> First: That Klankraft, with proper coordination with religion gives the only logical interpretation of life. Apart from religion, Klankraft would be worthless....
>
> Second: In order to fully carry out the real purposes of the Klan, we, as Klansmen, necessarily, must have religion to supply the needs for our soul.

Third: We need Klankraft just as bad as religion.... You can't do away with religion and have Klankraft. We as Klansmen must show our zeal for both to go forward.[6]

In a similar vein, a Kligrapp from an Ohio Klavern also touched on the relationship of the Klan and religion. He first asserted, "The principles upon which the order is founded are taken from the Twelfth chapter of Paul's letters to the Romans." He further stated, "It is not claimed, not intended that the Klan be a church, nor that it take the place of the church, but it is intended that the Klan be a powerful adjunct to the Protestant Church." The Klan official then went on to enumerate what the Klan stood for: law and order, freedom of speech, press, and conscience, free public schools, separation of church and state, and Protestant Christianity. Further, it was the "sworn duty of a Klansman to ... follow the teachings of Jesus Christ, the Klansman's Criterion of character."[7]

The ideology as stated above was again reinforced by the *Kourier Magazine* in a lengthy article entitled "Ideals and Principles of The Ku Klux Klan."[8] The paper enumerated four principles when expounding on the "CHRISTIAN IDEALS" of the organization. The first pointed to the Bible "as the basis" for the American Constitution. The Bible was of course "the most practical guide of right living, and the source of all true wisdom."[9] The next three principles were:

2. We teach the worship of God. For we worship the Lord thy God.
3. We honor the Christ, as the Klansman's only **criterion of character**. And we seek at His hands that cleansing from sin and impurity, which only He can give.
4. We believe that the highest expression of life is in service and in sacrifice for that which is right; that selfishness can have no place in a true Klansman's life and character; but that he must be moved by unselfish motives, such as characterized our Lord the Christ and moved Him to the highest service and the supreme sacrifice for that which was right.[10]

At the bottom of the same page as the above cited passage appeared was included a prayer in which assistance from God was sought to assist Klansmen "forsake the bad and choose and strive for the good"; that God assist in keeping "ablaze in each Klansman's heart the sacred fire of devoted patriotism," and again pointed to Christ as the "Klansman's criterion of character."[11]

In the same issue of the *Kourier Magazine* was included the preamble to the Klan constitution, as well as sections one, three, four, and six of the document. Included below is the preamble in its entirety. As written, one can easily see the rhetoric used to give the order a sense of grandeur. Included are references to the spiritual purposes of the order, its patriotic appeal, as well as a supplication for God's assistance.

> We, the members of this Order, citizens and probationers of the Invisible Empire, Knights of the Ku Klux Klan, in order to insure unity of organization; to guarantee an effective form of government; to perpetuate our great institution through patriotic and fraternal achievements; to preserve forever its holy principles; to continue and make vital its spiritual purposes; to achieve its laudable objects; to attain its lofty ideals; to consummate its mission and to promote effectively all things set forth in the Imperial Proclamation herein; do declare this Constitution of the Knights of the Ku Klux Klan, in lieu of the original Prescript of the Ku Klux Klan, as the supreme law of this society, and pledge our voice, our loyalty, our manhood and our sacred honor to enforce the same. In our endeavor toward the faithful fulfillment of this, our honorable mission, we solemnly invoke the guidance and blessings of Almighty God in behalf of our country, our homes, our race and each other, now, and unto generations yet unborn.[12]

At the end of the article, the paper included a benediction, again seeking the "blessings of God." In ending the prayer, the paper reversed the words of the order's designation of Invisible Empire to "Empire Invisible" in reference to God's Kingdom in seeking for it's dead, Christ's salvation for departed Klansmen: "and when death shall summon thy departure may the Savior's blood have washed thee from all impurities perfected [by] thy initiation, and thus prepared enter thou into the Empire Invisible and repose they soul in perpetual peace. Amen."[13]

In another Klan publication the issue of white supremacy was expounded. The paper declared the superiority of native born whites and in a patriotic vein recalled the Pilgrims, Daniel Boone, George Washington, Benjamin Franklin, Abraham Lincoln, and Robert E. Lee. It then stated: "Surely the blood of kings and potentates could be no more royal—no lineage more noble." The paper also professed the need to ensure white "blood not be polluted, but kept pure as a sacred heritage." In this manner the white race and America would "take its place at the pinnacle of all nations of the world where purity, Christianity, peace and prosperity reign supreme." This was "one of the ultimate desires of the Knights of the Ku Klux Klan."[14] This ultimate desire would always "be the earnest endeavor of the Knights of the Ku Klux Klan ... through Christ Jesus our Criterion of Character."[15]

An integral aspect of white supremacy dealt with miscegenation. For the Klan of the 1920s (as it still is for the present Klan), this was a critical and essential element in the maintenance of white supremacy. Miscegenation was seen as detrimental as this would weaken the white race. From a religious standpoint, this activity was seen as a direct affront to God's dictates. E. F. Stanton, minister and supporter of the Klan, explained that all plants and animals acted according to God's will. The exception was man: "Man is the only creature that mates wrongfully. Concerning the principal affairs of life, in some respects other creatures are wiser than man."[16] Stanton cited the prophets regarding mixed marriages and stated, "Klansmen are opposed to marrying strangers. A pure civilization cannot exist with impure blood." As a result of admonishments by biblical prophets, "the seed of Israel separated themselves from all strangers and stood confessed in their sins." Further, Jews "separated from Israel all the mixed multitude." The Klan, affirmed Stanton, was intensely involved in "freeing America from the crimson curse of marrying strangers. It is the crime of crimes in all ages and climes." Miscegenation was unequivocally "a dishonor to God and disgrace to Man." From Stanton's perspective, "For the purpose of being elevated the blacks enjoy mixing with whites." The results, however, were disastrous because "wreck and ruin, decay and death always follow."[17] A close review of Stanton's opinions (although not the only person to delve into this issue), demonstrates the link between the Klan of the 1920s and the issue of miscegenation and Seed Line theology that became a matter of extreme concern for later twentieth and early twenty-first century Klans and White Identity groups. This topic will be covered more extensively later.

In an article entitled "Sparks from *the* Fiery Cross," a writer for the *Fiery Cross* recounted the rise of the Klan in 1915. Climbing Stone Mountain in Georgia, William J. Simmons and his companions reached the top and there "chose enough stones to build an altar." A wooden cross is made "from a storm stunted pine" and a Bible, an American flag, a sword, and water are produced as part of the items used in the ceremony reviving the Ku Klux Klan. The cross is then set on fire. "The Fiery Cross!" The "symbol of the Scottish clans of old, the rally-sign of an ancient race of free, fearless, God-loving warriors who had represented the purest and proudest strain of blood the world has ever known." The men on top of the mountain: "reverently, in the glow of the symbolic Cross of Flame, they dedicated themselves to the cause and principles of Americanism and Protestantism. Their oaths they sealed with the Bible, the flag, the sword and the crystal clear water."[18]

The writer recounts how the Klan "saved" the South and preserved "white supremacy in these United States" after the Civil War. To the Klan was owed the salvation of the nation, and once its "mission" was completed the Klan was dissolved with the promise "that the Fiery Cross quickly would be rekindled should need for it arise." That need arrived in 1915. There was war in Europe, "unrest at home, social, industrial and racial disturbances. Churches stood empty, Bibles were unopened, and flagpoles erected for the Stars and Stripes were growing rusty from disuse."

On top of this, "thousands of aliens were roaming the land unchallenged, preaching their deadly doctrines of revolution and [un]godliness." In response to this "the Invisible Empire was awakened out of its long sleep. Its Fiery Cross relighted on the dark heights of Stone Mountain." There was an instantaneous reply and "the response to its Sacred summons was little short of magic." The Klan once again saved the nation, it swung into action as

> hurricanes created by religious minorities are battering the gallant old ruin this way; tornadoes caused by racial minorities are hammering her that way. Down— she is sinking, down, down. America is doomed. America is doomed.
> But wait a minute—
> The Ku Klux Klan is riding again. The Fiery Cross is ablaze. The Imperial Wizard has sent forth the Imperial Summons North, South, East and West, the Klansmen are rising. Like clouds forming against the sunset, their ghostly legions are falling into line. The bugles have sounded "Forward." The charge is under way. Right now, this instant the battle is booming.
> Don't worry about America. The Klan will save America. It always has. It always will.[19]

In another issue of the *Fiery Cross*, the Imperial Wizard, by this time (1940) James A. Colescott, sketched another instance in which the Klan saved America. Using the word introduced to the world by Germany, he referred to the "Roman blitzkrieg" in the election of 1928. In that year, according to Colescott, "the Catholic hierarchy decided to put an end to troublesome freedom-loving America by destroying her." To this end, "the Scarlet Mistress of the Seven Hills decided to destroy America by absorbing her into the Holy Roman Empire." Colescott portrayed Rome as involved in a plot to place Alfred E. Smith, the Democratic Party candidate and a Catholic, in the White House. As pictured by Colescott, "That absorption and destruction would be achieved by the simple expedient of placing a faithful prince of the Church at the head of the United States government." Once again "the fate of America looked hopeless. For the moment, it seemed inevitable that the Roman's [sic] would conquer. Then came the Ku Klux Klan." In the words of Colescott: "Like a phoenix rising from the ashes, the Klan, asleep for half a century, sprang to life. Overnight its white hosts were riding upon every road in the land. Its Fiery Cross, symbol of 100 per cent Americanism, blazed in every city, village and rural countryside." According to the Imperial Wizard, "Americans rallied to the Fiery Cross by the millions." Consequently, "the Ku Klux Klan sent America's enemies down in the most ignominious defeat ever recorded at the ballot box." By so doing, "The Catholic blitzkrieg of the United States had been smashed by the Ku Klux Klan." But it was now 1940 and Colescott saw another Catholic plot underway. With the exchange of envoys between the U.S. and the Vatican, the Imperial Wizard saw the Catholic Church and the Pope attempting to capture the White House "by way of the back door." And as for the chief executive, Colescott said, "Poor President Roosevelt—God pity him!" From Colescott's perspective the exchange of envoys was simply "part of the second papal blitzkrieg."[20]

In December of 1939 a "Christmas Greetings" was published in the Klan national paper. The piece dealt with the meaning of Christmas, the work of Christ, and His unselfishness towards mankind. Just as Christ worked unselfishly for humanity, so too did the Klan lift "high the Fiery Cross that America may see the light and direct her footsteps in the pathway of safety." In explaining what the Klan represented the paper said, "It is Christian, it is American, it is white, it is patriotic, it is unafraid, it is charitable, it is unselfish, it is Protestant, it is militant." The paper also called upon "Klanspeople" to "rededicate ourselves to the Holy service of our God, our country, our Klan, our homes and each other." In ending, the periodical declared: "Let us remember, and never forget, that from the teachings of Christ came our slogan: 'Not For Self, But For Others.'"[21]

At the Eighth Imperial Klonvokation held in 1936, Imperial Wizard Evans gave thanks "for the divine providence that permits us to come together once again in Klonvokation." He also praised the women of the Klan in whom "we have found inspiration to do a magnificent service to our God and our Country." He gave thanks to God for "that perfect union of minds and souls between the men and women of the Klan which will enable us to more effectively serve God and our Country." He also asserted: "The sign of the fiery cross, the insignia of the Klan" had brought people in America closer together. The Imperial Wizard declared it was the purpose of the Klan to keep America free and out of European entanglements; and, he proclaimed: "we will always be found fighting on the side of God and man."[22]

In the early 1950s, possibly as early as 1953, definitely by 1954, an exceedingly radical and bigoted Klan-supporting paper known as *The Aryan Knight Views*, later *Aryan Views and White Folks News* began publication in Waco, Texas. The paper was published in the form of a newsletter and appears to have ended publication perhaps in 1964 or 1965. Religion, the central issue of this work, was addressed by Horace Sherman Miller, publisher and editor. His views enveloped and presented Klan philosophies in such a manner that he referred to them as the Ku Klux Klan religion. In the first instance in which such a reference occurs, Miller is denouncing the Supreme Court decision of *Brown vs. Board of Education of Topeka* (1954). Extolling white supremacy, and exceedingly critical of desegregation, Miller accused the Court of being swayed by communists; of overstepping its legal bounds; of disregarding previous Court precedents; of ignoring and possible destruction of the Constitution, and, through its decision, bringing into question the legality of the Texas state government. He then stated, "Stand on the principle of the Aryan Race and the Ku Klux Klan religion, ready and willing to sacrifice our lives for the Constitution. Without it, enslavement is sure."[23]

In her work, *Gospel According to the Klan*, Kelly Baker emphasizes the need to accept the religious belief of organizations such as the Ku Klux Klan as valid, irrespective of how radical such beliefs may be:

> If supremacy movements maintained the legitimacy of their world views, then scholars must take seriously their claims no matter how extreme. The religion of the Klan should be seen as religion. The religious systems of the hate movement, believable or not, influenced their members and often supplied divine mandate for their racism, hate, and the purpose of the community.[24]

Additionally, irrespective of how the Klan may be viewed, their beliefs and actions are relevant and formed the basis for America's white nationalistic religion, inclusive of its racism, separatism, and biblical interpretations. Quoting Baker again:

> Klansmen and Klanswomen developed their own form of what they ought to do.... To see how morality influenced them gives a clear sense of how religion and nationalism were bound together for the order. It also demonstrates that religious people do not necessarily embrace principles that would better humanity. Rather, religious actors are complicated and contradictory, and they use their religious beliefs and actions for the benevolent as well as the malevolent. The Klan as a case study showcases how religion in the United States has not always been a force for civic good or progress, and adding the Klan to the American religious landscape illuminates the seamier side of American Christianity.[25]

In effect, the Klan, and its brand of religion is legitimate because it is their belief, as any belief is legitimate for any American religious mainstream denomination. Such was the case for Horace Sherman Miller.

Part of Miller's beliefs, as is the case for white supremacy groups, was his excessive anti–Semitism. He objected to the confirmation by the U.S. Senate of Joe E. Estes to a governmental post "because he is a member of an organization that uses the Kol Nidre prayer to make null and void his legal oath to the.... Constitution." Miller objected to the Jewish prayer recited on the eve of Yom Kipper. The prayer declared null and void all vows made rashly by members of the community during the past year. The vows, however, apply only to those made between man and God, not between individuals. Apparently Miller saw no difference and set forth a resolution addressed to the U.S. Congress concerning the Kol Nidre, Communists, and religions not conforming to his perspectives.

**Concurrent Resolution**

> Whereas Communist, et al, religions and other forms of invisible International, Universal, religions constitute a denial of the inalienable responsibilities of the Aryan Race and the Ku Klux Klan religion; and
> Whereas The Aryan Knight of the Ku Klux Klan religion of the United States have traditionally supported the aspiration so the legal oath to achieve self-government or independence against Communist oath taker and in their struggle against tyranny and domination of International, Universal invisible government; Now, therefore be it
> Resolved that House of Representatives (The Senate Concurring), That it is the sense of the Congress that the United States should administer no "Kol Nidre" policies or programs of the International, Universal, invisible religions but exercise its legal influence so as to support our Aryan Race and Ku Klux Klan religion.[26]

To Jews and Communists must be added Blacks (referred to as Mau Mau from an uprising by an African ethnic group in Kenya), who were seen as another of the many enemies of the Klan that were out to destroy America and the white race. The "Mau Mau monster," according to Miller,

> is out to destroy our Aryan Race and our Ku Klux Klan religion. It come from the Soviet pusher's hell beneath animality [sic].
> Many falsehoods have been and are being circulated against the Ku Klux Klan religion saying that we are narrow, bigoted and that we are for protecting our kind to exist. The Aryan Race and Ku Klux Klan religion has all ways been and still are champions of freedom. We believe in absolute liberty to protect our purity.
> We are for our Klan religion and do oppose corrupt doctrines and are against our Aryan Race and Klan religion cooperating with Talmudists because of their "Kol Nidre" Testament.[27]

Through his unorthodox interpretation of Klan religion, Miller asserted it was separate from Protestant forms. In the continuation of the above citation, Miller presented a broad assessment of what Klan religion meant:

> We are not for PROTESTANTS (Klansmen are not PROTESTANTS). We are not for co-existence with protestants as such. Because to co-exist with them would be telling you that protestantism is good when we definitely know that many of its doctrines are of the Talmud.
> We are not for protestant preachers and we are opposed to inviting them to our Klan's pulpits, because in so doing we would teach our Aryan Race that the teaching of the Talmud is important when it has caused the division among our Aryans in opposition to the Klan doctrine which we have learned with purity; avoid the protestants.
> We are against the Jew-Catholic-Christ Internationale, and we are against our Aryan youth co-existing with Mau Mau mongrelizers. Because it is the Internationale commune which seek to lead the Aryan youth away from pure Klan religion instead of to it. We are dedicated to teach our youth a good work. Do not ask the Aryan Race and Ku Klux Klan religion to co-exist with the Mau Mau mongrelizers.
> The Aryan Race must preach its pure gospel; we do preach our Aryan doctrine

and our Klan has a responsibility to exist and we are ready to fight for that privilege and protection for our 48 State Republics and our purity. We believe that much good has been done through the Klan religion, because we preach purity of race and religion. We believe that the great commission was given only to the Aryan Race and that in carrying out this commission of purity we do not co-exist with the Jew-Catholic-Christ Talmudists who are not willing to declare purity of race. We won't co-exist with false teachers.[28]

The importance of religion to Klan ideology is clearly apparent in separate studies by two scholars. William Vincent Moore in "A Sheet and a Cross: A Symbolic Analysis of the Ku Klux Klan," who completed a content analysis of 45 issues of the *Fiery Cross* from 1968 to 1972 (different than the *Fiery Cross* of 1939–1944), noted that of the six major themes identified in his research, Religion received 19.5 percent (third among the six themes studied), of the 100 points assessed. In order of assessed importance, the six themes were: Race 23.6 percent; Internal Communism 21.4 percent; Religion 19.5 percent; Conservatism 13.6 percent; Patriotism 11.9 percent; and External Communism 9.6 percent.[29] Moore's work studied the fundamentalism of the Klan as reflected in its emphasis on religion. This fundamentalism in turn leads to either an aggressive posture based on the need to revitalize those areas of American culture seen as having deteriorated, or a defensive posture in which the individual or group is seen as alienated from the prevailing principles of the dominant culture.[30] It is the second posture that is most clearly seen in modern white supremacist groups.

The second work is that of Juan O. Sánchez, "A Content Analysis of the Political Leadership of the Ku Klux Klan in the 1920s." In his work, Sánchez explored the success of the Klan based on language usage. In order to assess the Klan's leadership, a content analysis of 109 articles obtained from six Klan publications from the 1920s was accomplished. In Sánchez's analysis, six language categories were utilized to ascertain the Klan's use of either transactional or transformational language as a means of determining the organization's leadership style. (Transformation language is one that brings about a positive and uplifting transformation of an individual or group. Transactional language is one that represents an exchange; for instance, pay for work as means of achieving and end.) Tied to Transformational or Transactional language usage were the language categories/themes of Immigration, Law Enforcement, Religion, Education, Racism, and Klan. While the first five categories are easily understood, the category of Klan language dealt with language used for self-identification and self-promotion.[31]

Sánchez utilized dendrograms as a means to analyze the relationship between the thematic word clusters to transformational or transactional language. The principal dendrogram, which included the 109 articles, demonstrated the relationships of the six language themes to transactional and transformational language. The dendrogram demonstrated that Religion was the third language category in relationship to Transformational and Transactional language. In fourth, fifth, and sixth position were Education, Racism, and Klan language, respectively. On a percentage basis, religion was the fifth most utilized language category, but as noted, third in relationship to the type of leadership language utilized by the Klan.[32] A was the case in the study by Moore, the study by Sánchez demonstrated the significance of religion within the overall Protestant theology of the Klan. For Horace Miller, his brand of religion was exceedingly important.

In his stand against desegregation, Miller accused Texas Governor Allan Shivers of abandoning "constitutional government" and Chief Justice Earl Warren of overthrowing the Constitution. Miller asked whether Warren could "TAKE AWAY YOUR FREEDOM TO SEGREGATE FROM ME AND FORCE ME TO MONGRELIZE WITH YOU AGAINST TEXAS LAW?" He asserted that "DISCRIMINATING AGAINST ARYAN RACE & KLAN RELIGION" would lead to mob rule and bedlam.[33] According to Miller: "The Aryan Knight asserts experience has shown the DESEGREGATOR could not be trusted in respect to responsibility." He also declared: "The Aryan Race and the Ku Klux Klan religion will not give up our independence to protect ourselves. The TERRIBLE KNIGHTS ARE ABLE TO AND DETERMINED TO DO SO."[34] As seen by Miller: "The major task of the Ku Klux Klan Religion is to inculcate the Aryan principles of finest citizenship." The Klan stood within all legal bounds of the law; was loyal to the government whose responsibility was to "furnish the Power for Protection."[35]

According to Miller, a combination of Communists, Catholics, and Jews were subverting the U.S. government. Miller listed a number of questions, the answers of which, when answered by Klansmen in the proper manner, would demonstrate the Klan was protecting the government. Among the questions were the following:

> Do you take an oath and swear before a Ku Klux Klan JUDGE that the Romanist Church organization takes "Kol Nidre" oath to destroy non–Catholic power?
> Do you resist the Cannon law of Pope?
> Do you resist Talmudists, Communists, Fascists, & Internationalism?
> Do you deny that the Roman Catholic Church persecutes the Ku Klux Klan religion?
> Do you guarantee the freedom of the Aryan Race and their Ku Klux Klan religion to teach purity and safety?
> Do you campaign against intolerance and racial hatred and [the] Ku Klux Klan?
> Do you pursue and try to crush the Ku Klux Klan religion of purity and assist in their carnage and rape and give thanks for their massacre?

## II. Beyond 1930

Have you read the Texas Declaration of Independence?
Have you read the OATH OF ALLEGIANCE of the Ku Klux Klan religion?[36]

Miller then went into a diatribe of anti–Catholic rhetoric and interjected the following: "OBEY THE ARYAN GOD OF TRUTH, AND ROME SHUTS ITS DOOR IN YOUR FACE. OBEY THE GOD OF LIES, AND ITS DOOR STANDS WIDE OPEN FOR PROMOTION." To Miller, Catholics and Jews were "rogues and hypocrites." Neither had any redeeming value, and "there is no difference between the Roman Commune and the Talmudah Commune." The one irrefutable truth, as seen by Miller, was white supremacy and the Klan: "The reality of the Aryan Race and its Ku Klux Klan religion must be regarded as proved as certainly as anything in scientific research can be proved."[37] However, since the Klan had many enemies and America was in danger, there was a need to confront the antagonists. Miller thus declared: "It is time for the Aryan Race and the Ku Klux Klan religion to rise and ride as never before."[38]

In protecting their own, the Klan of course barred all others that did not fall into their classification of white. Seeking new members, Miller proclaimed: "NON ARYANS, Asians and Africans and coloreds excluded."[39] Miller asserted the duty of the Klan was towards their own: "The obligation of the Aryan Knights and the Ku Klux Klan religion is to attend first, last, and all ways to the welfare of our Kith, Kind and Kin."[40] In his invectives against African Americans and Communists who he saw as undermining the U.S. government, Miller stated, "Come on, come on, The Aryan Knight and the Ku Klux Klan religion want men that are not afraid of the threats of an alien, Mau Mau pushing, people."[41] To assist in defense of "Klan religion," Miller formed the "Aryan Protection Association (A.P.A.)." Of the 14 "principles" enumerated under the A.P.A., the first read: "The Aryan Church includes all white people; upholding The Aryan Baptist, Aryan Methodist, Aryan Presbyterian Churches, et cetera."[42] Following the last enumerated "principle" was the A.P.A. oath which stated,

> I most solemnly sweat [sic] and promise that I will use my influence to promote the interests of the Aryan Church of white people—Liberty, Quality & Fraternity—and will seek the unity of our Kith, Kin & Kind to multiply after their own Klan; that I will endeavor at all times to place the political positions of governments in the hands of Aryans. To all of which I do most solemnly promise and swear, so help me God.[43]

Miller also railed against communists of all stripes and declared: "The Aryan Race and the Ku Klux Klan religion are pledged to AMERICANISM TO DESTROY COMMUNISM."[44] He asserted: "This organization-religion described as the Aryan Knights Ku Klux Klan, Registered Under Texas

Lobby Law, and publishing The Aryan Views.... White Folk News ... are uncompromisingly not pro–Communist." He further declared: "NO MEMBER OF THE ARYAN KNIGHTS KU KLUX KLAN OR THE ARYAN VIEWS ... WHITE FOLK NEWS ... HAS EVER SERVED ... THE COMMUNIST PARTY ... THE MEMBERS AND I, MYSELF, OF SAID RELIGION ARE UNCOMPROMISINGLY PRO-AMERICAN."[45]

Miller, like other Klansmen, used the cross as a rallying and reference point for the organization. Apparently referring to Jews who were viewed by Miller as mortal enemies, he exclaimed: "ARYAN CULTURE UNDER THE FIERY CROSS: TO TEACH THE REMEDY, NOT THE FAULT ... AND TEACH THEM THIS ART.... THE REIGN OF THE KLAN ... TRIUMPH IN DEFEAT...." Miller saw the white race on the edge of death, "helpless amid rags and ashes under the beak and talon of the Vulture Race. An 'Invisible Empire' must arise from the field of death and challenge the Vulture Race to mortal combat." Miller asserted that "the great doctrine, led by the reincarnated souls of The Aryan Knights of the Ku Klux Klan Religion" under the guise of the "Invisible Empire" would once more "save the life of White People"; that in so doing it would "form another one of the most dramatic chapters in the history of the Aryan Race and its Aryan Church." Declaring the Klan was "winning one victory after another," Miller affirmed: "Never has the Aryan Knights Ku Klux Klan Religion carried a heavier load than it is carrying today under the Vulture Race."[46]

Much as other writers referred to the "sacred fire" that was kept alive by the Klan, so too, did Miller refer to the mythical "sacred fire" that Prometheus purloined from heaven and gave to man.[47] As seen from Miller's perspective:

> It seems to me that this fire—this sacred flame—stolen from heaven itself for the benefit of humanity and guarded by primitive man as his greatest treasure is a symbol—a symbol of the sacred fire of freedom. If so, we of the Aryan Knights Ku Klux Klan Religion, The Aryan Church, may well consider ourselves to be the keepers of the sacred fire. For surely the history of Planet Earth shows that where Aryanism flourishes the fires of freedom brightly burn. And when once a despot, a usurper, seeks to enslave his fellows, his first step is invariably to outlaw Ku Klux Klan organizations, [he] has TO BANISH THE KEEPERS OF THE SACRED FIRE.[48]

Having interjected a religious interpretation, Miller then adds the patriotic aspects consistent with Klan discourse.

> Surely in America the fires of freedom were kindled by Kukluxmen by the precious blood and agony of our Aryan forebears. Bunker Hill and Brandywine, Valley Forge, Saratoga and Yorktown (AND ALAMO) bear witness to the price paid for freedom's light and warmth and fiery cross. When once the Flame of Freedom burned brightly on our altars, a shrine was needed to protect this precious flame from the

savage elements and the no less savage hands of would-be despots and tyrants. So our Government was born to house our new-won freedom.[49]

Fire and the "fiery cross" was the centerpiece during the initiation ceremony of inductees into the Invisible Empire, it was placed on the "sacred altar" when these individuals were becoming "citizens." Kneeling on their right knee the neophytes were addressed by the Exalted Cyclops who said: "Sirs: Neath the Fiery Cross, which by its holy light looks down upon you to bless with its sacred traditions of the past, I dedicate you in body, in mind, in spirit and in life, to the holy services of our country, our Klan, our homes, each other and humanity." The Exalted Cyclops then approached each candidate and "baptizes" them by pouring a few drops of the "dedication fluid" on their backs, on their heads, tossing some upwards, and moving his hand in "a horizontal circular motion around the candidates head." As he does each step he says: "In Mind, In Body, In Spirit, And in Life."[50] Once the initiation ceremony is completed, the initiates are escorted to chairs provided for them and the Kladd addressed the new members with a short speech. In the address, inserted below, can be seen the two emotional philosophies of patriotism and religion used to create a sense of importance and belonging in the new members.

> Fellow Klansmen, you have been elevated to a high estate and vested with the most honorable title among men. Klansmen. You are now entitled to receive a full explanation of the mystic signs and symbols of the Klavern. First upon the altar is placed the sword. It represents the indomitable courage of our ancestors who used it to sever the bonds of Old World tyranny, and carve out a new nation dedicated to liberty and freedom. It also symbolizes the willingness of Klansmen to defend and protect with their lives, if necessary, the government of the United States of America against any aggressor who might attempt to destroy it through violence. The flag, placed upon the sword, is the emblem of our pure patriotism. Its red stripes symbolize the blood of our forefathers shed freely that we might have the blessings of freedom. The white stripes symbolize the purity of their motives in creating a nation in which God might be worshipped in accordance with the dictates of individual conscience. The stars in the field of blue symbolize the heavens from whence came the divine inspiration which welded our fifty states into one union, indivisible and indestructible. The Bible is placed on the flag to signify that we recognize our government can succeed only insofar as we follow Christ's mandate that we give ourselves 'as a living sacrifice, wholly acceptable unto God.' Next to the flag stand the vessel of pure water which consecrated you in mind, body and spirit. The cross signifies the suffering of Jesus Christ, the Klansman's Criterion of Character, for the redemption of mankind. The Fiery Cross symbolizes a Klansman's flaming zeal in the protection of the ideals which you have to-night pledged yourselves to cherish and defend.[51]

In the first "lecture" given to the new Klansmen they receive an overview of the organization concerning its inception and activities during Reconstruction. The lecture relies heavily on the Dunning School interpretation regarding Reconstruction (named after William Archibald Dunning). The Dunning interpretation of Reconstruction was race biased and stated the South was prostrated under Reconstruction, and that Black political leaders were incapable of governing. Under this scenario the Klan rose to protect civilization and restore order through needed extralegal sanctions. According to this perspective, and the Klan's interpretation, the people in the post–Civil War South were "pauperized, bleeding, prostrated and defenseless." The South was visited "with a pestilence ... more terrorizing than the seven plagues of Egypt." The southern people's cry was "full of intense anguish,—melancholy groans and manly men struck dumb, mingling with the sickening, penetrating sobs of distressed women and the plaintive cry of hungry, cladless child."[52] During Reconstruction,

> Carpetbaggers, the vultures of gluttonous greed, swooped down form their aerie on the lofty peaks of the mountains of national authority o'er the dismal plain of human helplessness, fastened their tortuous talons in the fleece of defenseless innocence and consumed with avaricious avidity the vital flesh of the people's sustenance; and the scalawags—the conscienceless, cadaverous wolves of treason—gnawed the bones remaining to a baleful state of ghastly bleaching.
> 
> The chastity of the mother, wife, sister and daughter was imperiled and their sacred persons were placed in jeopardy to the licentious longings of lust-crazed beasts in human form. Might ruled over Right. Life and living was made intolerable; the rasping, discordant notes of penury had displaced the heavenly harmony of domestic happiness and no man's home was secure.
> 
> Ignorance, Lust and Hate seized the reins of State, and riot, rapine and universal ruin reigned supreme; the highest form of cultured society was thrust down and its noble neck was forced under the iron heel of pernicious passion who yielded to a potent scepter of inquisitorial oppression, and the very blood of the Caucasian race was seriously threatened with an everlasting contamination.[53]

But everything was made right when "from over the mysterious borderland from the Empire of the Soul the Ku Klux came." The Klan was the "knight errantry in the highest, noblest and gravest form personified." It was the Klan that "dissipated the cruel storm of the American reconstruction." Of greatest importance was the standard under which they rode. "With a 'fiery cross,' symbol of the purest and most loyal patriotism as their beacon, the Ku Klux Klan road through the darkness of Reconstruction's night; they dispelled the dense darkness of that frightful night, and at the rising of the sun of a glorious day, they saw the shades of that awful night receding."[54]

The lecture ends by asserting:

> The Spirit of the Ku Klux Klan still lives, and should live a priceless heritage to be sacredly treasured by all those who love their country, regardless of section, and are proud of its sacred traditions. That this spirit may live always to warm the hearts of manly men, unify them by the spirit of holy clannishness, to assuage the billowing

tide of fraternal alienation that surges in human breasts, and inspires them to achieve the highest and noblest in the defense of their country, our homes, each other and humanity, is the paramount ideal of the Knights of the Ku Klux Klan.[55]

Under the United Klans of America of the 1960s, a manual was written wherein was established a guideline for local Klans to follow. The manual explained the methods by which the Klans could be successful in ensuring the spread and maintenance of their philosophies. One of the methods employed was the establishment of committees to deal with specific areas of concern such as budget, welfare, propaganda, publicity, law support, and so on. Of significance to this work is the "RELIGIOUS ACTIVITIES COMMITTEE."[56] In the following citation is included the stated purpose of the committee, the membership makeup, and the duties that fall upon the members.

> The weakness of Protestantism as a social power it its internal divisions. When united it is irresistible. Upon this Committee devolves the sacred duty of bringing co-operation among all Protestants for the great, joint, Protestant purposes of the Klan.
>
> **Members**
> A Chairman and four to six members appointed by the Exalted Cyclops after consultation with the Kludd. As many denominations as possible should be represented, so that the Klan can have a spokesman in every church.
>
> **Duties**
> (a) To promote the spiritual welfare of Klansmen.
> (b) To promote campaigns and programs to disseminate the principles of Protestantism
> (c) To assist the Publicity Committee in combating all anti–Protestant propaganda.
> (d) To assist the Propaganda Committee in watching the activities of religious sects which oppose the Klan principles and program of Americanism.
> (e) To keep in touch with Protestant ministers of the Klanton and announce to the Klan any special activities of the churches.
> (f) To co-operate with Protestant ministers in promoting religious instruction for American children.
> (g) To assist the poorer children in attending services.
> (h) To promote harmony within the ranks of Protestantism, and work for unified action by all Protestants on moral issues, for their mutual interests and for the good of the community.
> (i) To promote the reading of church publications in Protestant homes.
> (j) To co-operate with the Public Schools Committee in promoting the reading of the Holy Bible in the public schools.
> (k) To watch public libraries for anti-religious, anti-moral, anti–Protestant and deceitful or questionable literature, and recommend measures to have such literature removed from circulation.[57]

As may be noted from the duties listed, religion in the form of "Protestantism" played a crucial role in the philosophies of the Klan. Coupled with their view of Christ as their "Criterion of Character"; their belief in their inception by "divine origin"; and their "foundation" based upon the Bible, the Klan was indeed blessed. To assist in the spread of their philosophies the Klan invited "all men who can qualify" to become members and "join in our noble work ... and in disseminating the gospel of Klankraft."[58]

Klankraft continued to be an important avenue to impart Klan philosophies on the Internet. The Texas Knights of the Ku Klux Klan (TKKKK), like other Klan organizations, argued that they were fighting against what they viewed as reverse discrimination and to uphold white Christian values. The order was "unapologetic[ally] committed to the interests of, Christianity, ideas, and cultural values of the White Christian Majority." Utilizing verbiage similar to the Klan of the 1920s, the writer stated the organization's foremost objective was "to unite white persons, native-born, Gentile citizens of the United States of America, who owe no allegiance of any nature or degree to any foreign government, nation, institution, sect, ruler, person, or people."[59] And, like the Klan of the 1920s, Klankraft was the process through which members would reach a higher spiritual level:

> Spirituality is the ultimate aim of Klankraft. It believes in the reality of spiritual values and seeks to project them into the whole sphere of its influence. It emphasizes the reality of spiritual things, and seeks to build up belief in the reality of spiritual life. It endeavors to lay old upon the spiritual qualities in a man's being and develop these to the very highest. It would cultivate the highest ideals and aspirations. It would develop faith, courage, confidence, sympathy, responsibility for others, self-sacrifice and service. It would make these qualities operative in every aspect of human life and conduct. Its method is instruction, and its medium is the ritual. It recognizes that without the cultivation of the spiritual, a man possesses neither strong character nor a true life.[60]

Klankraft was no doubt used as a means to reach the goal of the TKKKK which was "to unite White Christians through the bond of brotherhood and make them aware of the problems facing our communities and country. We educate them on how and when to take action (in a nonviolent way)." Affirming that the organization was a "patriotic, fraternal, law abiding organization," the writer also stated the order's philosophy: "Our ideology is simple, self-preservation and the advancement of the White Christian America."[61]

Being White Christians, the White Kamelia Knights of the Ku Klux Klan (WCKKKK), as did the TKKKK, indicated they were a "Christian Identity Klan." Both organizations utilized the identical religious arguments relying on biblical interpretations to support their views. The WCKKKK starts by providing an explanation of Christian Identity:

> **Identity Christian** simply implies that we identify our race as being the true descendants of the Israelite people. I understand that most people have been educated to believe that the jewish people are God's chosen people. Christians have even gone as far as to call themselves judeo-christians, they become extremely hostile at the Klan whenever this subject is mentioned. But, we are followers of Christ and even if our beliefs are unpopular, they are still correct. I am constantly told that Christ was a jew. That Moses and Abraham were jews, but, this belief is incorrect.[62]

Using Genesis as the basis for the argument, the writer states that the seed of Abraham was to populate all areas of the earth; that Israel will benefit all the peoples of the world. The question is how Israel, a small nation, can assist other peoples? The writer rhetorically states, "Maybe God lied, for the jews that claim to be God's chosen people are one of the smallest groups of people on earth and its existence has only been possible though the help of other nations."[63] Having raised the question the writer then provided the answer:

> No, God does not lie and he keeps his promises. It is the Anglo-Saxon, Germanic and Scandinavian people that has created great nations and civilizations. Through our laws and technology we have helped raise the standard of living for all the people on earth. Through our great knowledge in farming and agriculture we have helped feed the world and have taught others how to feed themselves. There have been many mistakes concerning God's chosen people "Israel," due to the mistakes in translating the Bible, but for me, a follower of Christ, I look to Christ's own words to clarify this mystery.[64]

Further proof was added by the writer when he included a variety of biblical interpretations from the Old and New Testaments that, from the perspective of the WCKKKK, demonstrated the true chosen people are white Christians.

The religious philosophies of the Klan permeate their websites through their pronouncements. An Imperial Kludd of the Original Knight Riders, Knights of the Ku Klux Klan affirmed that society could not understand the true feelings of Klan members. Klansmen and Klanswomen, however, held deep beliefs which were included by the writer: "The four things that all legitimate Klansmen and Klanswomen hold nearest and dearest to their hearts are represented in their beliefs and in their ages-old slogans: 'For God, Country, Home, and Klan'; 'For Christ, Country, Kin, and Klan'; 'For God, Race, Family, and Nation,' and 'For our God, our Nation, our Culture, and our Heritage.'" To further emphasize the devotion of the members the writer ended with: "Clearly honor, integrity, courage, and duty beat in the hearts of Klansmen and Klanswomen."[65]

Charles Murray, the Imperial Wizard of the New Empire Knights of the Ku Klux Klan (NEKKKK), also provided a short explanation of some of that order's ideals. Stating the order had been formed in March of 2013 because he and others had become "sick of the modern Klan groups which exist today," Murray explained the reasoning and provided examples of what the order was not: "The New Empire Knights of the Ku Klux Klan wants to return the Klan to greatness. We are not Neo-Nazi, drunk skinheads or criminals. We are White Christians who love God, His Son Jesus and the white race. Our mission is to educate our white brothers and sisters on true Biblical teachings, the truth about Jews and to expose the enemies of our great race." Murray included the order's stand on some elements of society and a conservative perspective concerning women: "We are against drunks, child molesters, wife beaters, drug addicts, lazy people who refuse to work and criminals. Only white Christian men can join our ranks. While we respect white women, we feel white women should spend their time raising our children, educating them and being keepers of the home—just like the Bible commands." This new Klan group would, according to Murray, "set the new standards of the KKK."[66]

As an independent order, the Church of the National Knights of the Ku Klux Klan Realm of Kentucky (CNKKKKRK) provided their own sentiments. According to an overview on their website, the CNKKKKRK, "acting in its sovereign and independent charter, want to establish justice, secure the blessing of liberty to ourselves and secure a future for our White Children, invoking the favor and guidance of almighty God." Declaring it was praying "to see our kids delivered form the darkness," it also affirmed there was "an assault upon our White Christian Faith" by the federal government. The writer also asserted the organization was on a "crusade ... to wake up the White Race" in order "to take the federal government's control out of our lives." Claiming the "liberal government governs against us," the writer further maintained it did not represent "White Christians." In order to counter the detrimental governmental policies, and as part of the crusade in which the organization was involved, the CNKKKKRK sought "White Christian men and women who have the same morals and values and believe in positive Christianity." As the government did not represent "White Christians," as represented by the order, it was therefore up to the CNKKKKRK to alleviate the shortcomings: "WE must rebuild the foundation of our White Children. The Holy Bible and Christ in our lives, schools, and public office will enable our Children to learn and live in a positive way. I call upon you, Sons and daughters of White Christians, America and the world in defiance of tyranny and oppression from this liberal government." Adding encouragement through patriotic appeal, the writer included a rhetorical plea: "Pick up your cross and sword wisely in the defense of our flag. I call upon you. Lay your hand to the robe of the Klan. Lay your hand to the robe of the movement. You were born of a free heart. Have the courage to follow it."[67]

The above citations dealing with Klan websites demonstrates that the modern Klan, much as did the Klan of the 1920s, uses religious rhetoric as a means to incite an emotional response aimed at validating its religious and social philosophies and acquiring devotees. The tone of the rhetoric, in the estimation of the author, has become more radicalized due to anti-governmental undercurrents. However, regardless of the argument, whether anti–Black, anti–Jewish, anti-foreigner, anti-gay, or anti-government, the basis of the argument is still predicated on religion. Religion, through God, Christ, and the Bible still provides the means to substantiate and validate Klan philosophies. This key characteristic of the Klan has remained constant.

# 7

# *God's Divine Providence*

Initially published in 1916, the *Kloran*, the Klan "Bible" (it contains the rituals and ceremonies performed when the order is holding its meetings—its "Klonklave"), went through numerous reprints and in the process underwent minor changes. The 1934 edition, as did all previous editions, contained the *Klan Kreed*, a sort of "Lord's Prayer" which embodies the beliefs of the organization. These beliefs were, of course, established by God, and it was "the duty of men of kindred thought to unite fraternally for the fulfillment of these divine purposes; that by so doing they increase the fellowship of men and more effectively carry out the will of God; the Knights of the Ku Klux Klan is an Order in all ways conforming to these great principles."[1]

The principles under which the Klan operated were those propounded by Christ and delineated by God. This was reiterated during the Eighth Imperial Klonvokation held in 1936. Addressing the influence of Christ and God on Klansmen, a speaker reminded the membership that if they lived "in conformity with the teachings of Jesus Christ" they would "be molding the temple of Klankraft." In so doing Klansmen would "be building a haven for those who come after us." And the building would not be through selfishness, "but on the high ideals and doctrines of living which God has outlined for us."[2] God, however, had done much more than frame a mode of living for Klansmen. It was through "Divine Providence" that God "has blessed us in giving us as our leader [Hiram Wesley Evans] a man whose vision, whose foresight, whose integrity of character and steadfastness of purpose has led the Klan to the victories it has achieved in the past." The Klan also felt "that Almighty God has bestowed his approval upon the Knights of the Ku Klux Klan and its endeavors by preserving to us through all the vicissitudes which have beset him during his tenure of leadership as our beloved leader."[3]

As may be seen, the idea of divine origin remained a strong and central argument in Klan writings beyond the 1920s. This precept was reiterated even in prayer, as demonstrated in the following citation:

> God of all, author of all good: Thou who didst create man and so proposed that man should fill a distinct place and perform a specific work in the economy of Thy good government, Thou has revealed Thyself and Thy purpose to man, and by this revelation we have learned our place and our work. Therefore, we have solemnly dedicated ourselves as Klansmen to that sublime work harmonic with Thy will and purpose in our creation.[4]

This ideology was again reiterated in the Klan periodical, the *Fiery Cross*, in 1939. In November of that year the Grand Dragon of Indiana proclaimed Thanksgiving Day a "sacred day." According to the proclamation, "In the divine providence of Almighty God there is shortly to be given the organization the sublime privilege of consecrating itself anew on the first Thanksgiving Day which we as an organized Realm shall witness." Each klavern was to summon five of its officials in order to prepare "a program which shall fittingly exalt the noble traditions" of the day. Accordingly, "above all other things, emphasis should be placed upon our responsibility to our Father in Heaven and our solemn duty to reconsecrate ourselves as citizens and Klansmen to the furtherance of His mighty cause." In seeking God's assistance in their work every Klansman was to attend their respective churches at the same time during the day, thus, "throughout the realm of Indiana as the prayers of countless Klansmen rise to Heaven, may God grant unto this great work the guidance of his divine wisdom and the strength necessary to the fulfillment of those purposes symbolic of the cross in whose light we march to Christian patriotic victory."[5]

The Christian victory for which the Klan worked was of course not only for its own benefit, but for other Americans as well. As stated by the *Fiery Cross*: "We seek that which will give unto others those things which insure the rights, the privileges, the opportunities that contribute to human happiness." The paper exhorted its members to join physically and mentally and work for "a glorious tomorrow." Even against staggering odds the Klan was sure to win because it had God on its side for, according to the paper: "All the powers of darkness have failed to destroy the Ku Klux Klan. Through storm of hatred we have passed. For months it seemed as if we would be overwhelmed by satanic forces, but God was with us and, therefore, we today are stronger for our experiences."[6]

In a similar vein there appeared another article in 1940 in which an Oklahoma Klansman pointed to numerous historical instances in which revolts against tyranny were characterized as the "Spirit of the Klan." More specifically, it was in the "history of the white race" in which was evident the "spirit to band together in secret for their own protection." According to the Klansman, it was this spirit that motivated the early Christians to gather secretly in the catacombs, and it was the same spirit that led the English barons to force the Magna Carta upon King John. The spirit was also reincarnated by John Calvin, Martin Luther, and John Knox. From Europe the spirit came to America and was manifested in the Boston Tea Party. This spirit was finally given a designation; it was "the Reconstruction period which made famous the name by which this spirit has become known—the spirit of the Klan."[7]

Using words which invoked the classical and distorted Reconstruction interpretation of William A. Dunning, the writer elucidated on the "Klan spirit." It was this spirit which arose in the South to save the white race, the spirit which, according to the writer, was "reincarnated out of the agony of the blackest night that ever afflicted any people, from over the mysterious borderland of the spiritual Invisible Empire of the white race—the shrouded legions of the Klan came riding." It was this spirit whose purpose was "as pure as the snowy white of their robes ... with a sacred devotion that faltered not at danger ... rode ... to save their God-given heritage of racial integrity." When white supremacy was once again established the Klan "reverently locked safely away in their hollowed archives every visible evidence of their physical form until such time as they were needed again."[8]

Such a need arose once more in 1915. In that year "the spirit of the Klan materialized itself again and another reincarnation ensued." The enemy this time were the "criminal, alien, Nazi, Fascist, Bund, and Communist un–American influence" which "loosed their vicious and venomous campaign of scandal, vituperation and hate" against the Klan. But the Klan could not be destroyed because "it is as strong as our American Caucasian civilization: it belongs in essence to the realm spiritual." Furthermore, destruction could not take place because of the divine origin of the hooded order. This was so because "from the Spirit of the Klan has been born a 'Spiritual Purpose' that is wholly American, and to achieve this divine purpose the Klan rides on today as never before."[9]

A direct reference to the divine origin of the Klan appeared in the *Fiery Cross* in June of 1940. In a one paragraph article entitled "Ku Klux Klan Still on Guard" the paper asserted:

> George the Third tried to throttle America, but God raised up the Minute Men who trusted Him and kept their powder dry. A foreign church emperor and machine politics tried to throttle America, but God raised up the Ku Klux Klan which lighted the way for American voters. Red 'brain trusts', and subversive 'fifth columns' are trying to throttle America, but God still lives and the Ku Klux Klan still says that only Americans shall be placed on guard![10]

The *Fiery Cross* again stated the belief of the Klan's divine origin in 1941. The affirmation came from a Colorado Klanswoman whose article was carried in the paper. The writer expounded on the need for Klankraft. She pointed to various areas throughout the world in which there existed social and political turmoil, and voiced the need to educate American citizens as to their responsibilities. This need was of divine origin for, as stated by the writer, "it is our belief that the 'Order is born of God' and that it will not perish from the earth until it has accomplished the great mission for which it came into existence." In attaining the completion of its divinely assigned mission the Klan would "stand against foes without and enemies within." Because of divine origin, success by the Klan was assured. In the words of the writer: "To paraphrase a great militant hymn; 'Like a mighty army moves the Klan of God' and nothing can deter their onward march."[11]

Horace Sherman Miller, publisher and editor of the *Aryan Knight Views*, in an open letter to its readers printed the following:

> OPEN LETTER, Oct. 14, 1955
> TO GENERAL TIRE & RUBBER CO.
> Plant Manager Howard Korsmo,
> Waco CIO-URW President Howard D. Lynn Lorena
> Governor Allan Shrivers,
> President Dwight D. Eisenhower, Washington D.C. et al
> TO WACO AND TEXAS KLANSMEN, et al
> My dear Klansmen, EVERYWHERE:
>
> You know God gave Klansmen the holy klannish instinct for our creed of "Racial Privacy," for values, advice, direction, liberty and property. Our Government of La, [sic] guarantees that Klansmen do have Racial Privacy. And God-given and Government-Guaranteed Racial Privacy far surpasses all Jew-nigger-loving psychologists and so called professional CIO-URW ...[12]

The letter continued in a rambling fashion decrying desegregation, labor, communism, politicians, and race mixing. The paper's assertion of "God-given" instinct and "Racial Privacy" are key features of the Klan's very existence; they are fundamental attributes bestowed by God. This is reiterated in another newsletter when the paper stated: "Our ARYAN CHURCH is dedicated: 'TO KEEP THE ARYAN RACE PURE,' because it is the Command of God and we represent the original KKK.... A Klansman is only bound to the original group morally and spiritually, because our religion can become effective if all people of the white race UNITE and that is also a Command of God."[13]

The *Aryan Knights Views*, like other Klan supporting periodicals, asserted that the organization's existence was the work of God. The paper, in a vitriolic attack against Jews, Catholics and especially communists, proclaimed itself as God's chosen people:

> There is something evil with God's chozen, [sic] in such situations, when it is getting ALONG with the authorities of the State. And it is terrible for God's choZen to get the police authorities to crush K.K.K. idealism for all to see.
> K.K.K'.S HOLY POWER OVERRIDES GOD'S CHOZEN IDIOTS
> The secret of the strength of K.K.K. lays in the fact that there IS a holy authority behind our words. We do not enjoy any recommendations from God's choZen idiots, or the authorities in power. WE ARE KNOWN BUT TO GOD AND HAVE GOD'S BLESSING. A KUKLUX CAN ASK FOR NO MORE FROM THE HAND OF HEAVEN.[14]

God, however, had not only given the Klan life, dictated separation of the races, chosen them above all others, and given the white race supremacy, but He had also given them their own "holy water." In a Klan publication that describes the rituals and ceremonies of the order, its method of organization, and its constitution and by-laws, there is included the "Naturalization Ceremony" whereby an "alien" (anyone not a member but qualified to become one) is inducted into the order. The Exalted Cyclops, during the Dedication part of the ceremony,

> *holds up the vessel from the Sacred Alter* [sic], *containing the dedication fluid, and addresses the candidates as follows:*
> With this transparent fluid, life-giving, powerful, God-given fluid, more precious and far more significant than all the sacred oils of the ancients, I set you (*or each of you*) apart from the men of your daily association to the great and honorable task you have voluntarily allotted yourselves as citizens of the Invisible Empire, United Klans of America, Knights of the Ku Klux Klan...[15]

After the "God-given fluid" has been poured over the new members there is a "dedication prayer" in which is included the following:

> Now, oh, God! We, through thy goodness, have here dedicated with Thine own divinely distilled fluid these manly men at the alter kneeling, who have been moved by worthy motives and impelled by noble impulses to turn from selfishness and fraternal alienation and to espouse with body, mind, spirit and life, the holy service of our country, our Klan, our home and each other, we beseech Thee to dedicate them with the fullness of his (*or their*) sacred, solemn oath to our noble cause, to the glory of Thy great name. Amen![16]

As may be seen from the preceding passages, along with other previously mentioned "divine" precepts handed down by God, He also bestowed to the hooded order its "divinely distilled fluid" used in the "baptism" of new members.

Texas Klan leader Louis R. Beam, in a short pro–Klan monograph argued the Klan had to engage in active opposition to the federal government in order to re-establish "their Nation." The government, argued Beam, no longer protected "the descendants of those who created this nation." The Klan, therefore, was obligated to once again rescue the nation from a government that "seeks unlawfully to extinguish the descendants of those who conceived it." To that end, drawing on the Battle of the Alamo, Beam declared, "Thus, as Travis at the Alamo, *We* draw the line in the dust; *We* choose sides; and *We* force others to do so. Our friends and allies become clear—our enemies, even clearer. We force polarization of the people based upon what is necessary for the survival of our race."[17] Having identified the enemy that was out to destroy the racial descendants of the nation's fathers and the means to delineate between the opposing forces, Beam further separates the two based on good and evil and God's law:

> We thereby create, by our uncompromising stand against evil, a day and night, good and evil, right and wrong. Our very intransigency separates us from those who would knowingly or unknowingly lead us to defeat and destruction.
> Our goal—a Racial Nation of and by ourselves. No compromise, no concessions, no quid pro quo, no rest or cessation of effort and will until we have our National State.
> Those who work for our Nation are our allies; those who oppose it are adversaries.
> In one simple, masterful stroke everything becomes clear again: Right vs. wrong, good vs. evil, light vs. darkness, establishment or destruction, a future or no future.
> Ride, Klansmen! Carry upon your lips the scared cry: Our God and no other! His law and no other! Our Racial Nation or no nation![18]

Beam reiterates the Klan's position regarding the nation's origins and God's law: "The history of the Founding Fathers and our Nation is the history of a racially pure family. The Klan seeks to preserve that history and family. We cannot hope to be successful if we are in violation of God's Word."[19] Beam then emphasizes the unwavering opposition to what he viewed as an unlawful government hostile to God:

> The Klan concedes no authority to govern not lawfully obtained under our American Constitution. No usurpers of authority shall rule us. We further recognize that forces that are evil and contrary to God have infiltrated our government and stained our flag's honor. We pledge our lives, our fortunes and our sacred honor to recover our nation from these people—by whatever means and methods God makes known to us.[20]

Approaching the idea of divine origin from a different angle, Beam asserted the world was enmeshed in a struggle between good and evil; that the forces of good were represented by God and Christ and the bad by Satan. Beam, however, went further when he declared that communism was "an AGENCY of Satan." Since communism was aided by a supernatural force then it was only natural to "turn and ask assistance from the ONE source of SUPERNATURAL POWER that can overcome Satan."[21] Beam then interjected his interpretation concerning the Klan's divine connection when he stated:

> This is where and when we align ourselves with Almighty God, our Creator, our Savior, and our inspiration. We do not commit the popular blasphemy which says: "God is on our side," or "We are His Chosen people." Quite the contrary. WE have chosen GOD. We have placed ourselves under His Direction. We have become His Finite Instrument with which we earnestly pray, He will choose to save Christian Civilization. He is our Shepherd, our Foundation, our Strength, without which we will be hopelessly devoured by the Agents of Satan.[22]

The religious rendition continues when the creed and tenets of the organization are set forth:

### Credo of the Ku Klux Klan

We, the members of the Ku Klux Klan hold the following ideals to be truth beyond gainsaying, established by God, confirmed by the words Christ Jesus, and born [sic] out by the history of man.

Namely, that there is an elect that is especially gifted, bearing the inheritance of Heaven, coming from above to establish God's Kingdom on earth, who, like a branch engrafted in the Godhead of Christ, bears fruit for the altar of eternity of which no other race can attest. Also, that this elect is the White man who, from ancient times, has been called ARYAN, meaning "noble one." And, that as members of this supreme race, it is our blessed duty to be honorable before all men and chivalrous to all women and to follow our Lord Jesus who came to gather the lost sheep back into our Father's fold. Though we dispose our Satanic adversaries with a consuming vengeance, let us none-the-less remember our first love, our Father, and His sons and daughters, the members of our race, for we are members in the body of Christ, His living church and holy shrine that guards the priceless wisdom: Christ in you, the hope and glory.

We recognize the signs of the times, the growing clouds, the first volleys of thunder and the darkening horizon. And we know that this presages a darker time to come. But, though the darkness encases us, as bearers of the sacred flame of Race will march and are now marching, through hell's valley, cleaving the night into dawn. Our work is towards the RENAISSANCE, or rebirth, of the true understanding of our Aryan identity. For, once White men realize how precious the treasure of their blood is, then they will understand the heathen's frenzied attempt to rob him of this gift; then also will one White man fight like an army of thousands to protect the treasure that is his.

We further pledge our talents, our lives, and whatever God has given us to make this MOVEMENT a potent force. We know that in a MOVEMENT unity is the seal of strength, that unity is the expression of life, and that members of our race shall know us to be Christians by our love for one another.

Brethren, know that the victory of the Aryan-elect is foreordained, and that history is the inexorable movement towards finalizing the design of Divine Destiny which was before the beginning of the world. Therefore, we do not fear any man or group of men, for our Lord is known as "Emmanuel," or "God is with us." Having

God with us, what man or devil can withstand our might. Nor do we fear death, for what sting of death is there for the children of the Immortal God.

Armageddon draws nigh, and the saints of Christendom are being assembled to destroy the wolves in sheep's clothing who daily blaspheme our Lord in the synagogues of Satan. And, though we work amidst the seemingly hopeless chaotic ruins of our crumbling race, we are at peace in the prophecy that when Christ returns He will reward each according to his works and will say to His chosen, "Come, ye blessed of my Father, inherit the Kingdom prepared for you from the foundation of the world." Even so, amen.[23]

God, biblical teaching, revelations, white supremacy—the essence of the Klan's religious beliefs—all are incorporated in the above passage. The Ku Klux Klan *is* God's tool; it *is* the lost flock; it *is* the arm of the Lord; they *are* "the saints of Christendom," and to them will be given the Kingdom of Heaven, or so one is led to believe through Beam's religious rhetoric. Similar in vein is the following assertion by Jim Blair, Imperial Wizard of the Knights of the Ku Klux Klan in the 1980s.

> MY KLAN OATH BINDS ME NOT ONLY TO THE WORTHY AND HOLY TRADITIONS OF THE PAST, BUT TO KEEP THEM ALIVE FOR THE GENERATIONS NOT YET BORN. I MUST CREATE A SACRED UNFADING BOND BETWEEN MYSELF YOU KLANSLADIES AND KLANSMEN AND EACH OF YOU BETWEEN YOUR WHITE BROTHERS AND SISTERS. THE KLAN IN ALL ITS BEAUTY, GREATNESS AND POWER IS GOD'S BLUEPRINT AND PLAN TO SAVE OUR COUNTRY, ITS CHRISTIAN HERITAGE AND THE WHITE CHRISTIAN CULTURED CIVILIZATION. THE KLAN IS AN IMPREGNABLE SHIELD OF HONOR TO OUR GOD, OUR RACE AND OUR COUNTRY THAT CAN BE MAINTAINED ONLY BY THE MEMBERS OF THIS GREAT ORDER.[24]

With the advent of the Internet in the late 1980s to early 1990s, the Klan created its own web pages and continued to espouse its religious rhetoric. Through the remainder of the twentieth and into the twenty-first century, a more diverse set of organizations whose exceedingly conservative religious philosophies at times coincided, came into existence. Some were offshoots of already established organizations; others came into existence by virtue of different philosophies. These organizations include Christian Identity, White Pride, Ku Klux Klan, Seed Line, Covenant, Skin Heads, Aryan Nations, and a wide variety of other organizations.[25] Religion remains an integral part of the internet-based Klan. Web-based Klan organizations reference their beliefs as being encompassed within an organized church. The American Knights of the Ku Klux Klan, as did earlier groups, saw their activity as a means of protecting the nation and the white race while they crusade for God:

> Nothing in life is more satisfying and fulfilling than making a commitment to a great goal and then devoting one's talents and energies to its' achievements. As a member of the *Church of the American knights of the Ku Klux Klan,*

> You will be taking a hand in shaping the future of the White Race. Any White person, who can see the threat to the future of our race and refuses to stand up for his people, doesn't deserve to be counted among then!
>
> We, the *Church of the American knights of the Ku Klux Klan*, are the largest, most active, fastest growing Klan organization in the world today. We are not just another *"political party"* or *"supper club."* The Klansman and The Klanswoman of the Church of the American knights of the Ku Klux Klan are KRUSADERS for GOD, COUNTRY, and the WHITE RACE. The Ku Klux Klan is a way of life the members live every day. If you've had enough of what's going on in this society, contact us, and *BECOME A PART OF THE SOLUTION FOR OUR FUTURE!!!!*[26]

Another modern day Klan that refers to its organized faith is the Church of the National Knights of the Ku Klux Klan (CNKKKK). As do other contemporary white supremacist groups, the CNKKKK views whites as the true children of God (versus Jews). In obtaining church status the CNKKKK seeks to protect its first amendment rights regarding its written materials and support its beliefs regarding Blacks based on their biblical interpretation:

> In the year 2000, after much work, the Reverend Ray Larsen, Imperial Wizard of the NKKKK Inc. was able to get us a Church status. Does this mean we only allow religious people? NO! The reasons we became a Church are many. One of them is so we would be able to get our materials into places that we were not previously allowed, such as jails, and also we would be more securely protected under the First Amendment. It has also helped us in court cases, where being Klan would have not carried weight. Our becoming a Church has.
>
> What do we believe in our Church? We believe in the Bible before liberals translated it. We of the White Race came from Adam and Eve, not monkeys. The Bible clearly shows we are of one lineage, and makes reference to Beasts who walked on two legs. It also spoke of the wrongs of sleeping with these beasts. So we believe that blacks are not our Brothers and Sisters, but are beasts of burden. To accept evolution fully, is to say that we are equal with these animals, which history shows that we are not equal to, and in fact are superior to. While the Supreme Court has accepted animals to Vote and Marry with our race, we have not and never will accept this.[27]

As previously stated, it must be understood that a close association exists with mainstream American Protestantism and groups such as the CNKKKK, as being a member of the CNKKKK, "one must accept the tenants of the Christian religion. That means one must recognize that there is a God who created this beautiful world we live in." Like mainstream Protestantism, the CNKKKK does "not accept people who follow the occult, whether Paganism or Satanism," nor does it accept atheists. The organization is, however, amenable to working with non–Christians as long as they are also "fighting to maintain White Supremacy."[28]

It is the Imperial Knights of America (IKA) that provide a clear picture regarding their religious beliefs. In a lengthy proclamation the IKA outlines its "doctrinal beliefs as taught by the Holy Scriptures," which it states are the "basic digest defining the true faith once delivered to the saints." Quoting a wide variety of biblical scriptures to justify their beliefs, the IKA declares their belief in the Bible and God, and that "covenants, and prophecy of this Holy Book were written for and about a specific elect family of people who are children of YHVH God (Luke 3:38; Psalm 82:6) through the seedline of Adam." The IKA also states the scriptures are "written as a doctrinal standard for our exhortation, admonition, correction, instruction and example; the whole counsel to be believed, taught and followed (II Tim. 3:16. Acts. 20:27)." Much like mainline Christians, the IKA views Christ as "Yahshua the Messiah (Jesus Christ)," the son of God who will return to judge humanity. Turning to the issue of the God's chosen people, the IKA declares, "God chose unto Himself a special race of people that are above all people upon the face of the earth (Deut. 7:6; Amos 3:2). These [are the] children of Abraham through the called-out seedline of Isaac and Jacob (Psalm 105:6; Rom. 9:7)." Along with the Seed Line theology, the IKA also believe in the "New Covenant ... made with the Children of Israel."[29]

The "New Covenant" ideology encompassing the IKA's religious beliefs is delineated in one of the paragraphs of the proclamation:

> WE BELIEVE the White, Anglo-Saxon, Germanic and kindred people to be God's true, literal Children of Israel. Only this race fulfills every detail of Biblical Prophecy and World History concerning Israel and continues in these latter days to be heirs and possessors of the Covenants, Prophecies, Promises and Blessings YHVH God made to Israel. This chosen seedline making up the "Christian Nations" (Gen. 35:11; Isa. 62:2; Acts 11:26) of the earth stands far superior to all other peoples in their call as God's servant race (Isa. 41:8, 44:21; Luke 1:54). Only these descendants of the 12 tribes of Israel scattered abroad (James 1:1; Deut. 4:27; Jer. 31:10; John 11:52) have carried God's Word, the Bible, throughout the world (Gen. 28:14; Isa. 43:10–12, 59:21), have used His Laws in the establishment of their civil governments and are the "Christians" opposed by the Satanic Anti-Christ forces of this world who do not recognize the true and living God (John 5:23, 8:19, 16:2–3).[30]

The IKA continues by stating that their enemy is the Devil and his offspring "commonly called Jews today." Further demarcating the opposing sides, the IKA proclamation affirms that Adam "is the father of the White Race only." A key distinguishing feature between "God's chosen" (Adamic man) and all other races is that "Adamic man is made trichotomous, that is, not only of body and soul, but having an implanted spirit (Gen. 2:7; I Thes. 5:23; Heb. 4:12) giving him a higher form of consciousness and distinguishing him from all the other races of the earth (Deut. 7:6, 10:15; Amos 3:2)." In effect, God created and selected the white race, gave him a soul, but more importantly, a spirit—something that is lacking in non-white races. Having been chosen by God, they are opposed to miscegenation because this is "prohibited in God's natural divine order from ruling over Israel.... Race-mixing is an abomination in the sight of Almighty God, a satanic attempt meant to destroy the chosen seedline, and is strictly forbidden by His commandments." Finally, the IKA provides its statement regarding gender roles, asserting that "men and women should conduct themselves according to the role of their gender in the traditional Christian sense that God intended. Homosexuality is an abomination before God and should be punished by death (Lev. 18:22, 20:13; Rom. 1:24–28, 32; I Cor. 6:9)."[31]

Much as previously mentioned Klan organizations, the Invisible Knights of the Fiery Cross (IKFC) make the same pronouncements. Miscegenation is, according to the IKFC, "racial suicide ... in the name of equality." Along with the declaration that whites are superior to non-whites, the organization also asserts that race mixing "is Satan's goal to have us violate our Heavenly Father's law on mixing our seed with other people of the world." The organization further asserts that the federal government is assisting with the destruction of the white race because of its affirmative action programs. In addition, the IKFC argues that the federal government encourages non-white immigration, provides welfare to non-working immigrants, encourages race mixing in school, and that white children are being taught the races are equal. However, from the IKFC's perspective, "The inequalities of the Races have never been more apparent than that [sic] in the Bible." The IKFC then cites various biblical passages interpreted as God's admonition against race mixing and ending by referencing whites as the chosen people of God using a variant form of YHVH, God's name as used by the IKA: "We, the True Chose people of God, the True Tribes of Israel, are commanded not to Race mix. We are NOT EQUAL IN THE EYES OF YAHWEH."[32]

The argument against miscegenation is one of the most persistent of the Klan's philosophical dogmas. Virtually every modern-day right wing organization, whether Klan, White Christian or other Identity group is vehemently opposed to race mixing using God and biblical references to substantiate their beliefs. Taking a defensive stand, the Original Knight Riders, Knights of the Ku Klux Klan (OKRKKKK), argues that American society is incapable of understanding their beliefs. It then states as other orders have, that their mission is "God ordained":

> To it [society], anyone and everyone who claims to be, or professes to be, a member of the nearly 150 year-old hooded order called, the "Ku Klux Klan" couldn't

possibly have a heart; to Society, the Ku Klux Klan is only about prejudice and intolerance fueled by ignorance and hate. In Society's finite mind, any person who would don a white robe and hood and proudly call themselves a "Klansman" or "Klanswoman" would be incapable of feeling love or caring about anything or anyone; Klansmen and Klanswomen couldn't possibly believe that theirs is a God-ordained mission or that they have a Divine responsibility to enforce God's laws within this nation or wherever active "Klans" are established.

But, as is normally the case in this "politically-correct" yet "biblically-ignorant" 21st Century Society, it is the vast majority of the populace that is misinformed concerning the beliefs and loves held by the men and women who comprise the Ku Klux Klan and live within its vast and "Invisible Empire."[33]

To the Klan, the ills of society were caused by a government controlled by Jews, the Zionist Occupation Government (ZOG). It is because of Jews that race mixing is occurring: "The belief that a white race should mix within other races has been twisted and glorified by the Jews and the media. Everywhere we look we are exposed to inter-racial relationships and are shown that all is well and it is a wonderful thing." Citing Leviticus 19:19, the Exalted Cyclops of the OKRKKKK, the Klan official opined that animals were "examples of God's true meanings.... They have stayed true to God's word." This was so because animals did not "watch television, movies or read the newspaper. They are unaware and not brainwashed by the outside world to believe that it is ok to mix among races." Everything that was negatively impacting American society was due to the negative influence engendered by the ZOG. What was being advocated, according to the Exalted Cyclops, was "that it is ok to mix breed, pollute our country with mongrels, drug addicts and homosexuality, take prayer out of schools and anything else to destroy our great nation and our youth. This then becomes what people believe is the right thing to do, But then in reality all it is doing is what it was designed to do and that is destroy the pure and innocent." It was up to the Klan to ensure that the remnants of the "Aryan race" engage in ending the "nonsense" that is transpiring.[34]

From the same website, one of the Grand Dragons also commented on the religious philosophies and social governmental policies. Addressing "White Aryan American citizens" that "are tired of the other races taking advantage," of "having our rights trampled on, and fed up with the taking of our jobs by 'Affirmative Action' and other government-made reverse racism laws," the Grand Dragon stated, "We Klansmen and Klanswomen are very proud of our race and our heritage, you of the Aryan race should be too." The writer asserted that the "Klan saved this great nation before and it looks like we will have to save it again." The statement is in reference to the historical myth of nineteenth century Reconstruction Klan and its role in "saving" the South from Scalawags, Northern Republicans and the freed slaves. The Klan, according to the Grand Dragon, "was the first legal policing system in this nation. The Klan served and protected the citizens of this nation and tried to keep them from harm. The Klan separated good from evil." The writer also asserted that no such information is found in the history books used by the public education system because "Zionists don't want you to know. They control what our children's history, as well as all, books teach them."[35]

Asserting that the OKRKKKK is a Christian organization, the writer decried the ills of society and maintained that "the Zionists, liberals and all anti–American entities out there want this to be, the calculated destruction of America." It is only by paying close attention to what is happening on television that viewers will be able to fully grasp what is taking place. Furthermore, "we need to stop the 'glamorization' of race-mixing. It is unnatural, it goes AGAINST Gods laws. It is genocide to our people and whats [sic] worse, it's all engineered! It is not by accident that all this is happening, it's not just a 'fad' or a 'phase,' no, it is engineered and put in place by ZOG." Declaring that television portrays race mixing in a positive light, the writer stated that what in reality occurs is negative, especially for "the children born from these inter-racial relationships." The concern over the Blood Line is then addressed: "And what about our Aryan bloodline? What about the other races [sic] bloodline?" The writer then added, "Race mixing is a huge problem, someday we'll not have a beautiful blond haired, blue-eyed baby to be proud of. We will have no one left to carry on our ancestors [sic] roots and heritage.... There is no winner with race mixing. All races lose." God is then brought into the argument to provide divine justification: "God made us all different for a reason and it is mentioned in the Bible. We, as Klansmen and Klanswomen are strictly opposed to race mixing and do not allow it with our offspring, we teach them the pride of the Aryan race, the great country the White race built and the most valuable accomplishment our race has made." Along with the issue of race mixing, also addressed was homosexuality, another activity against God's laws. Finally, the issue of illegal immigration is addressed, with the writer affirming that

> the hordes of illegal aliens are taking yours and your children's jobs, collecting tax refunds there [sic] aren't entitled to, taking advantage of our system, coming here to have their babies, using our tax dollars to live on, bringing more violence, gangs and crime here, bringing diseases we had taken care of years ago back to us, bringing parasites causing us harm. They are killing kids, either molesting them, abducting them and torturing them, or killing them by driving drunk a thousand times over. They actually use and have more rights in our own country then we, the legal, tax-paying, law abiding citizens do![36]

To best understand the depth of the Klan's belief, the declaration "I am a Soldier" included on the OKRKKKK website (as well as others), demonstrates the commitment to God. Setting aside the knowledge that the declaration comes from the Klan, the statement could well apply to a crusader of the eleventh through thirteenth centuries, or to a statement by a member of a religious army from the Middle Ages. For that matter, substitution of Allah for God, Mohamed for Christ, and the Koran for the Bible could make the declaration appear to be that of an Islamic terrorist.[37] What must be understood is that religious beliefs are valid for the person advocating the beliefs. They are at the root of what drives the individual or group. Such beliefs are no different than those held by any of the major religious organizations, who, when threatened by outsiders, become defensive. This is no different for the Klan.

As a soldier, a weapon is needed in order to fight against the enemy and protect one's beliefs. The Aryan Nations, Knights of the Ku Klux Klan include the sword in their proclamation as a symbol of God's strength and laws, laws the Klan is to protect in defense of their "Racial Nation" as chosen by God:

> This unsheathed sword of the spirit of Israel, which is the word of God, represents the Law of YaHWeH. Its presence on our altar signifies that we as an organization, are solidly behind every life law the Father put in motion since the foundations of the earth were laid in place. The laws of kind after kind and remain ye separate. The law that we are to be a Holy people unto Him above all people upon the face of the earth. Disobedience to His Holy Word we believe, is the reason we stand in the political quagmire that our Holy Race finds itself captive to this very day.
>
> This sword also signifies that we are set for the defense of our flag the Aryan Nations standard and all that it symbolizes. YaHWeH's Holy Word says that we are His Battle-axe and weapons of war. (Jeremiah 51:20) Our Racial Nation and all of its Holy tenets, laws statutes and judgements are of our Heavenly Father. We believe the Aryan Nations is the true and divine Holy Race of YaHWeH, the lost sheep of the House of Israel. We swear to defend our Holy Race by all justifiable means and methods, from any encroachment whatever, from any source whatever, whether it be traitors within or enemies without. This sword is a constant reminder of our obligation to defend our race and enforce the laws of our God, through God ordained authorities and justifiable means, not by devils who have snuck in unawares. May we wield it wisely and well in defense of our race, our families, our homes, our liberties and our God.[38]

Within the above included citation, the Aryan Nations KKK referenced the organization's flag which it swears to defend. From their perspective Protestant America, the Constitution and the U.S. flag no longer represent white Americans. Within their religious beliefs as God's chosen "Holy White Race" the organization views current society as foreign to God's will. The writer interjected the analogy of captive Israel to paint itself as the modern White Israel living in captivity subject to a nation under Jewish influence, and a divine relationship with God who created the organization.

> The American flag or the United States constitution no longer represents the White race. Not one single thread of the American flag today represents any White man, woman or child. Not one word of this bastardized document that these modern day politicians call the constitution represent any member of the Holy White Race. It today represents defeat and failure for our people. Today we are a captive people, living in a captive land enslaved to the international monetary system and the mongrel race of Jews who created it. The nigger hordes they force our children to cohabitate with in the public school system, the religious institutions they boldly but erroneously call Christian churches and every facet of life here on American shores is more evidence of defeat and tribute.
>
> Today our complete and total patriotism is to the Aryan Nations and the banner for which she stands. The banner which represents the Twelve Tribes of Israel and our Holy Race. The Invisible Empire is Aryan Nations. We recognize that as our only authority. God the Father created Aryan Nations as a representative of our Father's Holy Christian Empire and as His battle-axe. His authority which is Aryan Nations is the Invisible Empire of the Aryan Nations Knights of the Ku Klux Klan. This is the position of the Aryan Nations Knights and has been it's [sic] position since it's inception as a division of Aryan Nations in 2003.
>
> Furthermore; We do not salute or pledge allegiance to a flag that we know represents our demise and total destruction. The American flag today represents just that for our Race.[39]

Although the various Klan organizations are in general agreement regarding their Christian Identity, their being the chosen race, their philosophies regarding Blacks and other minorities, their perspective regarding Jews, and their stand on homosexuality, there some are differences regarding the American flag and constitution. Whereas the Aryans Nations KKKK appear to completely reject the Constitution and invoke the Aryan Nations' flag as their standard, other groups regard the Constitution and flag as fundamental symbols and key elements of their ideology. For instance, the Church of the National Knights of the Ku Klux Klan (CNKKKK) regards the Constitution as "the finest system of government ever conceived by man."[40]

The Invisible Knights of the Fiery Cross argue that the federal government, through the Supreme Court, has "taken religion out of our classrooms."[41] Coupled with the suppression of religion, as viewed by the Invisible Knights, are the federal government's regulations regarding racial equality. Based on their religious and biblical interpretations the races, according to all Klan organizations, are not equal. Because of federal guidelines on race, the Invisible Knights argues, "the Federal Government no longer represents White Christian America."[42] Despite its argument "that the Federal Government has become an enemy to White America,"[43] within the "Klan Kreed," on its webpage the Invisible Knights state: "WE recognize our relation to the government of the United States of America, the supremacy of its Constitution, the Union of States there under, and the Constitutional Laws thereof, and we shall be devoted to the sublime principles of a pure Americanism and valiant in the defense of its ideals and institutions."[44] The same "Kreed" and statement is included on the website of the United Klans of America. The Traditionalist American Knights of the Ku Klux Klan, under the "PATRIOTIC IDEALS" section of their proclamation declare they "are sworn by a solemn oath to uphold and defend this immortal Constitution."[45] Lastly, the White Kamelia Knights of the Ku Klux Klan contain the same statements as the Invisible Knights declaring, as did the Invisible Knights, "the Federal Government no longer represents White Christian America."[46]

# 8

# *Christ, Eternal Emperor of the World Wide Invisible Empire*

Attacking immigration, the Grand Klokard of Kentucky stated that large numbers of Americans were "still in the dark, they have not received the real light of freedom from the horde of un–American aliens who have come upon our shores like human vultures and are trying to destroy that which our fathers fought, bled and died for." Representative of what the American forefathers stood for was, of course, the Klan. This was symbolized, according to the Klan official, by the light "burning in every city, town and hamlet through out [sic] our grand and glorious land, in the form of a fiery cross, the symbol of Christ, and the Ku Klux Klan."[1] Even though the principles for which America stood for were being upheld by the Klan, there still existed the danger posed "by the sinister workings of the enemy who do not work in the blessed light of day, but rather in the darkness—because they are evil."[2] However, there was still hope because the Klan, like Christ, was a savior: "The light of the world is Jesus, the light of America is the fiery cross of the K. K. K., long may it burn and far may the blaze be seen so that men who call themselves such, may rally around this symbol of true Americanism and receive a new birth—be born again, into the empire invisible."[3]

As pointed out in Chapter 3, the Klan justified its secrecy by demonstrating that Christ also used clandestine means to achieve His ends. It was the conditions of the times, according to the Klan, that led Christ to employ covert action. Addressing secrecy from this perspective, the *Kourier Magazine* justified secrecy on the part of the Klan when it stated: "Conditions often demand and justify secrecy of plans in the making. Banks do not reveal their plans until launched. Governments plan in secret for the good of their citizens. Secrecy is not necessarily evil. Christ resorted to secrecy from necessity. No one sees the root of a tree as it grows. It is the fruit that counts."[4]

By 1934, in the midst of the Great Depression, the Klan was also feeling the financial strain being visited upon the nation as a whole. Klan leadership was becoming concerned with the declining membership. A Great Kludd of Ohio asked the question in an article entitled "Shall We Quit or Shall We Fight?"[5] In asking the question, the Klan official answered by stating the hooded order had survived the abuses heaped upon it by its enemies. Although not directly comparing the organization to Christ, the citation below implies such a comparison.

> What is to be done? Have we a job? The Ku Klux Klan is an American organization (or is it and institution?). The Klan has been tried and tested, and it has always won. It was tried by the furnace of Religious Hatred, and it proved its might; tried by the fires of social ostracism, and it made friends; tried by the test of Ridicule, and had been vindicated; tried by prosecution as well as persecution, in society and in the courts, and has been exonerated from all blame, and its loyalty to our government and all its institutions has been established.[6]

By 1936 economic conditions were such that the Klan could no longer maintain publication of the *Kourier Magazine*. Even so, in its last issue before it ceased publication, the Klan portrayed itself, like Christ, abandoned by its own: "Crucified by the negligence of those whose battles it has fought for twelve years, it [the paper] is forced to retreat and leave the field to our common enemies."[7] So ended, for a short time, the publication of "the official organ of the Knights of the Ku Klux Klan."[8] For three years no official publication of the hooded order existed. In July of 1939 the Klan, under Imperial Wizard James A. Colescott, began publication of a newspaper under the name of *The Fiery Cross*.[9]

Throughout this period, Klansmen were urged to emulate Christ. Additionally, many times in Klan prayer and rhetoric, success of the order's objectives was asked for through Christ's intercession. Such was the case in a small eight-page pamphlet entitled *America for Americans*. The pamphlet included the standard Klan rhetoric of patriotism and white supremacy. Pointing to historical figures and incidents of prominence, the pamphlet declares that "it is and will always be the earnest endeavor of the Knights of the Ku Klux Klan to preserve this Great Nation for its native born through Christ Jesus our Criterion of Character."[10] Similar rhetoric was followed by Louis R. Beam when he proclaimed: "Christ has always been our Last Spiritual Hope. He is now become our Last Hope for earthly civilization and physical Life as we have come to know it under our governmental system of Equal Justice under the law."[11]

But the teachings of Christ could easily be reinterpreted by the Klan. The *Klansman*, a Klan newspaper published in Louisiana, wrote of George Pepper, the California Grand Dragon: "Pepper said the Klan believes in a segregated society based on free enterprise and the Bible, a book he claims clearly advocates racial separation." Quoting Pepper, the paper wrote: "Jesus said love thy neighbor, but He didn't say what neighborhood to live in."[12]

Preaching unity and good works through faith, a Klan periodical stressed the need to follow the leadership of Christ while at the same time describing the emblem worn on the robes of Klansmen. Through righteous living a Klan member could "help the cause of others in rightful need," while at the same time being "vibrant, colorful, honorable ... with the blessings of Christ."[13] Moreover,

> we as members of the Ku Klux Klan are united. Our beliefs remain constant in our souls everyday [sic]. It shines forth on our symbol. A White Christian cross on a red background superimposed with four K's around the cross. In the center is the drop of blood of Jesus Christ. This is all surrounded by a circle of unity. We must follow our age old traditions, never given in the compromises, following the leadership and fellowship of Jesus Christ.[14]

Of great concern to the Klan was the anti–Christ. The antithesis of Christ, from the Klan perspective, was to be found in other races, race mixing, or non–Christian religions. Turning to the emotional appeals of patriotism, the founding of the nation, religious freedom, and white supremacy, a writer asserted:

> Lets [sic] face the facts America only got to be as great a nation as it is because it was a Christian nation. The Constitution is being misinterpreted as is the Bible. America was founded by White Christians for a Christian nation. Freedom means nothing if imposed by anti–Christ races or false Gods and idols.
> 
> Freedom for what, ... to ... impose false religious means ... such as Moslem, Hindus, Jewish Faith, and such that seek to confuse people and distort the true Lord Jesus Christ....
> 
> True Christians have never been lambs lead to slaughter but brave men and women who stand united together as kinsmen in blood and spirit one God one people, against the anti–Christ. (Read) 2nd John 7–9 then ask yourself what race and religious people do not believe in Jesus Christ. This is the anti–Christ....
> 
> The true meaning of the Klan is friends and neighbors working together for Jesus sake as soldiers of Christian ways. When Christ was born three kings came to bring gifts to him henceforth the three K.K.K....
> 
> The entire basic's [sic] of the Klan law is taken from the Bible and in Rev. 7:9 we are spoken of, this is how our forefathers foreseen the protectors of our Christian nation. In the past our churches supported and united behind the Klan as some still do....
> 
> We should stand with God and do his work. The Klan will help Christians. The Klan is his army of Christians! Who will stand for the king Jesus Christ[?] We do!

Our white robes are our armor showing his light and truth (Jesus Christ). Upon our chest we bear the cross with drop of blood showing he died upon a cross for our sins so we might be saved and that each of us bear the same cross.[15]

Louis Beam, in *Essays of a Klansman*, pursued the same theme with regards to the Civil Rights Movement. To Beam, the white leaders of the movement were "only nominally in control," and were "under the influence of the false religion of humanism" and were "deeply involved in cultural self-destruction and negro sycophancy." The real leaders, however, were the "Jews who were one or more of the following: Zionist, anti–Christian, anti-white, communist, or practicing Talmudist. This latter group manipulated and directed the actions, policies, and efforts of the former group." Beam saw these groups as "working for such humanistic concepts as equality and brotherhood," but the ultimate objective was "advancing world Jewish domination, a purely racist concept." It was up to the Klan to counter what it viewed as efforts of by anti-white groups to subvert true Christian beliefs. According to Beam, "success from the viewpoint of Klansmen and allied groups can only be measured by the degree in which power is wrenched back from the anti–Christ Jew and his traitorous liege men."[16]

Another anti–Semite writer, Frazier Glenn Miller, in *A White Man Speaks Out*, also wrote disparagingly against Jews who he asserted controlled the U.S. federal government. Like Beam, Miller viewed non-whites who were being welcomed by the "Jew-ruled western world" as a threat to white Americans. Referring to the growth of minorities in the Midwest, Miller stated, "Multiplying like rats is perhaps too strong a phrase, but who can deny the similarity? Not only do the coloreds produce large families, the Whites there, and everywhere, are committing self-genocide through birth control and race mixing. Colored women make colored babies and White women do too."[17] Much like other Klan anti–Semites, Miller saw Jews as pursuing a one-world government. Jewish strength could be seen in Israel where "Jews dictate their will upon their Muslim neighbors."[18] Noting the differences between Israel and the U.S., Miller asked why white American could not emulate the Jewish state:

> There is a big difference, however, between Jew Israel and White America. Jew Israel is racist. They stick together. They fight for their own people. And, more important, they have the will to survive. Why can't we be like the Jews? Why can't we have the same racial pride, racial unity, and the will to survive as a people? If the Jews can have a Jewish state of their own, then why can't we have a White Christian state of our own?[19]

The perceptions concerning Jewish history, according to Miller, were due to Jewish control of the media. Specific to World War II, Miller asserted,

"Incidentally, The Holocaust is really the holohoax."[20] The Jewish media was seen as controlling what was written, ensuring the omission of information "not palatable to the World Jewish Agenda," and in the process providing an exceeding negative depiction of whites with the intent of annihilation:

> Weaken the White man. Make him ashamed of his history, forefathers, and Race. And, make his own children ashamed of their father. Put the White race on a guilt trip and never let them off. By making the White man weak, we become strong. Incite the colored peoples of the world to hate the White man. Study White history. Search out every detail of their associations with colored peoples, and accentuate everything negative and leave out everything positive.
> 
> At the same time, glorify the colored races. Accentuate everything positive and omit everything negative. Teach them that the White man is their enemy, and we Jews are their salvation and protectors, etc.
> 
> As a result of a half century of Jews-media anti–White hate propaganda, the violence against us by the colored races (and especially the Negroes) reached war-time proportions. The Negroes declared war against us, beginning in 1965, and this fact is proven by crime figures. Violent assaults against our people number in the tens of millions. And this carnage is the direct responsibility of the Jews who sicked [sic] them on us with their hate propaganda.
> 
> Make no mistake about it, the Jews intend to exterminate the White Aryan Race from the face of the earth. Their deep down guttural hatred for everything Aryan must be understood.[21]

Jews, according to Miller, "are masters of the big lie." At the forefront of changing American culture, Jewish lies included: "Racial diversity makes America strong. All men are created equal. America has always been a nation of immigrants. Abortion is a woman's right. The Germans murdered six million helpless innocent Jews. The great American melting pot. The Negroes built great civilizations in Africa. The White man invented slavery. No difference but skin color."[22] Miller asserted it has been through lies that Jews have achieved the amount of domination credited to them. Finally, according to Miller, America will be drastically changed because of the Jews: "And so fellow Aryans, it seems our kind is doomed to extinction. Thanks to the 'chosen people' our future generations will be mud-colored, kinky headed, slant-eyed, flat-nosed, small-brained, two-legged featherless creatures, ruled by the 'Jews.'"[23]

As has been done by many modern-day Klan organizations that are using the Internet to spread their version of religion, the Church of the National Knights Realm of Kentucky (CNKKKKK), has turned to biblical interpretation as a means of "proving" the Jews to be the spawn of the devil and whites to be the chosen people. The CNKKKKK's biblical interpretation regarding Jews claim Christ "identified them when He walked the earth and in His ministry called the Jews the children of the devil."

Reiterating the assertion, the CNKKKKK stated, "Jews are of their father the devil, and the lusts of their father they would do; that their father was a liar and a murderer from the beginning.... Jesus said they could not understand His speech, and that they had no spiritual capacity whatsoever.... And it remains that the Jews of today are the descendants of the forces that Jesus denounced in His time." Because Jews are descendants of the Devil "they should never be identified with the children of God!" According to the CNKKKKK's biblical interpretation, the Apostle Paul is said to have declared the Jews were against God, and thus are not the chosen people, nor do they belong to the twelve tribes: "The Jews are Hittites and Amalekites and Canaanites. They are red, black, yellow, and brown, as well as off-colored white. They have one thing in common: They are the offspring of Lucifer and the fallen angels which came with Lucifer."[24]

As viewed by the Klan, an anti-white, irreligious atmosphere had spread throughout the nation due to governmental policies. From the perspective of the Original Knight Riders, Knights of the Ku Klux Klan, "Our Ancestors built this great nation, and as white, Christian, legal American citizens and taxpayers, we feel as [sic] the quality of life for white Americans is deteriorating rapidly. Our own government has almost taken God completely away from us and is only interested in taking control of our lives."[25] Within the proclamation of the OKRKKKK by the order's Imperial Wizard, the organization, as do other such groups, proclaim their belief in God, the Bible, and Christ. The OKRKKKK, however, place Christ in a uniquely superior position within the members of the order as His subordinates. By so doing it ties itself directly to Christ providing the order a divine connection. The intent is to set aside differences among Klan organizations by declaring all such organizations as subordinate to Christ, the "Eternal Emperor."

> Now, therefore, I as the Imperial Wizard of the Original Knightriders, Knights of the Ku Klux Klan, speaking on behalf of ALL present-day orders, groups, and/or organizations using the name Ku Klux Klan, all being in one accord, do hereby proclaim that from this day forward, and until His eminent return (Revelations 19–22), that JESUS CHRIST IS NOW AND FOREVER MORE SHALL BE THE SPIRITUAL, ETERNAL EMPEROR OF THE WORLDWIDE INVISIBLE EMPIRE AND ALL RECOGNIZED, ORGANIZED KLANDOM.[26]

The connection to Christ was also made by the Aryan Nations Knights of the Ku Klux Klan. The organization made the association used and slightly modified the section that corresponded to the cross under the seven symbols of the Klan:

## 8. Christ, Eternal Emperor  149

Sanctified and made holy nearly nineteen centuries ago by the suffering and blood of fifty million martyrs who died in the most holy faith, it stands in every Klavern of the Aryan Nations Knights of the Ku Klux Klan as a constant reminder that Christ is our criterion of character, and His teachings our rule of life-blood-bought, holy, sanctified and sublime.

We have taken the cross, once a sign of ignominy, disgrace and shame, and have transformed it into a symbol of Faith, Hope and Love. We have added the fire to signify that Christ Is The Light Of The World. As light drives away the darkness and gloom so knowledge of the truth dispels ignorance and superstition. As fire purifies gold, silver and precious stones, but destroys the dross, wood, hay and stubble; so by fire of Calvary's cross we mean to purify and cleanse our virtues by burning our vices with the fire of His Sword. Who can look upon this sublime symbol, or sit in its sacred, holy light without being inspired with a holy desire and determination to be a better man? "By This Sign We Conquer."[27]

The organization addressed the concern regarding "lighting the cross" which it stated was "a religious ceremony" commemorating the martyrdom of Christ. Additionally, "the Aryan Nations Knights of the Ku Klux Klan light the cross as a warning signal to all men of the impending disaster that is facing our Nation if it continues on this present course without God." Explaining the difference between "lighting" and "burning" the cross, the writer declared, "The burning of a cross is an illegal act of violence against a person or a person's home, while invading their privacy with the intent to harass or intimidate." Cross "burnings" of the malicious sort was blamed on "juveniles, irate citizens or even the minorities themselves who do not understand the rules of the Klan, but wish to use the influence or the reputation the media has given the Klan to scare their victims, or glean favor and support from public opinion and law enforcement for themselves."[28]

What must be understood is that lighting the cross is viewed as a *religious ceremony* by the Klan. Here again, this activity is part of the beliefs as held and practiced by the organization. The symbol of the cross is used by both Klan and non–Klan, but it is seen from two entirely different perspectives. For the Klan the fire added to the cross is part of a religious ceremony signifying divine association with their belief in Christ and his teachings. But for those on whose property the cross is burned, the symbol is not Christ, love, or anything associated with religion, rather, it engenders fear, terror, and is directly associated with hatred and violence. Thus there exists a dichotomy regarding the most scared of symbols for Klan and non–Klan organizations, for Christian Klan people and non–Klan Christians. Further, both spectrums of the dichotomous symbolism associated with the cross are valid, and therein lays a crucial point with which American society has yet to come to terms. And before doing so, it must recognize that the beliefs of the Klan are part and parcel of American's racial and religious history, a history that justified American historical policies and actions against groups viewed as outside white American Protestant society. What the Klan says and does is nothing more than a reflection of that long social and cultural history.

Another organization that adamantly argued the differences between a cross lighting and a cross burning was the Knights Party. The arguments followed a similar strain; however, the Knights Party also stated that participation by Klan members in the lighting ceremony signified "a public declaration to Jesus Christ of their continued commitment to the Christian faith." And, like the Aryans Nations, the Knights Party blamed the media for distorting the significance behind a cross lighting at the same time blaming others for cross burnings. Of importance is the connection of the Klan's cross with that of mainstream Protestantism; again, this connection must be seen as an organic aspect of American's historical religious culture kept alive by the Klan's religious beliefs, however unsavory they may be.

> The cross lighting ceremony is another example of how the national media distorts the Klan image. They purposely use the word "burn" because of the negative image that is conjured up in the minds of many people. To them it is a desecration, a desire to destroy the cross. And any attempt by hoodlums to use the lighted cross as a symbol of hate or a threat is strictly NOT advocated by The Knights. These acts are cowardly and counter productive [sic] and are usually the actions of folks who watch too much late night television or Hollywood movies. Serious patriotic men and women never lower themselves to use the sacred cross in such a manner!
>
> And we should also point out that often "cross burnings" or other types of threatening actions including graffiti are often the acts of disturbed blacks, Asians, non-white Hispanics, homosexuals, or Jews who use the publicity for fund raising, to bolster sought after legislation, or even insurance scams!
>
> The Knights definitely does not burn the cross, but we do light the cross. The lighted cross of The Knights is no different than the average church that has a lighted cross either on top or in front of their church building. The light of the cross symbolizes the Light of Christ dispelling darkness and ignorance. It is the fire of the cross that reminds us of the cleansing "fire" of Christ that cleanses evil from our land. The fiery cross is a symbol that has long been popular with the Christian faith, for example the Methodist denomination uses the fiery cross as their symbol.[29]

Similar in nature is the material located on the website of the American Knights of the Ku Klux Klan (AKKKK). Like other Klans, the AKKKK harked back to the lighting signals used by Scottish tribes and as seen from the perspective of this and other organizations, the cross lighting is "a warning signal to all men of the impending disaster that is facing our Nation if it continues on it's [sic] present course without God." Furthermore, we also light the Cross, as a tribute to Jesus Christ in recognition of his sacrifice, and willingness to die for our sins. We endeavor to warn of the dangers of interracial mixing, and teach those who will listen and learn, the ways of the Klan. We feel it is our duty to prepare ourselves, and those of our race, for the hard road ahead, while the Government over this Nation turns like a rabid dog upon the very people who support it.

We of the American Knights of the Ku Klux Klan want you to understand that there is a difference between Lighting a cross and a Cross burning.

The lighting of a cross is a religious ceremony, performed in reverence to the Lord Jesus Christ, in recognition of his sacrifice.

The burning of a cross is an illegal act of violence against a person or a person's home, while invading their privacy with the intent to harass, intimidate, or do bodily harm. This act of burning a cross is usually performed by irate citizens who do not understand the rules of the Klan, but wish to use the influence of the Klan to scare their victims, by burning a cross usually less than ten feet tall in the persons yard or against the home.[30]

As may be noted, the American Knights of the Ku Klux Klan, as does the Knights Party, viewed the cross lighting as a "religious ceremony."

The Church of the National Knights Realm of Kentucky (CNKKKKK), has a similar pronouncement regarding the lighting of the cross, it makes note, as has been done by the Klan since the 1920s, that the cross "stands in every Klavern of the Ku Klux Klan as a constant reminder that Jesus Christ is our criterion of character and His teachings are our life blood, bought Holy, Sanctified, and Sublime." Giving the cross a sacred and religious symbolism associated with Christ's death, it then becomes the rallying point against the Klan's and America's perceived enemies: "This Old Cross was bathed in the blood of our Lord Jesus Christ and became transformed into the symbol of Faith, Hope, and Love. Today it is used to rally the Forces of Christianity against the ever increasing hordes of the Anti-Christ and the Enemies of America." Finally, as noted in previous quotations regarding the ceremonial aspect of the lighting, the CNKKKKK stated, "The Cross is never allowed to burn down, but is put out when the ceremony is complete."[31]

Whereas during the 1920s the Klan would, at times, compare itself to Christ, as time progressed throughout the last century and into the present, this aspect of the Klan's religious philosophies became somewhat diminished. The comparison can be said to have ended with the demise of the *Kourier Magazine* in 1936, no such comparison is noted in the *Fiery Cross* established in 1939. By then the principal enemies were communism, fascism and Nazism, Christ became the religious and symbolic leader of a Klan changed by world events. Christ continued to be the Klansman's Criterion of character and the light of the Klan's Christian world. Christ himself evolved within Klan philosophy becoming white with a diminished

Jewishness. His importance was also magnified through the lighted cross which gained much greater significance as part of the Klan's religious ceremony. Finally, Christ was used through the Klan's biblical interpretations to denigrate and remove the Jews as children of God; instead, they became the children of Satan—the anti–Christ.

# 9

# *Refining the Interpretation of the Bible*

In the 1930s the Klan continued with its emphasis on the Bible, especially the twelfth chapter of Romans. This chapter was "recognized throughout the Invisible Empire as the Klansman's Chapter."[1] Klansmen were to present themselves to the service of God as a means of carrying out His divine plan. To those Klansmen who would respond to Paul's appeals there was to be everlasting reward, for "God will without doubt derive temporal and eternal benefit."[2] A Klansman from New Jersey, as had other Klansmen, explained the six symbols of the Klan. Included among the six were "the **Holy Bible**, the **Cross**, the **Flag**, the **Sword**, the **Water** and the **Robe**." The Bible, according to the writer, was an "inestimable gift of **God** to man," it was the "**Book of Books**." It was to be found in every Klavern "open to the twelfth chapter of Romans ... it is a constant reminder of the tenets of the Christian." Emphasizing its importance, the writer declared, "This chapter is a Klansman's law of life."[3]

Emphasis on the Bible as an integral part of what the Klan stood for was consistently included in the *Kourier Magazine*. In a section entitled "Just Kluxing," the paper would include short paragraphs commenting on Klan philosophy or warnings against America's perceived enemies. In one such paragraph the paper included the house divided quote of Christ and stated, "The Klan is for a united America, standing on the national Constitution, holding forth a Bible, and overshadowed by the Stars and Stripes."[4] This emphasis was reiterated by a Klan official from Virginia in a letter sent to the *Kourier Magazine*. Stating that the churches in Virginia were poorly attended and in financial straits, the Klan official requested letters from area citizens to ascertain how the Klan could assist. The letter contained the usual rhetoric concerning the Klan's ideology including references to the Bible: "The principles upon which the order is founded are taken from the twelfth chapter of Paul's letter to the Romans." Stating the intent of the Klan was to "be a powerful adjunct to the Protestant Church," the official declared that along with the flag and the Constitution was the "Holy Bible" as "keystones of Klan principles."[5]

The idea of white supremacy was a philosophy long interpreted as originating from the Bible. In a lengthy article that expounded on the "Ideals and Principles of the Ku Klux Klan," the *Kourier Magazine* stated: "THIS IS A WHITE MAN'S ORGANIZATION, exalting the Caucasian Race and teaching the doctrine of White Supremacy."[6] In the section that covered the Klan's philosophy concerning race, the paper asserted:

> WE STAND FOR WHITE SUPREMACY. Distinction among the races [is] not accidental but by design. This is clearly brought out in the one book that tells authoritatively of the origin of the races. This distinction is not incidental, but is of the vastest import and indicates the wisdom of the divine mind. It is not temporary but is as abiding as the ages that have not yet ceased to roll. The supremacy of the White Race must be maintained, or be overwhelmed by the rising tide of color.[7]

In the second part of the same section, the paper again firmly emphasized the Klan's principle of white supremacy. It adamantly proclaimed the need to maintain white men in positions of authority and stated the Klan would not allow a transfer of power to "blacks or a color, or to permit them to share its control"; that such a transfer or sharing was "an invasion of our sacred constitutional prerogatives and a violation of divinely established law."[8] Established law was, of course, based on biblical interpretation. In an article questioning the equality of man, a Klan supporter affirmed the differences among all living creatures, including man. Blacks, of course, were seen as intellectually inferior and morally degenerate; additionally, "entire races and ethnic groups are fundamentally different from each other—in a qualitative sense." Citing Genesis, such differences had been, according to the writer, designed by God: "God knew what he meant when he ordained slavery back in Genesis 9:25–27."[9]

The ideology of racial inequality, based on God's design, could easily be applied to society at large. Under this religious perspective, the Klan maintained its activism against governmental programs of the 1950s and beyond whose aim was desegregation and social integration. The Klan in effect wanted to maintain separation of the races. George Pepper, Grand Dragon from Fontana, California, stated the order remained "steadfastly opposed to school busing, affirmative action programs and communism." Interjecting the Bible, Pepper conveyed the Klan's religious construct when he stated the Klan believed "in a segregated society based on free enterprise and the Bible," the book Pepper claimed, "clearly advocates racial separation." Interjecting Christ as well, the Klan official further stated, "Jesus said love thy neighbor, but he didn't say what neighborhood to live in."[10]

A segregated society meant race mixing would not occur. As emphasized time and again, this aspect of Klan ideology was based on biblical interpretation. In interpreting the biblical adage of "love thy neighbor," a Klan supporter asked whether this meant "God wanted white people to marry black people and have half-breed children which can only lead to destruction of all races and we would end up with only one race." Asking rhetorically whether God had made a mistake, the writer then stated, "Read the Bible, I Kings Chapter 11 and Leviticus 20:24 and you will see that God did want races to separate. There are hundreds of verses in the Bible which will prove this." Stating that exceptions exist, the writer pointed to King Solomon and his many lovers. However, despite the activities of King Solomon, the writer emphasized the King's error, asserting: "if you read I Kings Chapter 11 you will see that it was against God's commands."[11]

The *Fiery Cross*, established in 1939, published the organization's official pronouncements. As the official mouthpiece of the Klan, it continued with the religious assertions pertaining to God, Christ, and the Bible. In a message to the Klan membership, James A. Colescott, the new Imperial Wizard, affirmed that the Bible was the most published book; it was the "limitless storehouse of Divine Law and human wisdom." Colescott further asserted that "Americans constantly ... read reread, study and love ... the Holy Scriptures." And, in conversation with a minister, Colescott stated, "the Twelfth Chapter of Romans is one of the best known writings in the Bible. You see it i[s] the book upon which the Ku Klux Klan is based."[12]

Also based on biblical interpretation was the burning of the cross, or lighting, as emphasized by the Klan. Arguing against those that viewed the Klan's lighting of the cross as desecrating and sacrilegious, a writer pointed to various places in the Bible where God used fire. According to the writer, "Fire is often used in the Bible as a symbol of God (Deuteronomy 4:24)." Continuing with the citations, the writer noted how Christ was "compared to fire (Malachi 3:2)," and how the Holy Ghost was also "compared to fire (Matthew 3:11)." The writer then turned to Exodus where God spoke through the burning bush. As a form of destruction in Genesis, God used fire to destroy Sodom and Gomorrah, and fire was also used in Leviticus where God destroyed the brothers Nadab and Abihu due to sacrificial profanity. Continuing, the writer pointed to Chronicles where fire fell on Solomon's temple, and Kings where fire fell on Elijah's altar, so too, was Elijah take to heaven "in a chariot of fire." Finally, the writer cites Genesis 3:24 after Adam and Eve are driven from the Garden of Eden; thereafter God placed an angel with a flaming sword to deter re-entry. Finally, the writer turns to Hebrews 12:29 and reiterates his argument stating: "after careful study of these few scriptures that God and fire go hand-in-hand at times! Indeed, 'Our God is a consuming fire.'"[13]

After the 1954 Supreme Court decision of *Brown v. Board of Education*, the United Klans of America became even more adamant regarding white supremacy. The organization included its principles in a five-page pamphlet wherein the organization viewed the court's decision as a major error, claiming the decision nullified "the sovereignty of all states."[14] The National Association for the Advancement of Colored People (NAACP), was declared by the Klan to be "a subversive organization, and is infiltrated with Communistic ideologies." The writer then asserted the Klan was committed to the protection of "American principles" and its biblical beliefs:

> We the Klan will never allow ou[r] blood bought liberties to be crucified on a Roman cross: and we will not yield to the integration of white and Negro races in our schools, or anywhere else.
> We will follow the teachings of the Bible, and not the unwise and one-sided rulings of the U. S. Supreme Court which is not in keeping with the Constitution of the United States of America.[15]

Along with the above statements, the document included the Klan's often stated beliefs that Christianity was "founded on the teachings of Christ." Further, "an infidel or a person who rejects Jesus Christ and His teachings, cannot be a true Klansman."[16] Delving then into the issue of race, the writer, as had been done by countless other Klan officials and supporters, affirmed the concept of white supremacy and declared the Klan was "not anti–Negro, it is the Negro's friend." However, despite this friendship, "the Klan is eternally opposed to the mixing of the white and the colored races. Our creed: Let the white man remain white, the black man black, the yellow man yellow, the brown man brown, and the red man red. God drew the color line, and man should so let it remain, read Acts 17:26 if you please."[17] A more emphatic statement against miscegenation reminded readers of previously existing law that prohibited interracial marriage. Society, however, had changed, but this did not change God's law: "This was based on God's Sacred Word, the Holy Bible, which says that interracial marriage is a sin. Genesis 1:11 says '…after his own kind.' Ezra, in 2, 9, and 10, also warns us not to race mix."[18]

In the *Klansman,* a Klan periodical, were also espoused the Klan's distinctive social and religious beliefs. In an editorial, Klan convert and evangelist the Reverend Gene Neil, ex-military, ex-public defender from Florida, and ex-convict, denounced minorities as murderers and rapists. Declaring that a race war was imminent, he urged white Americans to arm themselves in order to "survive the terrible years to come." Proclaiming himself a Christian who opposed violence, he nevertheless cited Luke 23:36 and stated, "But just before Jesus was crucified—when He knew the heathens were going to try to take over the world—He warned His Christian disciples to take up swords. In fact, He told them that if they did not already have a sword they should sell one of their garments and go purchase a sword (Luke 23:36). The day of the sword is at hand. The day of the Ku Klux Klan is now."[19] In a subsequent editorial, Neil again tied the Bible to the Klan's ideological stand. Attacking Blacks, homosexuals, and communists as purveyors of crime, and in defense of his Christianity and Klan membership, Neil stated, "The Invisible Empire Knights of the Ku Klux Klan is not only a sound Christian organization—founded upon and guided by fundamental Bible teachings—but, perhaps of almost equal importance, it is the only Christian organization in the world today actively and effectively fighting communism, homosexuality, X-rated schools, crime, terrorism and racial and sexual perversion." He then stated his motivation for being a member of the hooded order; it was, according to Neil, "the only Christian organization and that is why—as a Bible believing Baptist evangelist and as a flag-waving American patriot—I am a proud member and eager supporter of the Klan."[20]

In another article in the *Klansman*, the concept of faith was delved into with the ultimate objective to affirm the belief that white Americans were the chosen people of God. It was faith in Christ and the gospel that would lead to "faith in ourselves." Referring to Genesis, the writer stated Ham was cursed because of "race-mixing." Hatred of the Jews, according to the writer, was due to God's blessings," their "genealogy," and "racial purity." Part of the key to the belief in whites being God's chosen people is Exodus which deals with the Jews in captivity. In Deuteronomy 7:1–3; 7:16; and 20:17 the Israelis gain ascendency in Canaan, but fail to completely subjugate all its enemies. In Judges 1:27–36, according to the writer, the failure by the Jews is a failure to obey God's instructions. Then citing Numbers 33:55 and Judges 2:3, the tribes not subjugated by the Israeli now become "pricks in the eyes of the Israel tribes." These "pricks in the eyes," are "high taxes for welfare programs," and "the sin of race-mixing and destruction of lineage purity." Referring back Deuteronomy 4:7–8, the writer now identifies the United States as the referenced "great and mighty nation ... now being destroyed by atheist court rulings, worldly sins, forced race-mixing" and "having turned from God's word." Combining Genesis 27:28 and 49:25–26, as well as Deuteronomy 8:7–9, the writer references the mineral riches and abundance of food as again meaning the United States. Then referencing Hosea 1:10; 11:2, and Chronicles 7:14, these biblical citations are indications of the "Christians called sons of God." The mandates to teach the gospel to nations found in Genesis 28:14 and Isaiah 43:10–12, 21 is a reference to what the United States has been doing. Also from Isaiah 28:14 the reference to a new language is interpreted to be English. And in Luke 1:77, 2:32, and Hebrews 8:10–13 and 9:14–17, the new covenant church means Christians. From Samuel 7:10, Chronicles 17:9, and the entire chapter of Isaiah 41, and 49:12, the reference to a new homeland is once again the U.S. Then from Isaiah 42:16–19, Hosea 1:9, 10; 2:6, and Romans 11:25, 26, comes the biblical assumption that white Americans were unaware of their true identity as God's chosen people. The final citation is from John 8:33 where the Israeli claim to be of "Abraham's seed" and never having been in bondage. At this point the writer brings the argument to its conclusion: "Note: therefore, having never been in bondage, the Jews could not possibly be true Israel. Our eyes are opened, we understand. Praise the name of Jesus."[21]

In another article claiming white Americans are the true children of God, in this case Caucasians, the writer begins his argument by stating, "If you are a Caucasian, you are also Israelite according to Webster and the Holy Bible." Citing Webster's Encyclopedia of Dictionaries with a publication date of 1958, the writer affirms the work, on page 64, states, "Caucasian pertains to the white race originating from the Caucasus Mountains near the Black Sea." Turning then to Kings 15:15 the writer declares the Bible states "Israel would be scattered north of the river Euphrates." This came about when, according to 2 Kings 17:6; 18:9–11, in 721 BC the Jews "were taken captive and driven by the Assyrians into the Caucasus Mountains located between the Caspian and Black Seas." The final citation in the article references Hosea 2:6 claiming that the blocking of the path with "thorns" meant that "God was making it clear that the tribes were not to return to Palestine. As Israel left the mountains and migrated into Europe, and finally to North America, they became known as CAUCASIANS."[22]

The ideological belief that white Christians are God's chosen and are the lost tribes of Israel was also pursued in yet another article entitled "White Christian Roots." As in the previous cited work, the argument was that the lost tribes of Israel migrated to Northern Europe and from there to the Americans, specifically the U.S. In setting the argument, the writer stated the usual; that the Klan believes "in the tenets of the Christian religion," and in Christ as the Son of God. According to the writer, to understand the connection between the Klan and Christianity, "one must realize that the White Caucasian's roots are deeply inbedded [sic] in Bible history and in Christianity, and that had it not been for the White Race, Christianity would not be established all throughout the world as it is today." The loss by the "White" Jews of their relationship with God came about as follows: "During the time of the 19 Kings and 7 Dynasties, the 10-tribed Kingdoms of Israel, which had since split from the biblical nation of Judah, sinned greatly against God by rejecting His everlasting covenant (Exodus 31:12–18)." As a result of this, according to the writer, "they lost the knowledge of God their Creator, and they lost all Hebrew languages and customs."[23]

Tracing, in Leviticus 26, the Israeli defeat and captivity by Assyria to the Caucasus Mountains, the writer claims that Israelites, "within 100 years, they migrated North by Northwest and eventually became 'lost.' The 10-tribed Kingdom of Israel became the 'Lost 10 Tribes of Israel.'" These lost tribes, according to the author, were the tribes of Ephraim and Manasseh. The writer claims a different set of Israeli were conquered and sent into captivity to Babylon. It is this set of Israelis that return to Jerusalem and who tampered "with the Mosaic Laws ... giving us the anti–Christ religion of Judaism." Meanwhile, the Israelis that had traveled to Northern Europe continued their travels to England and eventually the U.S. These separated or "lost" tribes "reaped their rewards according to the prophesies of Genesis 48 and 49. History has proven—without a doubt that Ephraim and Manasseh are representatives of the countries known today as Great Britain and the United States ... countries founded by, nurtured by, and developed by the White Caucasian Race." These countries, based on the writer's biblical interpretation, have received the blessings "described in Genesis 48:14–16 and Genesis 49:22." Based on the interpretative explanations Ephraim and Manasseh, "received the right to the name of Israel ... and their descendants were never Jews." Further, it was to these tribes "that Jesus Christ was referring to when he told His disciples in Matthew 10:6 'But go to the lost sheep of the House of Israel.' It was in these 'lost 10 tribes' (also referred to as 'Gentiles in the Bible) that the seed of Christianity was to be nurtured."[24]

A threat to white Americans as God's chosen was the anti–Christ. This was identified in an article in the *Klansman* as other religions that did not believe in Christ and communists who had taken control of

America from within. Like other pro–Klan writers, the author of the article asserted America was a Christian nation. However, "the Constitution is being misinterrupted [sic] as is the Bible. America was founded by White Christians for a Christian nation. Freedom means nothing if imposed by anit-Christ [sic] races or false Gods and idols." The author claimed that such forces had "committed the worst of crimes against God." Americans, however, would rise against its enemies because "true Christians have never been lambs lead to slaughter but brave men and women who stand united together as kinsmen in blood and spirit, one God, one people, against the anti–Christ. (Read) 2nd John 7–9 then ask yourself what race and religious people do not believe in Jesus Christ. This is the anti–Christ." The writer then invoked the birth of Christ to provide validity to the organization: "When Christ was born three kings came to bring gifts to him, henceforth the three K.K.K." The writer also asserted, "Romans 12 is our code and the circle of life our stand [sic] for he came from the east." Invoking the Bible the writer further stated, "The entire basics of the Klan law is taken from the Bible and in Rev. 7:9 we are spoken of, this is how our forefathers foreseen [sic] the protectors of our Christian nation."[25]

By the late 1980s the Christian Identity movement had gained greater momentum, this ideology was also defended by the Klan through biblical interpretation. West Virginia Grand Dragon Gregory Beckett, in defense of the ideology against negative publicity by newspapers, emphasized: "The movement bases its beliefs on the teachings of the divinely inspired word of God. Its basic belief is that white, Anglo Saxons are the 'lost' ten tribes of Israel and are the 'chosen people' spoken of in the Bible." Emphasizing the religious aspect of the movement, Beckett noted the perspective of some ministers: "It seems that many so-called clergymen think that 'Identity' is a perversion of authentic religious values and a source of bigotry, racism and anti-semitism [sic]. (Note that the word 'values' is not the same as 'beliefs')." Beckett also argued that criticism of the movement was directed by religious leaders who espoused "the world religion of Secular Humanism," and by "the anti–Christ Satanic Seed, the so-called 'chosen ones,' the infernal Jews." Such leaders, asserted Beckett, "have long distorted the word of God Almighty and have led astray millions of our racial kinsmen." The ideology held by the Klan was the true faith because opponents to the movement had caused the order's racial kinsfolks "to believe the false doctrine that all men are created equal, and that the Church of God allows interracial and homosexual marriage and relationships." Accordingly, such teachings had "distorted and changed all of God's laws." It also misrepresented Christ who "came only 'but unto the lost sheep of the *House of Israel* (Matthew 15:24) to that of one which encompasses *all* mankind."[26]

Arguing that religious opponents were destroying the nation with their irreligious dogmas, Beckett then cited the biblical reference of false prophets: "Well did the prophet speak of modern day 'preachers' in Jeremiah 50:6: 'My people hath been lost sheep, their shepherds have caused them to go astray.' The 'Shepherds' of today condemn the Identity Movement because it follows and obeys the word of God and calls those into account who do not—Shepherd and Sheep alike!" Offering advice to the religious leaders of "the world religion of Secular Humanism" who preach "from their Synagogues of Satan," and to their followers, Beckett stated, "Read Matthew 7:15 and follow suit. And to you Sheep that follow those Shepherds, read Matthew 7:15–20." To further underscore the seed line belief of the Identity Movement, Beckett asserted the opposition of the Jewish "Satan Seed" was based on biblical misinterpretation and desire by Jews to maintain their special status: "For too long has the 'Seed of the Woman' mistaken the 'Seed of the Serpent,' as depicted in Genesis 3:15, for that of 'the chosen seed.' When the true 'seed' is recognized, 'that which was, will no longer be.'" As final justification for the Identity ideology, Beckett quoted Mathew 5:11 and 10:22 wherein the true believers are persecuted for their beliefs.[27]

White supremacy was but one of the many philosophies espoused and supported through biblical interpretation. Web-based Klan organizations were just as adamant on this point as was the Klan of the 1920s. The entire Bible was the correct path that was to be followed by the organization; such was the pronouncement of the Original Knight Riders, Knights of the Ku Klux Klan. Further, based on their beliefs, they were right while others were wrong.

> The men and women of the Invisible Empire, Original Knight Riders, Knights of the Ku Klux Klan further believe and accept the Holy Bible as being the infallible, unerring Word of God, written by men divinely inspired by the Holy Ghost to do so, and that the Word is written in a literal, yet symbolic, fashion; the Holy Scriptures are accepted as their "official guidebook and road map on the path of life" (Hebrews 4:12).
>
> Regardless of what modern-day theologians, bible scholars, or "politicrats" may state, the men and women of the Invisible Empire, Original Knight Riders, Knights of the Ku Klux Klan believe that the Ten Commandments, all biblical ordinances, principles, laws, edicts, and mandates of Almighty God as spelled out in scripture do not change. Like the Holy Trinity, they are everlasting—"politically-correct" or not. True Klansmen and Klanswomen will defend them and obey them at all costs (Malachi 3:6; Hebrews 13:8). As was written by the First Era Klansmen: "While I breathe, I trust the cross—with God as my leader and my sword as my companion."[28]

Invoking Christ as a means to legitimize the philosophy and attract adherents, the pronouncement ended with and appeal for support, "Don't you want to be on the winning side? For more information on how to accept Jesus Christ as your personal Lord and Savior and on how you too may become an active participant in the White Liberation Movement by joining this organization, please write to our national headquarters or call our hot line."[29]

The Aryans Nation, Knights of the Ku Klux Klan also addressed the Bible in their proclamation. Much as the Klan of the 1920s and the Original Knight Riders, Knights of the Ku Klux Klan, the Aryans Nation KKK, and for that matter as do some major Protestant orders, viewed the Bible as the literal word of God, and the guideline of life's rules, especially for the Klan:

> This Book Divine signifies that there is a God. No sane man of reasonable Intelligence can look upon the sacred volume without thinking of YHVH as its author, Righteousness as its aim, and eternal life as its end. It is a constant reminder that YHVH is our Father. Life is our opportunity, and heaven is our home. It reveals the way of life, the cause of death. It is a LAMP unto our feet, a light unto our pathway and the only sure guide to right living. It is the book of books and reveals the only true God who is called YaHWeH.
> 
> In a Klavern you will always find this wonderful book opened at the twelfth chapter of Romans. This is the most practical and the most complete chapter in the whole Bible on the CHRISTIAN living. It is a constant reminder of the tenets of the Christian faith, and is a Klansman's law of life. Every Klansman should read it the first thing every morning and endeavor to live by it during the day. 'I BESEECH YOU THEREFORE BRETHREN BY THE MERCIES OF GOD,' that you follow its teachings.[30]

Along with the Bible, the proclamation also referenced the white robe worn by the Klan. As has been pointed out, in their white robes the totality of the Klan represented the multitudes referenced in Revelations. Wearing of the robe signified a closeness and similarity to Christ, a cleanliness that would be approved by God upon entering heaven:

> This white robe is also a symbol of the robe of righteousness to be worn by the Saints in the Kingdom of Heaven we shall establish here on earth. The sage apostle, a prisoner on the Island of Patmos, peered into the portals of the Great Beyond, and caught a glimpse of that Saint robed in white which was the righteousness of Christ. Taking Christ as our criterion of character, and endeavoring to follow His teachings, Aryan Nations Knights wear this white robe to signify that they desire to put on that white robe which is the righteousness of Christ, in that Empire Invisible which is our Holy Aryan Nations, the Sanctified Race of YaHWeH, that lies out beyond the vale of death where there will be no more parting and no more tears.
> 
> A lying scoundrel may wrap his disgraceful frame in the sacred folds of a Knight's robe, but as the scripture says, a whited sepulcher is still full of dead mens [sic] bones. Therefore, as we seek to be Holy Aryan Knights, may we through the grace

## 9. Refining the Interpretation of the Bible   163

of God and by following His Christ, be able to hide the scars and stains of sin with the righteousness that is Christ when we stand before His Great White Throne.[31]

The emphasis on the Bible can be clearly seen in the proclamations located on the websites of the Imperial Knights of America, Kingdom Identity Ministries and the New Empire Knights of the Ku Klux Klan. The three sites include the same proclamation and it is probably found on the sites of other white supremacist and Christian Identity groups. The proclamation is said to be "a brief statement of our major doctrinal beliefs as taught by the Holy Scriptures." The pronouncements include the religious philosophies of these groups and is replete with biblical references regarding their belief in God, His selection of a chosen people, Christ as the Redeemer and Savior, His return on judgment day, redemption for "individual Israelites," baptism and resurrection, the Covenant made by God, Christ as their High Priest, and His bond to the twelve tribes of Israel.[32]

It is at this point that the biblical interpretations of these groups bring into play their version regarding a "special race of people" from the "seedline of Isaac and Jacob." Included among the beliefs is that a covenant "was made with the Children of Israel," who, based on their tenets, are the "White, Anglo-Saxon, Germanic and kindred people" who are "God's true, literal Children of Israel." (See Appendix A for the full text as provided by Kingdom Identity Ministries.) According to their doctrines, "Only this race fulfills every detail of Biblical Prophecy and World History concerning Israel and continues in these latter days to be heirs and possessors of the Covenants, Prophecies, Promises and Blessings YHVH God made to Israel." Further, the white race is the "chosen seedline making up the 'Christian Nations'" and is set apart from all others as it "stands far superior to all other peoples in their call as God's servant race." It is this chosen race that is identified as the true "descendants of the 12 tribes of Israel," who "have carried God's Word, the Bible, throughout the world" and "have used His Laws in the establishment of their civil governments and are the 'Christians' opposed by the Satanic Anti-Christ forces of this world who do not recognize the true and living God." Placing the finishing touches on their belief as the chosen race, the proclamation includes the Klan's belief in "the Devil or Satan and called the Serpent" and his descendants who are "commonly called Jews today."[33] Within this ideology, Jews are the masters in a world conspiracy designed to destroy Christianity and the white race. As the leaders of the conspiracy, Jews are utilizing non-white minorities to achieve their ends.[34] The conspiracy, according to some believers, involved Jewish invention of Christianity as a means to undermine the Roman Empire, and is currently being used to achieve integration and miscegenation.[35]

Along with the above stated philosophies, the various elements of a religious Manifest Destiny can be gleaned from the Klan's religious statements. The entire proclamation serves as an excellent source document for deconstructing the Klan's religious ideology and understanding the order's intimate relationship to mainstream Protestant America. This is not to say that the proclamations mirror the same philosophies of mainstream America, rather, the manner in which the Klan links itself to God, to Christ, and through biblical references, is the same methodology used by modern-day preachers and Televangelists. The format would be easily recognized by non–Klan Protestants seeking religious explanations from the Bible. The methodology is similar, the message, however, is different.

As has been pointed out, a relationship exists between the thinking of mainstream Christian fundamentalists and Klan ideology. This can be determined by the statement of the Reverend Bailey Smith. On August 22, 1980, Smith, a member of the Moral Majority and then the President of the Southern Baptist Convention, stated God did not hear the prayers of Jews. According to Smith:

> It's interesting to me at great political battles how you have a Protestant to pray and a Catholic to pray and then you have a Jew to pray. With all due respect to those dear people, my friend, God Almighty does not hear the prayer of a Jew. For how in the world can God hear the prayer of a man who says that Jesus Christ is not the true Messiah? It is blasphemy. It may be politically expedient, but no one can pray unless he prays through the name of Jesus Christ.[36]

Despite criticism from other Christian leaders, Smith never apologized for his comment. But Smith is not the only Christian leader that has been derogatory against Jews. In 2003 Albert Mohler, president of Southern Baptist Theological Seminary in Louisville, Kentucky, compared Judaism to a "deadly tumor,"[37] and stated that Christians needed to continue evangelizing Jews in order to convert them to the true religion. These are but two examples of such beliefs, beliefs that, when stated by mainstream fundamentalist Christians, simply strengthen the religious ideology and pronouncements of the Klan. Even more harm is done when political leaders silently support, openly acquiesce, or rhetorically state similar pronouncements for political gain.

# Summary: Thoughts and Connections

Klan printed material from the 1920s to the present point to the organization's use of religion as a means to obtain legitimacy and recognition. Elements of the population in 1920s American society who saw the need for a religious crusade to cleanse the nation were easily recruited by the Klan. To such individuals it was important to address real or perceived ills, foreign and domestic, immoral and un–American. Using rhetoric that created an emotional response imbued with a spiritual motivation, the Klan attacked any group or issue it deemed threatening to the country. Its close association, indeed its stated divine connection with God, Christ, and the Bible, gave it an easily recognizable enticement with which mainstream Protestants could identify. The fervent religious motivation to engage in uplifting society, in becoming involved in beneficial societal activity, in the cleansing and establishment of a morally respectable government, in protecting women, home and country, as portrayed by the Klan, no doubt created a desire to participate in these worthwhile activities.

As a means to engage and showcase the Klan's strength and presence, the organization used both language and symbols, especially the cross, to provide for itself a legitimate footing within mainstream America and Protestant groups. However, the historical cultural prejudices deeply rooted in American society served to create identifiable scapegoats upon whom the Klan vented its religiously inspired bigotry. Through religious rhetoric extending back to Europe, colonial America, early nationhood, the nineteenth and twentieth centuries, and the first two decades of the twenty-first century, the Klan carved for itself a place in the American conscience. Using God, Christ, and the Bible, the Klan reinforced and solidified America's cultural history, especially so in the 1920s, regarding race, religion, and nativism. It vociferously reiterated the cultural and religious history of the nation as a means to obtain acceptance of its ideology, an ideology deeply rooted in the nation as a whole. It was through God that America and the Nordic race came into existence. The Klan, and by extension its religious and racial philosophies, were also created by God, and it was up to the Klan to ensure that God's creations were protected through the divine authority placed upon them. By arguing that such authority had been bestowed upon them by God, the Klan touched on an emotional tie with other Americans who also wanted to become part of the divine inspiration. The fundamentalist fervor of the time lent impetus to people's desires to engage in God's work, and God's Klanishness could spread itself upon those engaged in such activities.

Christ, who suffered for man, as the Klansman's example, was used to provide validity to Klankraft, racial uniqueness, and an ideology that placed the organization and individual Klansmen in a Christ-like position. The identification with Christ, his teachings, his Klannishness, his betrayal, his sacrifice, provided a societal position for Klansmen in which their actions were seen as serving for the betterment of the nation. Couched in messianic rhetoric, the Klan could justify its actions because it, like Christ, was misunderstood and persecuted. To claim that the Klan followed Christ's teaching also provided easy connection to mainstream Protestantism, which the Klan professed to be strengthening. Ministers seeking avenues to engage and enlarge their congregations saw the Klan as an organization that could assist in reviving Protestant enthusiasm and passion. Thousands of ministers joined the order to strengthen Protestantism, increase their congregations, or increase their pocketbooks. Regardless of the reason, it was through religion, through God, through Christ, that the Klan attained enormous success. This is not to say that other social issues that the Klan pursued were not as equally important, however, the religious incentives established by the Klan's philosophies should receive the same amount of validity regarding the success of the order.

As further proof of its divinely ordained mission, the Bible was used to explain the Klan's prophesied origination. Biblical interpretations were used to demonstrate the evilness of the Catholic Church; to identify the Scarlet Woman; to paint Catholics as engaged in a conspiracy to overthrow American institutions, and America itself. Biblical passages were construed in such fashion so as to identify the Klan as an integral part of biblical history, a history that prophesied its divine origin or its rise as dictated by evolving circumstances. The Bible, God's word, dictated the separation of races, the supremacy of the white race, indeed it was the basis for everything, from a religious standpoint, that the Klan professed to believe. Being God's word, it had to be upheld, for to do otherwise would be treason to God.

God, Christ, the Bible, and what the Klan wrote was based on religious freedom. Time and again the Klan argued for the freedom to privately interpret the word of God as one of its principle tenets. That freedom was eventually used to the extreme to explain and justify Klan philosophies involving every facet of their beliefs. The Klan's own interpretation of God's word and of Christianity provided the rationalization and validity to espouse a white supremacy that could be traced back to European Nordic races, something that modern day White Racialist and White Identity groups are most adept at accentuating. Further, by interweaving dogmatic religious interpretations, Middle Eastern, European, and early colonial history inclusive of settlers who arrived seeking religious freedom, and national heroes from the founding fathers onward, individuals whose whiteness and Protestantism was stressed, the exclusion of any non-white and any role played in America's history by such groups was completely and conveniently ignored. America was a white man's country; Catholics, Jews, and any non-white element had no claim and needed the white man's consent to be part of American society and politics. Everything was overlaid with religion because through divine providence, through prophecy and through the Bible, the nation and God's chosen race came into existence; America was Israel and the Israelites were white Protestants as rationalized through Seed Line ideology.

Although its genesis extends to Europe and American settlement, the ideology of white supremacy and American biblical uniqueness received enormous impetus in the 1920s through Klan spoken and written material. From the fundamentalist ideology prevalent during the period, the connection to God was not difficult to make. Wrapping the rhetoric in the form of a crusade and the maintenance of God's divine decisions, the Klan shrouded itself under the mantle of God and Protestantism. It incorporated other issues that were important to American society of the time—patriotism, immigration, education, race, law and order, morality— and through its rhetoric these issues were enveloped in religion. Religion, because of its significance at the time, was the most opportune methodology. Previous historical interpretations have viewed this aspect of Klan rhetoric as religious intolerance, but to not ascribe any value to the order's emphasis on what it considered its beliefs, the basis for the organization, is to view this as simple propaganda. This work has demonstrated that religion has been an integral aspect of Klan philosophies for over one hundred years.

Indeed, a review of works on the Klan during Reconstruction will find the same religious ideology. The expansion and refinement of that ideology, however, has taken place during the twentieth and twenty-first centuries. The concept of Aryanism, White Israelites, Adamic Seed Line ideology, and all sundry philosophies associated with this ideology have been more fully developed to the point that the Bible has become the true basis for these doctrines. A simple review of the religious proclamations and biblical interpretations referenced throughout the book will suffice to understand the extent and importance of religion to the Klan. As previously stated, whether this emphasis on religion is indeed an intrinsic, fundamental, and essential element of their philosophies or whether it is used to justify bigotry, prejudice, and violence is difficult to ascertain. By the same token, how different is the Klan to other groups who are perceived to maintain extremist religious ideologies such as Islamic extremists, Davidians, or fundamentalist Mormons? Even when viewed as an extremist's perspective, the beliefs of these groups are provided more validity than those of the Klan; somehow, radical religious ideologies are accepted as part of these group's dogmas, but those of the Klan do not have the same amount of perceived legitimacy. Be that as it may; whether or not the Klan's religious ideology is perceived as valid or not, that the organization proclaims it, and has proclaimed it for over one hundred years, should provide such beliefs even partial validity.

As has been previously stated, what is evident over the past one hundred years is the evolving nature of the Klan's philosophies. During the 1920s the organization asserted numerous times that its existence was attributed to God. It was through God's divine will that the order received its mission to protect American ideals and strengthen Protestantism. The organization not only came into existence through God, He also provided His protection and His guidance. An integral part of God's divine will was white supremacy arrived at through God-ordained separation of the races. By the early 1950s, throughout the remainder of the twentieth and into the twenty-first century, the argument regarding the divine origin of the Klan, although reiterated on occasion, was no longer the emphasis. Rather, as a result of *Brown v. Board of Education of Topeka* (1954), which overturned *Plessy v. Ferguson* (1896), the key issues became separation of the races and miscegenation. The inflexibility on this issue became even fiercer throughout the Civil Rights Movement and to the present. Separation of the races and race-mixing, were, and is still seen, as violation of God's law, and like other Klan ideology, the Bible is used as the vehicle to support this dogma. However, the obstinacy, especially so after *Brown v. Board of Education of Topeka* makes it appear that the Klan shifted their emphasis not because of religious ideology, but because of simple prejudice and bigotry. Reestablishment of segregation became a paramount issue and the experience with biblical interpretation dictated the direction the Klan took in order to religiously substantiate their position. Be that as it may, to the Klan, all of God's laws, as interpreted by the various organizations, must be upheld regardless of the changes occurring in American society. In so doing, the Klan views itself as living based on God's word, that it does so gives the order its determination, its resoluteness to the point of obstinacy and inflexibility. However, how different is this than is the case with Islamic terrorist, Davidians, or Mormon fundamentalists?

As noted in the in chapter on Christ, post–1920s, during the 1920s the Klan on many occasions compared itself to Christ. Christ was their example, Christ was Klannish and created his own Klan, indeed, Christ was a Klansman. By the late twentieth and early twenty-first century these ideologies had been collapsed into two basic principles. Christ continued to be the standard by which Klansmen measured themselves and aspired to emulate. Christ also became white, losing his Jewishness, and through Klan biblical interpretation He condemned Jews who have now become the devil's spawn. Sundry to these ideologies is Christ's dying on the cross which has become the central part of the order's ceremony when lighted. Christ remains central to the order's ideology by virtue of being the central figure in the rise of Christianity. And regardless of the fact that Christ was born and died a Jew, it is not the Jewishness that is emphasized, rather, it is His role in establishment of Christian beliefs, beliefs the Klan is sworn to uphold against its perceived enemies, beliefs based on the order's biblical interpretations.

With respect to the Bible, it has been the key fundamental feature of Klan ideology that has undergone the most change. Not so much in the beliefs as interpreted, rather, the extent to which the Bible has been used to expand and support the Klan's beliefs. The Bible, as the basis of religious beliefs for millions of Christians across the world, and which has be interpreted in innumerable ways, has been dissected and interpreted by the Klan for the Klan. All areas of Klan ideology have been expanded through biblical interpretations as a means to provide itself religious validity, a validity that in many respects is no different than that of mainstream denominations. The validity, however, is based on an American cultural history that was very much alive and part of mainstream culture up through the 1960s. But as society has progressed beyond the Civil Rights Movement and younger generations have come of age in a society that is much more open and whose diversity is much more accepted, the Klan has retrenched itself in a culture that harks back to a time when the social structure was dominated by white perspectives that viewed non-whites as inferior and who were successfully marginalized. That marginalization has given way to an inclusiveness that creates a sense of diminished importance, of diminished opportunities. What the Klan has done through its religious and social philosophies is to create a world based more on a religious, rather than social self-marginalization. Through its biblically based religious interpretations and philosophies, interpretations and philosophies arrived at by all groups who base their beliefs on religion, a sense of right and wrong, of truth and falsehood is developed. Once these religiously based philosophies are refined to maturity, as may be seen for the Klan, the groups see themselves persecuted for what they believe is the maintenance of their understanding of "God's laws."

Having stated what is included above, how much has really changed within that significant portion of American society that espouses, either verbally or through quiet acquiescence, the Klan's religious ideology? Here, it may appear that a deviation from the thesis of the work is taking place. However, what is attempted is to demonstrate the underlying religious connection between Klan ideology and mainstream religious and political leaders and groups. Mainstream America must understand that the Klan simply reflects what America once was; that its philosophies were at one point mainstream American philosophies. The Klan represents an archaic America, an America that has changed with time. The Klan represents "the good old days" of a repressive, prejudiced and bigoted America. That repressiveness, that prejudice, that bigotry had a basis in a cultural history deeply influenced by religion. And it is religion that the Klan uses to justify its beliefs. To understand that connection allows us to review and analyze some of Imperial Wizard Hiram Wesley Evans' statements gleaned from his 1926 contribution to the *North American Review*:

> As to charges that the Klan brought race and religion into politics, that simply is not true. That was done by the very people who are now accusing us, because we are cutting into the profits they had been making in politics out of *their* races and *their* religion. Race and religion have been used by the aliens as political platforms. The Klan is in no way responsible for this condition. We merely recognize it when others dared not, and we fight it in the open. Our belief is that any man who runs for office or asks political favors, or advocates policies or carries on any other political activity, either as a member of any racial or religious group, or in the interests

of or under orders from such a group or of any non–American interest whatever, should be opposed for that very reason. The Klan's ambition is to get race and religion out of politics, and that cannot be done so long as any profit is exploiting them. It therefore fights every attempt to use them.[1]

The statements by Evans can in effect be placed squarely on any politician that, by their pandering to conservative religious groups of any religious stripe, attempts by and through that support to obtain funding in pursuit of religious agendas whose ultimate objective is to overlay the group's religious views on American society. Religion, in and of itself, is part and parcel of the cultural wars that have been eating away at American society and creating groups such as the Tea Party whose obstructionist policies, politically, bring the nation to a standstill. Such obstructionism is no different than the ideologies of the Klan whose policies are such that stopping any further perceived erosion of American ideals is preferable than to be in violation of "God's laws." Groups or individuals who resort to race or religion as a means to pursue political agendas are simply utilizing practices with a long history in American politics. In so doing such groups or individuals are both parroting what the Klan does, albeit in a less overt manner, and providing such organizations encouragement to pursue their religiously based philosophies.

The second comment points to the perennial aspect of the Klan. Stating that the hooded order had gained the "leadership in the movement for Americanism," Evans asserted the Klan's influence:

> Except for a few lonesome voices, almost drowned by the clamor of the alien and the alien-minded "Liberal," the Klan alone faces the invader. This is not to say that the Klan has gathered into its membership all who are ready to fight for America. The Klan is the champion, but it is not merely an organization. It is an idea, a faith, a purpose, an organized crusade. No recruit to the cause has ever been really lost. Though men and women drop from the ranks they remain with us in purpose, and can be depended on fully in any crisis. Also, there are many millions who have never joined, but who think and feel and –when called on— fight with us. This is our real strength, and no one who ignores it can hope to understand America today.[2]

Here again is the relationship between the Klan, mainstream Protestant America, and the nation's cultural history. Such association could be easily comprehended in the 1920s, though it is much more difficult today. However, the similarity of thinking is still alive in America's cultural undercurrent and political arena. Still at the forefront is the issue of immigration, of "taking back our country," the divide between liberals and conservatives. The Klan of the 1920s and exceedingly proactive conservative groups today, are not that different in their ideology. It is for this reason that the Klan has survived and will continue to do so for the foreseeable future.

A third comment involves the conservative perspective regarding elements in American society that are seen as leeches living off governmental programs. In this instance, Evans's comment is similar to Mitt Romney's "47 percent" speech reflective of the conservative wing of Republican Party, and Tea Party philosophy that again points to the cultural wars that have become an insidious aspect of American politics. For Evans, it was American liberalism that was to blame for the perceived problems leading the nation asunder:

> The plain people now see that Liberalism has come completely under the dominance of weaklings and parasites whose alien "idealism" reaches it logical peak in the Bolshevist platform of "produce as little as you can, beg or steal from those who do produce, and kill the producer for thinking he is better than you." Not all liberalism goes so far, but it all seems to be on that road. The average Liberal idea is apparently that those who can produce should carry the unfit, and let the unfit rule them.[3]

In any time period in American history when the country, from the point of view of conservative elements, appears to be teetering on disaster due to societal changes, there arise groups who claim to be working for the benefit of the nation. A variety of arguments are utilized as a basis for their perspectives, and within the arguments scapegoats are identified as elements that are assisting in the deterioration of American cultural ideals. Such was the Klan of the 1920s, such is the Klan of today, and such is mainstream religious and political rhetoric and action. However, these ideological arguments are vocalized by a wide variety of groups throughout America. The similarity of the arguments, especially when enveloped or driven by religious ideology determines the philosophical similarities and at times an inter-group association, be they Klan organizations or mainstream organizations with similar dogmas. Unrelated groups, however, may be driven by the same religious ideology (this would include political action groups represented by sub-elements within political parties), but at different levels of emphasis and activity. The fundamental basis for such ideology, however, is excessive fear associated with a changing society that engenders a feeling of disorientation and displacement alleviated through rationalized religious beliefs.

Despite the Klan's interpretations, their beliefs are such that marginalization is inevitable. American society and the world is changing, but the Klan's ideology remains rooted in an ever more archaic social and religious cultural perspective that once permeated American society. And although there remain threads of that perspective, a perspective that is evident in the religious and political rhetoric of excessively conservative groups and leaders, greater society appears to be moving towards a more accepting culture, especially so by virtue of the multiplicity of ethnic/racial groups. That excessively conservative views are advocated by religious leaders is understandable, much like the Klan it is based on their religious beliefs and the beliefs of their followers. However, when political leaders support, acquiesce, or vocalize the same or similar rhetoric for political gain, it serves only to provide validity to rhetoric or beliefs that are counter to the fundamental principles on which the nation was founded. Such utterances serve only to provide organizations like the Klan who profess, based on their beliefs, a desire to uphold a narrow interpretation of what the Constitution means; what rights and guarantees it provides and to whom, and use biblical interpretations to justify such beliefs. It is the unsolicited rhetorical support of political leaders that provides the Klan a partial basis to keep its restrictive social and religious ideology alive.

That ideology is extensively shared through the use of the Internet, a luxury the Klan of the 1920s did not have. A review of Klan websites will quickly demonstrate how these like-minded organizations have incorporated the same expanded religious arguments; arguments that have been extensively refined through biblical interpretations to confront the changing social and political policies deemed prejudicial to whites. Some websites include links to branches located in multiple states and to other Klan groups. Some include links to Christian Identity, Blood Line and other white supremacist organizations. There are various unifying factors that create a sense of group identity for both similar and disparate ideologies held by the organizations.

First and foremost is the white supremacist ideology given much greater credence through expanded biblical interpretation with emphasis on the White Christian and Seed Line concept. While some websites delve into the anti–Jewish argument as a means to bolster the argument, some do not and simply state their belief in white supremacy. Added to this argument is the biblical interpretation of separation of the races, eugenics and miscegenation. These beliefs lead to opposition to mainstream religions, especially Protestant, and an anti-governmental stance. In both instances this is due to a more inclusive society based on anti-discrimination and anti-segregationist governmental policies. Opposition to mainstream Protestant denominations is due to the perception of having caved in to governmental policies, policies deemed as detrimental to whites. Another area of keen and shared interest among the websites is the opposition to gay rights. Here the opposition is principally against the government for its anti-discrimination policies. In all instances the opposition is grounded on a religious basis through biblical interpretation that charges Klan opponents as being in violation of God's laws.

While the Internet may serve as a vehicle to share and disseminate Klan religious ideologies, it also serves as a means to counter what many see as bigotry and prejudice. This can be seen in Klan blogs where some opposition to its philosophies appears. Additionally, there are a variety of opposition organizations that maintain their own websites providing extensive information on the Klan, the prime example being the Southern Poverty Law Center, co-founded by Morris Dees.

Regardless of how the Internet, visual, or printed materials are used, the fundamental question is whether the Klan has used religion to provide itself legitimacy. It is the belief of the author that more than enough material has been presented to clearly demonstrate this has been the case for at least one hundred years—since the inception of the twentieth century Klan in 1915. With respect to the Klan of the 1920s, from the perspective of the author, why support for the organization dropped so precipitously beginning in 1924 needs to be explored. The extent of its extralegal activities most certainly posed a threat to rule of law and created a strong backlash that led to increased public, political, and judicial opposition. Undoubtedly political defeat in various states, along with legislative action against the order, played a role. However, from a moral and thus religious perspective, if one does a study of Klan leadership there is clear evidence that Klan leaders were lacking in the virtues they were publically extolling. The most evident example is that of David C. Stephenson, Indiana's Grand Dragon who was eventually sent to prison for murder (see David Chalmers' *Hooded Americanism*). In many instances Klan leaders at all levels, including Evans and Simmons, were more preoccupied with monetary gains and the maintenance of power than the preservation of moral standards. Whether the religious foundation, including divine origins of the Klan was actually believed by its leaders is questionable. However, their insistence on this, the pronouncements of like assertions by supporters, especially by Protestant ministers and other religious leaders, certainly provided the Klan an aura of religiosity. That it did provided the fervor that has assisted in its persistence. However, it is believed that disillusionment due to the moral failings of Klan leadership played a significant role in its rapid decline.

The success of the 1920s Klan should not be measured by the amount of money made by its leaders and hangers on, or the numerical membership attained; rather, its success should be measured by its persistence and the refined and expanded biblical interpretations of modern day Klans. Everything can be explained and justified using religion; religion provides the means to obtain substantive legitimacy, this is evident worldwide. And just as the Klan of the 1920s obtained that legitimacy, so too, does the current Klan. Further, referencing the first amendment of freedom of religion provides the Klan the basis for its religious legitimacy, a legitimacy that many in the United States appear unwilling to bestow.

That similar legitimization is provided to other groups but not the Klan may be rooted in white America's unwillingness to face its cultural history. Hundreds of thousands of families had relatives who joined the Klan of the 1920s, but today many of their descendants find this aspect of American history rather distasteful. Through personal experience while conducting research, descendants of families whose ancestors were Klan members were typically reluctant to discuss their forefather's philosophies or activities. This reluctance appeared to be out of concern over possible social rebuff or economic reprisal, especially against a family owned business. In either case, it is believed the reluctance was also associated with the growing awareness of social and demographic changes and the fact that racially charged words or actions are simply no longer the norm. Regardless of changing social and demographic trends, or current mainstream thinking, the issue is that the Klan of today, as did the Klan of the 1920s, uses religion as a means to legitimize their philosophies. For better or for worse, it is a legitimacy that must be accepted, even if it is accepted grudgingly.

# Appendix A: Doctrinal Statement of Beliefs

*Author's Note:* The Doctrinal Statement of Beliefs in Appendix A was provided by the Kingdom Identity Ministries as found on their website (http://www.kingidentity.com/doctrine.htm); however, it is also found on the websites of other Klan groups. There are various similarities with mainline Protestant thinking including the belief in God and Christ and that the Bible is the true word of God. However, a close reading of the Beliefs also identifies the Klan's dogmatic philosophies of whites being the chosen people of God through Abraham (the seedline ideology); that whites represent the 12 lost tribes of Israel; that Jews are the descendants (seedline) of the devil; that whites should separate (segregate) themselves from non-whites; that they are superior to non-whites and that miscegenation as well as homosexuality is against God's law. As can be easily determined, all beliefs are based on biblical interpretations and therein lay the basis for the religious interpretation of the Klan. The interpretive beliefs have been overtly vocalized for 100 years and refined over that time until having reached its present form. Close scrutiny of the Beliefs provides and insight into how the Klan uses biblical interpretations to substantiate its philosophies. The proclamation is also found on the website of the New Empire Knights of the Ku Klux Klan. Of interest is that the same proclamation is also found on the website of the British Klan, the Kingdom Identity Ministries, where they claim, as does the U.S. Klan, that America fulfills biblical prophecy.

All text in appendices is verbatim.

The following is a brief statement of our major doctrinal beliefs as taught by the Holy Scriptures. This list is not exhaustive, but a basic digest defining the true faith once delivered to the saints. For a further explanation of our beliefs and the implications of these truths, please contact us.

WE BELIEVE in YHVH the one and only true and living eternal God (Isa. 44:6); the God of our fathers Abraham, Isaac and Jacob (Exo. 3:14–16), the Creator of all things (1 Cor. 8:6) who is omnipotent, omnipresent, unchangeable and all-knowing; the Great I Am who is manifested in three beings: God the Father, God the Son, and God the Holy Spirit, all one God (Deut. 6:4).

WE BELIEVE the entire Bible, both Old and New Testaments, as originally inspired, to be the inerrant, supreme, revealed Word of God. The history, covenants, and prophecy of this Holy Book were written for and about a specific elect family of people who are children of YHVH God (Luke 3:38; Psalm 82:6) through the seedline of Adam (Gen. 5:1). All scripture is written as a doctrinal standard for our exhortation, admonition, correction, instruction and example; the whole counsel to be believed, taught and followed (II Tim. 3:16. Acts. 20:27).

WE BELIEVE Yahshua the Messiah (Jesus the Christ) to be the incarnate begotten son of God, the Word made flesh (John 1:14), born of the Virgin Mary in fulfillment of divine prophecy (Isa. 7:14; Luke 1:27) at the appointed time, having had His eternal existence as one with the Father before the world was (John 17:5, 21–22).

WE BELIEVE in the personally revealed being of God the Holy Spirit, the Comforter (John 15:26, 16:7), who was sent by God the Son to glorify Him (John 16:14) and teach us all truth (John 14:26, 16:13; I Cor. 2:10–12) according to promise (Ezek. 36:25–27; Acts 2:33; Eph. 1:13–14). The Holy Spirit is sent to dwell in (I Cor. 3:16; John 14:17) the members of the body of Christ, giving unto each different gifts (I Cor. 12) empowering them to witness (Acts 1:8) of sin, of righteousness, and of judgment (John 14:17; I Cor. 2:14), which God sent forth to His sons (Gall. 4:6), thus identifying the children of Israel (Isa. 44:1–3, 59:20–21; Haggai 2:5; Rom. 8:16) in this world.

WE BELIEVE that God the Son, Yahshua the Messiah (Jesus Christ), became man in order to redeem His people Israel (Luke 1:68) as a kinsman of the flesh (Heb. 2:14–16; Rom. 9:3–5)/ died as the Passover Lamb of God on the Cross of Calvary finishing His perfect atoning sacrifice for the remission of our sins (Matt. 26:28); He arose from the grave on the third day (I Cor. 15:4) triumphing over death; and ascended into Heaven where He is now reigning at the right hand of God (Mark 16:19).

WE BELIEVE in the literal return to this Earth of Yahshua the Messiah (Jesus Christ) in like manner as He departed (Acts 1:11), to take the

Throne of David (Isa. 9:7; Luke 1:32) and establish His everlasting Kingdom (Dan. 2:44; Luke 1:33; Rev. 11:15). Every knee shall bow and every tongue shall confess that He is King of kings and Lord of lords (Phil. 2:10–11; I Tim. 6:14–15).

WE BELIEVE Salvation is by grace through faith, not of works (Eph. 2:8–9). Eternal life is the gift of God through the redemption that is in our Savior Yahshua (Jesus Christ) (Rom. 6:23) who will reward every man according to his works (Rev. 22:12).

WE BELIEVE membership in the church of Yahshua or Messiah (Jesus Christ) is by Divine election (John 6:44, 65, 15:16; Acts 2:39, 13:48; Rom. 9:11, 11:7; II Thes. 2:13). God foreknew, chose and predestined the Elect from before the foundation of the world (Psalm 139:16; Jer. 1:5; Matt. 25:34; Rom. 8:28–30; Eph. 1:4–5; II Tim. 1:9; Rev. 13:8) according to His perfect purpose and sovereign will (Rom. 9:19–23). Only the called children of God can come to the Savior to hear His words and believe; those who are not of God, cannot hear his voice (John 8:47, 10:26–27).

WE BELIEVE Yahshua the Messiah (Jesus the Christ) came to redeem (a word meaning purchase back according to the law of kinship) only His people Israel (Psalm 130:7–8; Isa. 54:5; Matt. 10:5–6, 15:24; Gal. 4:4–5) who are His portion and inheritance (Deut. 32:9).

WE BELIEVE individual Israelites are destined for judgment (II Cor. 5:10; Heb. 9:27) and must believe on the only begotten son of God, Yahshua the Messiah (Jesus Christ), in whom only there is salvation (Acts 4:12), that they be not condemned (John 3:18; Mark 16:16). Each individual Israelite must repent, putting off the old corrupt man and become a new creature (Eph. 4:22–24; II Cor. 5:17) walking in the newness of life (Rom. 6:4). This spiritual rebirth (John 3:3–6; I Peter 1:23) being necessary for a personal relationship with our Savior.

WE BELIEVE in water baptism by immersion according to the Scriptures for all true believers; being buried into the death of Yahshua the Messiah (Jesus Christ) for the remission of our sins and in the likeness of His resurrection being raised up into the newness of life (Rom. 6:3–6). Baptism being ordained of God a testimony to the New Covenant as circumcision was under the Old Covenant (Col 2:11–13).

WE BELIEVE Yahshua the Messiah (Jesus Christ) to be our only High Priest (I Tim. 2:5; Heb. 3:1, 6:20, 7:17, 24–25) and head over His body of called-out saints, the Church (Rom. 12:5; I Cor. 12:12, 27; Eph. 1:22–23, 4:12, 5:23, 30; Col. 1:18, 24). His bride, the wife of the Lamb, is the twelve tribes of the children of Israel (Isa. 54:5; Jer. 3:14; Hosea 2:19–20; Rev. 21:9–12).

## Appendix A

   WE BELIEVE God chose unto Himself a special race of people that are above all people upon the face of the earth (Deut. 7:6; Amos 3:2). These children of Abraham through the called-out seedline of Isaac and Jacob (Psalm 105:6; Rom. 9:7) were to be a blessing to all the families of the earth who bless them and a cursing to those that curse them (Gen. 12:3). The descendants of the twelve sons of a Jacob, called "Israel," were married to God (Isa. 54:5), have not been cast away (Rom. 11:1–2), have been given the adoption, glory, covenants, law, service of God, and promises; are the ones to whom the messiah came (Rom. 9:4–5) electing out of all twelve tribes those who inherit the Kingdom of God (Rev. 7:4, 21:12).

   WE BELIEVE that the New Covenant was made with the Children of Israel, the same people the Old Covenant was made with (Jer. 31:31–33; Heb. 8:8–10) in fulfillment of the mercy of promised our forefathers (Luke 1:72).

   WE BELIEVE the White, Anglo-Saxon, Germanic and kindred people to be God's true, literal Children of Israel. Only this race fulfills every detail of Biblical Prophecy and World History concerning Israel and continues in these latter days to be heirs and possessors of the Covenants, Prophecies, Promises and Blessings YHVH God made to Israel. This chosen seedline making up the "Christian Nations" (Gen. 35:11; Isa. 62:2; Acts 11:26) of the earth stands far superior to all other peoples in their call as God's servant race (Isa. 41:8, 44:21; Luke 1:54). Only these descendants of the 12 tribes of Israel scattered abroad (James 1:1; Deut. 4:27; Jer. 31:10; John 11:52) have carried God's Word, the Bible, throughout the world (Gen. 28:14; Isa. 43:10–12, 59:21), have used His Laws in the establishment of their civil governments and are the "Christians" opposed by the Satanic Anti-Christ forces of this world who do not recognize the true and living God (John 5:23, 8:19, 16:2–3).

   WE BELIEVE in an existing being known as the Devil or Satan and called the Serpent (Gen. 3:1; Rev. 12:9), who has a literal "seed" or posterity in the earth (Gen. 3:15) commonly called Jews today (Rev. 2:9; 3:9; Isa. 65:15). These children of Satan (John 8:44–47; Matt. 13:38; John 8:23) through Cain (I John 2:22, 4:3) who have throughout history always been a curse to true Israel, the Children of God, because of a natural enmity between the two races (Gen. 3:15), because they do the works of their father the Devil (John 8:38–44), and because they please not God, and are contrary to all men (I Thes. 2:14–15), though they often pose as ministers of righteousness (II Cor. 11:13–15). The ultimate end of this evil race whose hands bear the blood of our Savior (Matt. 27:25) and all the righteous

## Doctrinal Statement of Beliefs

slain upon the earth (Matt. 23:35), is Divine judgment (Matt. 13:38–42, 15:13; Zech. 14:21).

WE BELIEVE that the Man Adam (a Hebrew word meaning: ruddy, to show Blood, flush, turn rosy) is father of the White Race only. As a son of God (Luke 3:38), made in His likeness (Gen. 5:1), Adam and his descendants, who are also the children of God (Psalm 82:6; Hos. 1:10; Rom. 8:16; Gal. 4:6; I John 3:1–2), can know YHVH God as their creator. Adamic man is made trichotomous, that is, not only of body and soul, but having an implanted spirit (Gen. 2:7; I Thes. 5:23; Heb. 4:12) giving him a higher form of consciousness and distinguishing him from all the other races of the earth (Deut. 7:6, 10:15; Amos 3:2).

WE BELIEVE that as a chosen race, elected by God (Deut. 7:6, 10:15; I Peter 2:9), we are not to be partakers of the wickedness of this world system (I John 2:15; James 4:4; John 17:9, 15, 16), but are called to come out and be a separated people (II Cor. 6:17; Rev. 18:4; Jer. 51:6; Exodus 33:16; Lev. 20:24). This includes segregation from all non-white races, who are prohibited in God's natural divine order from ruling over Israel (Deut. 17:15, 28:13, 32:8; Joel 2:17; Isa. 13:14; Gen. 1:25–26; Rom. 9:21). Race-mixing is an abomination in the sight of Almighty God, a satanic attempt meant to destroy the chosen seedline, and is strictly forbidden by His commandments (Exo. 34:14–16; Num. 25:1–13; I Cor. 10:8; Rev. 2:14; Deut. 7:3–4; Joshua 23:12–13; I Kings 11:1–3; Ezra 9:2, 10–12; 10:10–14; Neh. 10:28–30, 13:3, 27; Hosea 5:7; Mal. 2:11–12).

WE BELIEVE sin is transgression of God's Law (I John 3:4; Rom. 3:31, 7:7) and that all have sinned (Rom. 3:23). Only through knowledge of God's Law as given in His Commandments, Statutes and Judgments, can we define and know what sin is. We are to keep and teach the laws of God (Matt. 5:17–19) on both a personal and national basis.

WE BELIEVE God gave Israel His Laws for their own good (Deut. 5:33). Theocracy being the only perfect form of government, and God's divine Law for governing a nation being far superior to man's laws, we are not to add to or diminish from His commandments (Deut. 4:1–2). All present world problems are a result of disobedience to the Laws of God, which if kept will bring blessings and if disregarded will bring cursings (Deut. 28)

WE BELIEVE men and women should conduct themselves according to the role of their gender in the traditional Christian sense that God intended. Homosexuality is an abomination before God and should be punished by death (Lev. 18:22, 20:13; Rom. 1:24–28, 32; I Cor. 6:9).

WE BELIEVE that the United States of America fulfills the prophesied

(II Sam. 7:10; Isa. 11:12; Ezek. 36:24) place where Christians from all the tribes of Israel would be regathered. It is here in this blessed land (Deut. 15:6, 28:11, 33:13–17) that God made a small one a strong nation (Isa. 60:22), feeding His people with knowledge and understanding through Christian pastors (Jer. 3:14–15) who have carried the light of truth and blessings unto the nations of the earth (Isa. 49:6, 2:2–3; Gen. 12:3). North America is the wilderness (Hosea 2:14) to which God brought the dispersed seed of Israel, the land between tow seas (Zech. 9:10), surveyed and divided by rivers (Isa. 18:1–2, 7), where springs of water and streams break out and the desert blossoms as the rose (Isa. 35:1, 6–7).

WE BELIEVE the ultimate destiny of all history will be the establishment of the Kingdom of God upon this earth (Psalm 37:9, 11, 22; Isa. 11:9; Matt. 5:5, 6:10; Rev. 21:2–3) with Yahshua our Messiah (Jesus Christ) reigning as King of kings over the house of Jacob forever, of this kingdom and dominion there shall be no end (Luke 1:32–33; Dan. 2:44, 7:14; Zech. 14:9). When our Savior returns to restore righteous government on the earth, there will be a day of reckoning when the kingdoms of this world become His (Rev. 11:15; Isa. 9:6–7) and all evil shall be destroyed (Isa. 13:9; Mal. 4:3; Matt. 13:30, 41–42; II Thes. 2:8). His elect Saints will be raised immortal at His return (I Cor. 15:52–53; I Thes. 4:16; Rev. 20:6) to rule and reign with Him as kings and priests (Rom. 8:17; II Tim. 2:12; Rev. 5:10; Exodus 19:6; Dan. 7:18, 27)

# *Appendix B:*
# *The Seven Sacred Symbols of the Klan*

*Author's Note:* Appendix B demonstrates how the Klan interwove and used God, Christ and the Bible to create a positive image of themselves. The seven symbols interweave religion and patriotism as a means of providing legitimacy and as a recruitment tool to attract new members. The cross and water still form part of the religious ceremonial aspects of the Klan. Note also the use of fire in "lighting" the cross, again, part of the religious ceremony claimed by the Klan of the 1920s and the Klan of today. This version of the seven symbols comes from the December 26 issue of the *Imperial Night-Hawk*. Later versions removed the section dealing with the mask after anti-masking laws were passed throughout the nation. In order to keep the symbols at seven, fire was elevated to a separate section and symbol. The following text is taken from the *Imperial Night-Hawk*, December 26, 1923.

## The Bible

This Book Divine signifies that there is a God. No sane man of reasonable Intelligence can look upon the sacred volume without thinking of God as its author, righteousness as its aim, and eternal life as its end. It is a constant reminder that God is our Father. Life is our opportunity, and heaven is our home. It reveals the way of life, the cause of death. It is a lamp unto our feet, a light unto our pathway and the *only* sure guide to right living. It is the book of books and reveals the *only true God.*

In a Klavern you will always find this wonderful Book opened at the twelfth chapter of Romans. This is the most practical and the most complete chapter in the whole Bible on the Christian living. It is a constant reminder of the tenets of the Christian faith, and is a Klansman's law of life. Every Klansman should read it the first thing every morning and endeavor to live by it during the day. "I beseech you therefore brethren by the mercies of God," that you follow its teachings.

## *The Cross*

Out of the wonderful story of the sacred pages of this old Book Divine comes the sad, sweet story of Calvary's rugged but holy cross. This old cross is a symbol of sacrifice and service, and a sign of Christian religion. Sanctified and made holy nineteen centuries ago by the suffering and blood of fifty million martyrs who died in the most holy faith, it stands in every Klavern of the Knights of the Ku Klux Klan as a constant reminder that Christ is our criterion of character, and His teachings our rule of life-blood-bought, holy sanctified and sublime.

It was once a sign of ignominy, disgrace and shame, but being bathed in the blood of the lowly Nazarene, it has been transformed into a symbol of Faith, Hope and Love. It inspired the Crusaders of the Middle Ages in their perilous efforts to rescue the Holy Land from the Heathen Turks; and is today being used to rally the forces of Christianity against the ever increasing hoards [sic] of anti–Christ, and the enemies of the principles of pure Americanism.

We have added fire to signify that "Christ is the light of the world." As light drives away darkness and gloom, so a knowledge of truth dispels ignorance and superstition. As fire purifies gold, silver and precious stones, but destroys the dross, wood, hay and stubble; so by the fire of Calvary's cross we mean to purify and cleanse our virtues by burning out our vices with the fire of His word. Who can look upon this sublime symbol, or sit in its sacred, holy light without being inspired with a holy desire and determination to be a better man? "By this sign we conquer."

## *The Flag*

This old flag, purchased by the blood and suffering of American heroes, represents the price paid for American liberties. It is the symbol of the Constitution of the United States of America, free speech, free press, free schools, freedom of worship, and all Constitutional laws, both state and national.

Its red is the blood of American heroes. Its white symbolizes the purity of American womanhood and the sanctity of American homes. Its blue is but a patch of America's unclouded sky, snatched from the diamond-studded canopy that bends over our native land. Its stars represent an aggregation of undefeated states bound together in an inseparable union.

> "Its red is the red of the sunset evening glow,
> Its white is the white of the winter's driven snow,
> Its blue is the blue of the ocean, sea and sky,
> Its stars the states of a union that must not die."

It has never been trailed in the dust, trampled in the mud, or defeated in battle. It has never led a retreat or been hauled down at the command of an enemy. It is the greatest and most glorious flag that ever floated in a breeze or waved over land or sea. It was purchased by the sacrifice and blood of our fathers, and we most sacredly vowed that we will uphold and defend it with our sacred honor, our property, our blood and our lives. May we ever be true to our vow. Under its fluttering folds, as it floats in the gentle breeze in every Klavern, the Knights of the Ku Klux Klan will forever defend the principles of pure Americanism, and thus perpetuate the sacred memory of our venerable and heroic dead.

Who can stand under these Stars and Stripes, remembering the sacred traditions that entwine its holy past, without feeling that sublime patriotism that inspired our noble sires to die for our own, our native land?

## The Sword

This unsheathed sword of steel is a symbol of law enforcement. It represents the military, or enforcement powers of our government, from the president on down to the constable. Its presence on our sacred altar signifies that we, as an organization, are solidly behind every enforcement officer in the land, to "help, aid and assist in the proper performance of their legal duties." We stand unconditionally and unqualifiedly for the just and impartial enforcement of law, and for the defence [sic] and protection of all rights and privileges of all citizens alike, regardless of race, color, creed, lineage or tongue.

This sword also signifies that we are set for the defence of our Flag and all that it symbolizes, against the attack and invasion of every foreign power, government, sect, ruler or people in the whole world. We believe in America for Americans and are sworn to defend it by all justifiable means and method, from any source whatever, whether it be traitors within or enemies without. This sword is a constant reminder of our obligation to defend our country and enforce its laws, through duly constituted authorities and justifiable means and methods. May we wield it wisely and well in defense of our country, our home, our flag, our liberties and humanity.

## *The Water*

"This God-given, powerful, life-giving fluid, more precious and far more significant than all sacred oils of ancients," is a symbol of the purity of life and the unity of purpose. With this divinely distilled fluid we have been dedicated and set apart, in body, in mind, in spirit and in life, to the sacred, sublime and holy principles of Klankraft. In this dedicatory service we are solemnly admonished to keep our character as transparent and as clear and clean as the liquid in this glass. A drop of ink or blood in this crystal fluid will have the same effect as sin in our lives. May we keep our record clear and transparent free from the sin-stains of evil and wrong doing.

As water is useful to human life, so may we, as Klansmen, be useful to humanity. As drops of water mingle and intermingle, thus becoming one solid mass, may we, as Klansmen become so united, each with the other that we will become one solid mass, or one body in Klankraft. Thus we see the water is a beautiful symbol of unity, usefulness and purity. Who can fail to learn from these drops of water, the lesson of real Klannishness, and of brotherhood is a common service to mankind?

## *The Robe*

"The distinguishing marks of a Klansman are not found in the fiber of his garment or in his social, political financial standing; but they are spiritual, wisdom, a chivalric head, a compassionate heart, a prudent tongue and a courageous will: all devoted and consecrated to our race, our homes, our Klan and each other."

We use the robe to signify that we do not judge men by the clothes they wear, and to conceal the difference in our clothing as well as our personality. There are no rich or poor, high or low, in Klankraft. As we look upon a body of Klansmen robed in white we are forcibly reminded that they are on a common level. By this means we also help to conceal out identity, which is an essential element principle of Klankraft.

This white robe is also a symbol of that robe of righteousness to be worn by the Saints in the land of the Yet-to-Come. The aged apostle, a prisoner on the Island of Patmos, peeped into the portals of the Great Beyond, and caught a glimpse of the saints robed in white, "which was the righteousness of Christ." Taking Christ as our criterion of character, and endeavoring to follow His teachings, Klansmen wear this white robe to signify that they desire to put on *that white robe which is the righteousness of Christ*, in that Empire Invisible that lies out beyond the vale of death where there will be no more parting and no more tears.

"A lying scoundrel may wrap his disgraceful frame in the sacred folds of a Klansman's robe and deceive the very elect, but *only* a Klansman possesses a Klansman's heart and a Klansman's soul." Therefore, as we seek to cover here our filthy rags and imperfect lives with the robe of a Klansman, may we through the grace of God and by following his Christ, be able to hide the scars and stains of sin with the righteousness of Christ when we stand before His Great White Throne.

## The Mask

That hated mask, the terror of every crook in the land, how they cry, "take off the mask." But they don't know what they say. They do not understand why we wear it or what it means. "If they only knew."

In the first place it helps to conceal our membership. We are a great secret service organization to aid the officers of the law and we can do our best work when we are not known to the public. By this means we see and hear everything. We know the criminal but he does not know us. By our secret membership we gather a world of evidence and help gather a world of evidence and help to gather thousands of crooks into the meshes of the law that would otherwise escape.

It is also a symbol of unselfishness. With the mask we hide out individuality and sink ourselves into the great sea of Klankraft. Not as individuals, but as Klansmen, "we sacrifice to serve." Our motto is "Non Silba Sed Anthar—not of self but for others. Therefore we hide self behind the mask that we may be unselfish in our service.

Who can look upon a multitude of white robed Klansmen without thinking of the equality and unselfishness of that throng of with robed saints in the Glory Land? May the God of Heaven, Who looks not upon the outward appearance, but upon the heart, find every Klansman worthy of the robe and mask that he wears. Then when we "do the things we teach" and "live the lives we preach," the title of Klansman will be *the most honorable title among men.*

Thus with our symbols we seek to emphasize and impress the sacred, sublime and holy principles of Klankraft. With God as our Father, Christ as our Criterion, the Bible as our guide, the cross as our inspiration, and the flag as our protection, we mean to march on to a triumphant victory for the principles of right in the Knights of the Ku Klux Klan.

# Chapter Notes

## Introduction

1. C. P. Roney, *Is The Knights of the Ku Klux Klan Scriptural? A Biblical, Sane and Dignified Discussion of the Principles, Ideals and Policies of the Order* (Shreveport, LA: M. W. Drake, 192?), 1.
2. Ibid., 2.
3. Ibid., 15–16.
4. "Imperial Wizard Outlines Klan Objectives before Immense Gathering in Ohio," *Imperial Night-Hawk*, July 18, 1923.
5. *Imperial Night-Hawk*, October 3, 1923.
6. Walter C. Wright, "A Klansman's Criterion of Character," *Imperial Night-Hawk*, February 6, 1924.
7. Lem A. Dever, *Confessions of an Imperial Klansman: Hot Tar and Feathers* (Portland, OR: Lem A. Dever, 1924), 5.
8. Ibid., 7.
9. Ibid., 22.
10. Ibid.
11. W. M. Likins, *Patriotism Capitalized or Religion Turned into Gold* (Uniontown, PA: The Watchman Publishing Company, 1925), 83.
12. Ibid., 121.
13. Ibid., 211.
14. Ibid., 65–67.
15. Kelly J. Baker, *Gospel According to the Klan: The KKK's Appeal to Protestant America, 1915–1930* (Lawrence: University Press of Kansas, 2011), 12.
16. Charles C. Alexander, *The Ku Klux Klan in the Southwest* (Norman: University of Oklahoma Press, 1995), 84.
17. Kenneth T. Jackson, *The Ku Klux Klan in the City, 1915–1930* (New York: Oxford University Press, 1967), 18.
18. Ibid., xv.
19. Baker, *Gospel According to the Klan*, 14.
20. Ibid., 18.
21. Glen Michael Zuber, "Onward Christian Klansmen! War, Religious Conflict and the Rise of the Second Ku Klux Klan, 1912–1930" (PhD diss., Indiana University, 2004), 1.
22. William Vincent Moore, "A Sheet and a Cross: A Symbolic Analysis of the Ku Klux Klan" (PhD diss., Tulane University, 1975), 115–116.
23. Zuber, "Onward Christian Klansmen," 189.
24. Ibid.
25. Baker, *Gospel According to the Klan*, 13.
26. Moore, "A Sheet and a Cross," 119.
27. Ibid., 258.

## Chapter 1

1. Hiram W. Evans, "The Attitude of the Knights of Ku Klux Klan toward the Roman Catholic Hierarchy," *Imperial Night-Hawk*, March 28, 1923.
2. "Texas Klansman Outlines Principles Upon Which the Knights of the Ku Klux Klan Is Founded," *Imperial Night-Hawk*, April 4, 1923.
3. "Klan a Patriotic, Benevolent, Fraternal Organization of Christian Americans," *Imperial Night-Hawk*, April 9, 1924.
4. "Kansas Klansmen in State Meeting at Wichita Plan Future Progress," *Imperial Night-Hawk*, July 25, 1923.
5. "Grand Dragons and Great Titans Hold Successful Meeting at Asheville, N.C.," *Imperial Night-Hawk*, July 25, 1923.
6. "Thousands Rally to the Klan in Texas," *Imperial Night-Hawk*, October 31, 1923.
7. "The Definition of Klankraft and How to Disseminate It," *Imperial Night-Hawk*, November 7, 1923.
8. *Kourier Magazine*, December 1924, 21.

9. E. F. Stanton, *"Christ and Other Klansmen" or "Lives of Love": The Cream of the Bible Spread Upon Klanism* (Kansas City, MO: S. T. Harper, 1924), 8.
10. John Michael Paul, "God, Race and Nation: The Ideology of the Modern Ku Klux Klan" (master's thesis, University of North Texas, 1999), 56–58.
11. "The Definition of KlanKraft and How to Disseminate It," *Imperial Night-Hawk*, November 7, 1923.
12. Ku Klux Klan, *Klansman's Manual* ([Atlanta, GA: Ku Klux Klan], 1924), 16.
13. Ibid., 18.
14. Ibid., 19.
15. Ibid., 80.
16. Ku Klux Klan, *Papers Read at the Meeting of Grand Dragons Knights of the Ku Klux Klan at Their First Annual Meeting held at Asheville, North Carolina, July 1923* (Atlanta, GA: Ku Klux Klan, 1923), 38.
17. Ibid., 40.
18. "Let Us All Sacrifice to Serve," *Imperial Night-Hawk*, February 14, 1924.
19. "Christian Citizenship: The Gospel According to the Klan," *Imperial Night-Hawk*, November 14, 1923.
20. "Christian Citizenship: The Gospel According to the Klan," *Imperial Night-Hawk*, November 28, 1923.
21. "Life Demands Service! Sacrifice," *Imperial Night-Hawk*, November 21, 1923.
22. "Women of Ku Klux Klan Aid and Support Endeavors of Klansmen," *Imperial Night-Hawk*, August 8, 1923.
23. Ibid.
24. Ibid.
25. Claire C. Ward, "Where There Is No Vision the People Will Perish," *Imperial Night-Hawk*, April 9, 1923.
26. Ku Klux Klan, *Papers Read at the Meeting of Grand Dragons*, 126. The article was republished in the May 30, 1923, and April 9, 1924, issues of the *Imperial Night-Hawk*.
27. Ibid., 129.
28. "Restricted Franchise," *Imperial Night-Hawk*, December 19, 1923.
29. "The Seven Symbols of the Klan," *Imperial Night-Hawk*, December 26, 1923.
30. Ibid.
31. Ibid.
32. Ibid.
33. Ibid.
34. "What the Symbols of the Ku Klux Klan Mean to Me," *Kourier Magazine*, December 1926, 16–17.
35. Aryan Nation, Knights of the Ku Klux Klan, "The 7 Sacred Symbols of the Aryan Nations Knights of the Ku Klux Klan," accessed April 10, 2014, http://www.aryannationsknightskkk.org/why_light_the_cross.html.
36. William Vincent Moore, "A Sheet and a Cross: A Symbolic Analysis of the Ku Klux Klan" (PhD diss., Tulane University, 1975), 287.
37. Moore, "A Sheet and a Cross," 291.
38. "Klansmen, Stop and Take Stock: Build for the Year 1924," *Imperial Night-Hawk*, January 2, 1924.
39. "Further Similarities between the Primitive Church and the Ku Klux Klan Movement," *Imperial Night-Hawk*, October 29, 1924.
40. Walter C. Wright, "The Klan a Distinctive Organization; a Benefit to Every Community," *Imperial Night-Hawk*, April 2, 1924.
41. Glenn Michael Zuber, "Onward Christian Klansmen! War, Religious Conflict, and the Rise of the Second Ku Klux Klan, 1912–1928" (PhD diss., Indiana University, 2004), 370–371.
42. Kelly J. Baker, *Gospel According to the Klan: The KKK's Appeal to Protestant America* (Lawrence: University of Kansas Press, 2011), 37.
43. Zuber, "Onward Christian Klansmen," 375–376.
44. Walter C. Wright, "The Relationship of the Protestant Church to Citizenship," *Imperial Night-Hawk*, May 7, 1924.
45. "Similarity between the Primitive Church and the Klan," *Imperial Night-Hawk*, September 17, 1924.
46. "California Klansmen Meet in Richmond," *Imperial Night-Hawk*, July 23, 1924.
47. "National Dedication Services atop Stone Mountain Held Thanksgiving Night, November 17, 1924," *Kourier Magazine*, January 1925, 10–11.
48. Paul, "God, Race and Nation," 77, 80, 112.
49. Howard L. Bushart, John R. Craig and Myra Barnes, *Soldiers of God: White Supremacists and Their Holy War for America* (New York: Kensington Publishing, 1998), 35–38.
50. Kenneth T. Jackson, *The Ku Klux Klan in the City, 1915–1930* (Chicago: I. R. Dee, 1992), 15.
51. Baker, *Gospel According to the Klan*, 20.
52. "A Message from the Imperial Wizard," *Kourier Magazine*, February 1925, 1–2.
53. "A Statement from the Editor," *Kourier Magazine*, February 1925, 14.
54. "Come Now, Let Us Reason Together," *Kourier Magazine*, March 1925, 1.
55. Ibid., 3.
56. "The Klan: Protestantism's Ally," *Kourier Magazine*, August 1925, 9–12.

57. Ibid., 12.
58. Ibid., 13.
59. Hiram W. Evans, "The Klan's Mission—Americanism," *Kourier Magazine*, November 1925, 4.
60. "What Christmas Means to the Klansman," *Kourier Magazine*, December 1925, 1.
61. Ibid., 1–2.
62. "Why I Joined the Klan," *Kourier Magazine*, December 1925, 12–13.
63. Zuber, "Onward Christian Klansmen," 238–244.
64. Charles C. Alexander, *The Ku Klux Klan in the Southwest* (Norman: University of Oklahoma Press, 1995), 87. The same figure was included on page 16 in Martin Gitlin's *The Ku Klux Klan: A Guide to an American Subculture* (Santa Barbara, CA: Greenwood, 2009).
65. "The Need of the Ku Klux Klan," *Kourier Magazine*, March 1926, 26–28.
66. "The Need of the Ku Klux Klan," *Kourier Magazine*, April 1926, 11–12.
67. "Spiritual Rebirth of the Klan," *Kourier Magazine*, April 1926, 30–32.
68. Baker, *Gospel According to the Klan*, 24.
69. Ibid.
70. Hiram W. Evans, "The Destiny of the Klan," *Kourier Magazine*, August 1926, 5.
71. "Klan Activities in the States," *Kourier Magazine*, August 1926, 7.
72. "Appreciation of Dr. Hiram W. Evans," *Kourier Magazine*, September 1926, 7.
73. "Evangelistic Klankraft in Alabama," *Kourier Magazine*, February 1928, 22–23.
74. "What Is the Klan? Is It A Religion?" *Kourier Magazine*, February 1927, 14.
75. Ibid.
76. Moore, "A Sheet and a Cross," 283.
77. "What Is the Klan? Is It A Religion?" *Kourier Magazine*, February 1927, 14.
78. Ibid.
79. Ibid., 14–15.

# Chapter 2

1. Ku Klux Klan, *Papers Read at the Meeting of Grand Dragons Knights of the Ku Klux Klan at Their First Annual Meeting held at Asheville, North Carolina, July 1923* (Atlanta, GA: Ku Klux Klan, 1923), 10.
2. "Imperial Wizard Outlines Objectives before Immense Gathering in Ohio," *Imperial Night-Hawk*, July 18, 1923.
3. "Kansas Klansmen in State Meeting at Wichita Plan Future Progress," *Imperial Night-Hawk*, July 25, 1923.
4. "Elect New Wizard," *Dawn*, December 9, 1922.
5. Ku Klux Klan, *Proceedings of the Second Imperial Klonvokation Held in Kansas City, Missouri Sept. 23, 24, 25 and 26, 1924* ([Atlanta, GA]: Ku Klux Klan, 1924), 55.
6. Ibid., 56–58.
7. Ibid., 92.
8. Ibid., 60 and 63.
9. Ibid., 69.
10. Glenn Michael Zuber, "Onward Christian Klansmen! War, Religious Conflict and the Rise of the Second Ku Klux Klan, 1912–1928" (PhD diss., Indiana University, 2004), 258–259.
11. Zuber, "Onward Christian Klansmen," 260.
12. Ku Klux Klan, *Proceedings*, 79.
13. "A Klansman's Obligation to His God, His Home, Country and Fellow Citizens," *Night-Hawk*, September 19, 1923.
14. "Elwood Ind., Klan Aids Revival," *Night-Hawk*, February 14, 1924.
15. *Night-Hawk*, April 23, 1924.
16. "The Conflict of the Ages," *Night-Hawk*, July 16, 1924.
17. "Inspirational Address," *Kourier Magazine*, March 1926, 16.
18. Ibid., 17.
19. "Evangelist Praised by Klansmen of Falfurrias, Texas," *Imperial Night-Hawk*, March 26, 1924.
20. John Michael Paul, "God, Race and Nation: The Ideology of the Modern Ku Klux Klan" (master's thesis, University of North Texas, 1999), 106.
21. Ibid., 111.
22. Howard L. Bushart, John R. Craig and Myra Barnes, *Soldiers of God: White Supremacists and Their Holy War for America* (New York: Kensington Publishing, 1998), 35–38.
23. Leroy A. Curry, *The Ku Klux Klan Under the Searchlight: An Authoritative, Dignified and Enlightened Discussion of the American Klan* (Kansas City, MO: Western Baptist Publishing Company, 1925), 7–8.
24. Ibid., 27.
25. Ibid., 27–28.
26. "Bramble Bush Government," *Kourier Magazine*, December 1924, 11–12.
27. Ibid., 13–14.
28. Ibid.
29. Women of the Ku Klux Klan, *The Truth about the Women of the Ku Klux Klan* (Little Rock, AR: Parke-Harper, 192?), 3–4.
30. Ibid., 4–5.
31. Ibid., 6.
32. Hiram W. Evans, "The Klan's Fight for Americanism," *American Review*, March-April-May 1926, 3–4.
33. Ibid., 16–17.
34. Ibid., 18–20.

35. Ibid., 30.
36. Ibid., 31.
37. D. B. W., "A Klan Meditation," *Kourier Magazine*, February 1927, 19–20.
38. Ibid., 20–21.
39. Ku Klux Klan, *Proceedings of the Second Imperial Klonvokation*, 36–37.
40. "Bramble Bush Government," *Kourier Magazine*, December 24, 1924, 17.
41. Ibid.
42. Ibid.
43. Hiram Wesley Evans, "The Klan Mission—Americanism," *Kourier Magazine*, November 1925, 4.
44. Kelly J. Baker, *Gospel According to the Klan: The KKK's Appeal to Protestant America, 1915–1930* (Lawrence: University of Kansas Press, 2011), 37.
45. Ibid., 76.
46. Hiram Wesley Evans, "The Klan Mission—Americanism," *Kourier Magazine*, November 1925, 8.
47. Ibid., 9.
48. Ibid., 10.
49. Ibid., 11.
50. Ibid., 11–12.
51. "Address of Imperial Official," *Kourier Magazine*, December 1924, 24–27.
52. "The Bible and Protestantism," *Kourier Magazine*, June 1925, 21.
53. "Sacred Obligation of a Klansman," *Kourier Magazine*, August 1925, 26.
54. E. F. Stanton, *"Christ and Other Klansmen" or "Lives of Love": The Cream of the Bible Spread Upon Klanism* (Kansas City, MO: S. T. Harper, 1924), 72.
55. Ibid., 77.
56. "Onward Christian Klansmen," *Kourier Magazine*, January 1926, 2–3.
57. Ibid., 4–5.
58. Hiram Wesley Evans, "The Destiny of the Klan," *Kourier Magazine*, July 1926, 1.
59. Ibid.
60. Ibid.
61. Ibid., 2.
62. Ibid., 3.
63. Ibid., 7.
64. J. F. H., "An Awakened Citizenship," *Kourier Magazine*, August 1927, 20–21.
65. Wilson D. Bush, "Improvements in Klan Ritualism," *Kourier Magazine*, September 1928, 58–63.
66. Ku Klux Klan, *Papers Read at Meeting of Grand Dragons*, 65.
67. Ku Klux Klan, *Proceedings of the Second Imperial Klonvokation*, 44–46.
68. Ku Klux Klan, *Proceedings of the Fourth Imperial Klonvokation Held in Chicago, Illinois July 17, 18 and 19, 1928* (Chicago, IL: Knights of the Ku Klux Klan, 1928), 14.
69. Ibid., 19.
70. Ibid., 47–48.
71. Ibid., 51–52.
72. "In Defense of Mask and Secrecy," *Colonel Mayfield's Weekly*, June 17, 1922.
73. Ibid.
74. "God in the Klan," *Kourier Magazine*, February 1927, 18.
75. Stanton, *"Christ and Other Klansmen,"* 67.
76. Ibid., 67–68.
77. "Women of Ku Klux Klan Aid and Support Endeavors of Klansmen," *Imperial Night-Hawk*, August 8, 1923.
78. "Klanswomen Adopt Creed at Meet of National Officers," *Imperial Night-Hawk*, May 14, 1924.
79. Alma Bridwell White, *The Ku Klux Klan in Prophecy* (Zarephath, NJ: The Good Citizen, 1925), 130.
80. Ibid., 133.
81. Ibid., 135.
82. Alma Bridwell White, *Heroes of the Fiery Cross* (Zarephath, NJ: The Good Citizen, 1928), 187.
83. Ibid., 8.
84. Ibid., 10.
85. Ibid., 12.
86. Ibid., 14.
87. Ibid.
88. Ibid., 35–38.

## Chapter 3

1. "Christian Citizenship: The Gospel According to the Klan," *Imperial Night-Hawk*, November 28, 1923.
2. "Eyes of the Nation Are on Knights of the Ku Klux Klan," *Imperial Night-Hawk*, December 26, 1923.
3. Alma Bridwell White, *The Ku Klux Klan in Prophecy* (Zarephath, NJ: The Good Citizen, 1925), 32.
4. "Aiming at the Bull's Eye," *Kourier Magazine*, December 1924, 29.
5. William Joseph Simmons, *The Ku Klux Klan: Yesterday, Today and Forever* ([Atlanta: Ku Klux Klan, 1916]), 6–7.
6. "An Estimate of Modern Klan-Kraft," *Kourier Magazine*, April 1926, 21.
7. Ibid., 22–23.
8. "Texas Klansman Outlines Principles upon Which the Knights of the Ku Klux Klan Is Founded," *Imperial Night-Hawk*, April 4, 1923.
9. E. F. Stanton, *"Christ and Other Klansmen" or "Lives of Love": The Cream of the Bible Spread Upon Klanism* (Kansas City, MO: S. T. Harper, 1924), 40.
10. William Vincent Moore, "A Sheet and a Cross: A Symbolic Analysis of the Ku Klux

Klan" (PhD diss., Tulane University, 1975), 295–296.
11. Leroy A. Curry, *The Ku Klux Klan under the Searchlight* (Kansas City, MO: The Western Baptist Printing Company, 1924), 226.
12. Ibid., 228.
13. Ibid., 235.
14. Ibid., 240.
15. "The Seven Symbols of the Klan," *Imperial Night-Hawk*, December 26, 1923.
16. Ibid.
17. "With the Editor, Illuminated Crosses," *Kourier Magazine*, December 1926, 16–17.
18. "The Seven Symbols of the Klan," *Imperial Night-Hawk*, December 26, 1923.
19. "The Reincarnation of God," *Kourier Magazine*, January 1925, 7–8.
20. Ibid., 8.
21. Ibid., 9.
22. Ibid.
23. "Klan Activities in the States," *Kourier Magazine*, August 1926, 6.
24. Ku Klux Klan, *Papers Read at the Meeting of Grand Dragons Knights of the Ku Klux Klan at Their First Annual Meeting held at Asheville, North Carolina, July 1923* (Atlanta, GA: Ku Klux Klan, 1923), 108.
25. "Klansmen, Stop and Take Stock: Build for the Year 1924," *Imperial Night-Hawk*, January 2, 1924.
26. "Address of Imperial Official," *Kourier Magazine*, December 1924, 23.
27. Ibid., 24.
28. "Life Demands Service! Sacrifice!" *Imperial Night-Hawk*, November 21, 1923.
29. H. K. Ramsey, "Our Best Klonvokation," *Kourier Magazine*, September 1928, 56.
30. Rev. James Hardin Smith, "What Would Jesus Say?" *Dawn*, no. 8, December 16, 1922.
31. James K. Warner, "Let Us Pray for Our Enemies," *Dawn*, February 10, 1923.
32. White, *Klan in Prophecy*, 127–128.
33. Ku Klux Klan, *Proceedings of the Second Imperial Klonvokation Held in Kansas City, Missouri Sept, 23, 24, 25 and 26, 1924* ([Atlanta, GA]: Ku Klux Klan, 1924), 155–158.
34. Ibid., 159–161.
35. Ku Klux Klan, *Why You Should Become a Klansman: Of Interest to White, Protestant, Native-Born Americans Who Want to Keep America American* ([United States]: Knights of the Ku Klux Klan, 1924), 1- 2.
36. Walter C. Wright, "A Klansman's Criterion of Character," *Imperial Night-Hawk*, February 6, 1924.
37. Ibid.
38. Ibid.
39. Ibid.
40. Ibid., 3.
41. Kelly J. Baker, *Gospel According to the Klan: The KKK's Appeal to Protestant America, 1915–1930* (Lawrence: University of Kansas Press, 2011), 48–50.
42. "Grapes and Wild Grapes," *Kourier Magazine*, March 1925, 30–31.
43. Kenneth T. Jackson, *The Ku Klux Klan in the City* (New York: Oxford University Press, 1967), 302.
44. Stanton, *"Christ and Other Klansmen,"* 7–9.
45. Ibid., 33.
46. Ibid., 34.
47. Ibid., 34–35.
48. Ibid., 36–37.
49. "A Diagnosis and a Remedy," *Kourier Magazine*, April 1925, 6.
50. Hiram W. Evans, "Message from the Imperial Wizard," *Kourier Magazine*, June 1925, 1.
51. "Secrecy," *Kourier Magazine*, August 1925, 2.
52. Ibid., 3.
53. Ku Klux Klan, *A Fundamental Klan Doctrine* ([n. p.: Knights of the Ku Klux Klan], 1924), 3.
54. Ibid., 4–5.
55. Ibid., 6.
56. Ibid., 8.
57. "The True Spirit of American Klansmen," *Imperial Night-Hawk*, May 16, 1923.
58. Ibid.
59. Stanton, *"Christ and Other Klansmen,"* 6.
60. "The Man Every American Should Know," *Kourier Magazine*, September 1926, 2–3.
61. Ibid., 4.
62. T. O. "I Am," *Kourier Magazine*, February 1927, 23.
63. William Joseph Simmons, *The Ku Klux Klan: Yesterday, Today and Forever* ([Atlanta: Ku Klux Klan, 1916]), Title Page. The subtitle of the pamphlet was also included as a phrase on the front page of *The Dawn*, the Chicago based pro–Klan newspaper.
64. E. J. A., "An Open Letter to Knights of the Ku Klux Klan," *Kourier Magazine*, May 1927, 16.

# Chapter 4

1. "Dr. Evans, Imperial Wizard, Defines Klan Principles and Outlines Klan Activities," *Imperial Night-Hawk*, January 23, 1924.
2. "The *Kourier* Says," *Imperial Night-Hawk*, October 22, 1924.
3. "Klan Funeral Witnessed by Seven

Thousand in Portage, Pa.," *Imperial Night-Hawk*, March 5, 1924.
4. Howard L. Bushart, John R. Craig, and Myra Barnes, *Soldiers of God: White Supremacists and Their Holy War for America* (New York: Kensington Publishing, 1998), 7.
5. Ibid., 23.
6. "Christian Citizenship: The Gospel According to the Klan," *Imperial Night-Hawk*, November 21, 1923.
7. "Jesus the Protestant," *Kourier Magazine*, February 1925, 3–6.
8. "Christian Citizenship: The Gospel According to the Klan," *Imperial Night-Hawk*, December 12, 1923.
9. "The Seven Symbols of the Klan," *Imperial Night-Hawk*, December 26, 1923.
10. "A Klansman's Criterion of Character," *Imperial Night-Hawk*, February 6, 1924.
11. "Klan a Patriotic Benevolent, Fraternal Organization of Christian Americans," *Imperial Night-Hawk*, April 9, 1924.
12. "A Klansman's Criterion of Character," *Imperial Night-Hawk*, February 6, 1924.
13. Ibid., 3–4.
14. "The Twelfth Chapter of Romans as a Klansman's Law of Life," *Imperial Night-Hawk*, March 5, 1924.
15. Ibid., 7.
16. Ibid.
17. "Who Are Those in White Robes?" *Kourier Magazine*, June 1925, 18–19.
18. Ku Klux Klan, *Papers Read at the Meeting of Grand Dragons Knights of the Ku Klux Klan at Their First Annual Meeting held at Asheville, North Carolina, July 1923* (Atlanta, GA: Ku Klux Klan, 1923), 52; "Hope Is Born in Hearts of All Real Klansmen," *Imperial Night-Hawk* II, no. 7 (May 14, 1924): 6.
19. Hiram W. Evans, "The Klan Spiritual," *Imperial Night-Hawk*, October 22, 1924.
20. Rev. J. P. K., "The Stone that Smote the Great Image," *Kourier Magazine*, January 1927, 24–27.
21. Ibid., 27.
22. "The Open Door," *Kourier Magazine*, February 1927, 4–5.
23. Ibid., 5.
24. Alma Bridwell White, *Heroes of the Fiery Cross* (Zarephath, NJ: The Good Citizen, 1928), 9.
25. "The First Man to Mask," *Imperial Night-Hawk*, May 7, 1924.
26. Ku Klux Klan, *Proceedings of the Fourth Imperial Klonvokation Held in Chicago, Illinois July 17, 18 and 19, 1928* (Chicago, IL: Knights of the Ku Klux Klan, 1928), 8–9.
27. Alma Bridwell White, *The Ku Klux Klan in Prophecy* (Zarephath, NJ: The Good Citizen, 1925), 3.
28. Ibid., 6.
29. Ibid., 7 and 10.
30. Ibid., 14.
31. Ibid., 17–18.
32. Ibid., 22–26.
33. E. F. Stanton, *"Christ and Other Klansmen" or "Lives of Love": The Cream of the Bible Spread Upon Klanism* (Kansas City MO: S. T. Harper, 1924), 73.
34. Ku Klux Klan, *Proceedings of the Fourth Imperial Klonvokation Held in Chicago, Illinois July 17, 18, and 19, 1928* (Chicago, IL: Knights of the Ku Klux Klan, 1928), 19.
35. White, *Ku Klux Klan in Prophecy*, 37–39.
36. Ibid., 50.
37. Ibid., 54.
38. Ibid., 55–57.
39. Ibid., 70–72.
40. Ibid., 100–101.
41. Ibid., 103 and 106.
42. Ibid., 109 and 111.
43. Ibid., 118.
44. Ibid., 130–131.
45. Leroy A. Curry, *The Ku Klux Klan under the Searchlight* (Kansas City, MO: The Western Baptist Printing Company, 1924), 27–30.
46. Ibid., 30–33.
47. Ibid., 34–35.
48. "Honorable Klannishness," *Kourier Magazine*, May 1925, 31–32.
49. Ku Klux Klan, *Proceedings of the Fourth Imperial Klonvokation*, 8.
50. "Kourier Essay Contest," *Kourier Magazine*, December 1929, 30–32.

# Chapter 5

1. Glenn Michael Zuber, "Onward Christian Klansmen! War, Religious Conflict, and the Rise of the Second Ku Klux Klan, 1912–1928" (PhD diss., Indiana University, 2004), 249.
2. Daisy Douglas Barr, "The Soul of America," *Imperial Night-Hawk*, July 25, 1923.
3. Rev. W. H. Stephens, "The Fiery Cross," *Imperial Night-Hawk*, August 22, 1923.
4. *Kourier Magazine*, August 1925, 13.
5. *Kourier Magazine*, August 1925, 29.
6. W. F. R., "A Klansman's Prayer," *Kourier Magazine*, June 1926, 21.
7. "God in the Klan," *Kourier Magazine*, February 1927, 18.
8. H. E. R., "Transformation," *Kourier Magazine*, October 1927, 22.
9. E. C., "The Fiery Cross," *Kourier Magazine*, April 1928, 32.
10. "Our Dr. Jekyll and Mr. Hyde," *Kourier Magazine*, October 1931, 24.

11. B. W. B., "The Fiery Cross," *Kourier Magazine*, November 1931, 24.
12. "Soul Winning," *Kourier Magazine*, April 1932, 6.
13. "The Firm Foundation," *Kourier Magazine*, April 1932, 9.
14. "Awake! Awake!" *Kourier Magazine*, April 1932, 10.
15. "The Fiery Cross," *Kourier Magazine*, April 1932, 16.
16. "Awake Klansmen," *Kourier Magazine*, June 1932, 16.
17. J. N. M.., E. C., *Kourier Magazine*, June 1932, 39.
18. "A Krusader," *Kourier Magazine*, June 1932, 47.
19. "Klan Haven," *Kourier Magazine*, June 1932, 47.
20. C. A. B., "A Klansman," *Kourier Magazine*, July 1932, 18.
21. J. H. E. M., "Shall We Quit or Shall We Fight?" *Kourier Magazine*, February 1934, 11.
22. *Kourier Magazine*, October 1936, 4.
23. "God Give Us Men," *Kourier Magazine*, October 1936, 13.
24. "Priest or Kluxer?" *Dawn*, June 2, 1923.
25. S. E. Bauchle, "The Goat," *Dawn*, March 17, 1923.
26. "Hearsay," *Dawn*, May 26, 1923.
27. "Song of the Klan," *Kourier Magazine*, May 1932, 6.
28. "Onward Klansmen!" *Kourier Magazine*, January 1932, 8.
29. "Patriot's Battle Hymn," *Dawn*, June 2, 1923.
30. J. W. T., "A Klan Hymn," *Kourier Magazine*, October 1931, 25.
31. Ku Klux Klan, *Proceedings of the Second Imperial Klonvokation Held in Kansas City, Missouri Sept, 23, 24, 25 and 26, 1924* ([Atlanta, GA]: Ku Klux Klan, 1924), 136.
32. Ku Klux Klan, *Ku Klux Klan Song Book: Ten Stirring Songs for Real Americans* (Hammond, IN: The Hoosier, 1923) 2.
33. Ibid., 3.
34. Ibid., 4.
35. Ibid., 7.
36. Ibid., 9.
37. Ibid., 11.

# Chapter 6

1. "The Klan Creed," *Kourier Magazine*, January 1932, 16.
2. "Opening Prayer," *Kourier Magazine*, February 1932, 19.
3. "The Country That Has Forgotten God," *Kourier Magazine*, March 1932, 18.
4. Ibid., 81–19.
5. "Our Klan Klard: What does it Mean to You?" *Kourier Magazine*, March 1932, 136.
6. "Religion and Klankraft," *Kourier Magazine*, July 1932, 14.
7. "To the Ministers of the Gospel in Ohio County," *Kourier Magazine*, February 1934, 45.
8. "Ideal and Principles of the Ku Klux Klan," *Kourier Magazine*, October 1936, 14.
9. Ibid., 19.
10. Ibid.
11. Ibid.
12. Ibid., 20.
13. Ibid., 22.
14. "America for Americans," *Fiery Cross*, September 1939, 1.
15. Ibid., 4.
16. E. F. Stanton, *"Christ and Other Klansmen" or "Lives of Love": The Cream of the Bible Spread Upon Klanism* (Kansas City, MO: S. T. Harper, 1924), 12.
17. Ibid., 2.
18. "Sparks From the Fiery Cross," *Fiery Cross*, September 1939, 4.
19. Ibid.
20. J. A. Colescott, "Imperial Wizard's Message," *Fiery Cross*, March 1940, 8.
21. "Christmas Greetings Klansmen," *Fiery Cross*, December 1939, 4.
22. Ku Klux Klan, *Proceedings of Eighth Imperial Klonvokation, Knights of the Ku Klux Klan, Held in Philadelphia, Pa., Sept., 25–26-27,1936* (n. p.: Knights of Ku Klux Klan, 1936), 20–22.
23. *Aryan Knight Views*, No. 148, 5. The newsletter would later be titled *The Aryan News—White Folks News*. Due to inconsistencies by the publisher, dates and pages are not always included. Citation will typically be by newsletter number; where dates and pages can be discerned they will be included.
24. Kelly J. Baker, *Gospel According to the Klan: The KKK's Appeal to Protestant America, 1915–1930* (Lawrence: University Press of Kansas, 2011), 30.
25. Ibid., 241.
26. *Aryan Knight Views*, No. 192.
27. *Aryan Knight Views*, No. 168.
28. Ibid.
29. William Vincent Moore, "A Sheet and a Cross: A symbolic Analysis of the Ku Klux Klan" (Tulane University, PhD Diss., 1975), 244–245.
30. Ibid. 250–251.
31. Juan O. Sánchez, "A Content Analysis of the Leadership Language of the Ku Klux Klan in the 1920s" (PhD Diss., Our Lady of the Lake University, San Antonio, TX, 2009), 54.
32. Ibid., 65, 68.
33. *Aryan Knight Views*, No. 154.

34. *Aryan Knight Views*, No. 158.
35. *Aryan Knight Views*, No. 140.
36. *Aryan Knight Views*, No. 170.
37. Ibid.
38. *Aryan Knight Views*, No. 160.
39. Ibid.
40. *Aryan Knight Views*, No. 162.
41. *Aryan Knight Views*, No. 168.
42. *Aryan Views—White Folks News*, No. 485, October 1, 1959.
43. Ibid.
44. *Aryan Knight Views*, No. 155.
45. *Aryan Views—White Folks News*, No. 539, March 15, 1960.
46. *Aryan Views—White Folks News*, No. 464, May 5, 1959.
47. *Aryan Views—White Folks News*, No. 470, August 12, 1959.
48. Ibid.
49. Ibid.
50. Ku Klux Klan, *Kloran. Klan in Action. Constitution.* ([Tuscaloosa, AL]: Imperial Press, 1968), 13.
51. Ibid., 13–14.
52. Ibid., 15.
53. Ibid., 15–16.
54. Ibid., 16.
55. Ibid.
56. Ibid., 30.
57. Ibid.
58. Ibid., 38.
59. Texas Knights of the Ku Klux Klan, "Welcome," accessed June 19, 2014, http://www.texaskkk.com/.
60. Ibid.
61. Ibid.
62. White Kamelia Knights of the Ku Klux Klan, "Christian Identity," accessed March 21, 2014, http://www.wckkkk.org/identity.html.
63. Ibid.
64. Ibid.
65. Original Knight Riders, Knights of the Ku Klux Klan, "The Heart of a Klansman," accessed April 23, 2014, https://www.originalknightriders.net/.
66. New Empire Knights of the Ku Klux Klan, "Who We Are," accessed May 15, 2014, http://newempireknights.wordpress.com/about/.
67. Church of the National Knights of the Ku Klux Klan Realm of Kentucky, "We the People," accessed June 20, 2014, http://cnkkkkkentucky.webs.com/.

# Chapter 7

1. Ku Klux Klan, *Kloran: Knights of the Ku Klux Klan*, 7th ed. (Atlanta, GA: Knights of the Ku Klux Klan, 1934), 2.
2. Ku Klux Klan, *Proceedings of Eighth Imperial Klonvokation, Knights of the Ku Klux Klan, Held in Philadelphia, Pa., Sept., 25–26-27, 1936* (n. p.: Knights of Ku Klux Klan, 1936), 48.
3. Ibid., 89–90.
4. *Kourier Magazine*, October 1936, 10. No title; this was simply a prayer inserted at the bottom of the page.
5. "Klansmen Asked to Thank God for Blessings Received," *Fiery Cross*, November 1939, 3.
6. "The Klan in Action," *Fiery Cross*, January 1940, 6.
7. "Klan Embodies Spirit Which Has Always Won over Tyranny," *Fiery Cross*, April-May 1940, 6.
8. Ibid.
9. Ibid.
10. "Ku Klux Klan Still on Guard," *Fiery Cross*, June 1940, 2.
11. "What a Privilege It Is to Be a Citizen of the United States," *Fiery Cross*, First Quarter, 1941, 7.
12. "Open Letter," *Aryan Knight Views*, No. 205, October 14, 1955.
13. "To the White People Everywhere," *Aryan Knight Views*, No. 453, July 4, 1959.
14. *Aryan Knight Views*, No. 496, November 1, 1959.
15. United Klans of America, *Kloran. Klan in Action. Constitution.* ([Tuscaloosa, AL]: Imperial Press, 1968), 13.
16. Ibid.
17. Louis R. Beam, Jr., *The Klansman's Handbook: Being a Compendium of Ku Klux Klan Ideology, Organizational Methods, History, Tactics, and Opinions*, (n. p.: First Printing 1979, Revised and republished by Aryan Nations, 1982), 7–8.
18. Ibid., 8.
19. Ibid., 16.
20. Ibid.
21. Ibid., 32.
22. Ibid., 32–33.
23. Ibid., 35–36.
24. "MEET Jim Blair, Imperial Wizard Knights of the Ku Klux Klan," *Klansman*, (December/February 1984/85): 3.
25. For an extensive overview of modern day White Supremacist organizations who espouse Seed Line and Covenant theology see Howard L. Bushart, John R. Craig and Myra Barnes, *Soldiers of God: White Supremacists and Their Holy War for America* (New York: Kensington Publishing, 1998).
26. American Knights of the Ku Klux Klan. "Making Your Life Count," accessed March 27, 2014, http://www.kukluxklan.info/presents/americanknights/making_your_life_count.htm.
27. Church of the National Knights of the

Ku Klux Klan, "Why Are We a Church?" accessed March 27, 2014, https://sites.google.com/site/cnkrealmofky/what-we-believe.
28. Ibid.
29. Imperial Knights of America, "Our Beliefs," accessed March 27, 2014, http://www.kkkk.net/ourbeliefs.html.
30. Ibid.
31. Ibid.
32. Invisible Knights of the Fiery Cross, "Race Equality," accessed April 10, 2014, http://www.kukluxklan.us/Imperial_Wizard_Notes.html.
33. Original Knight Riders, Knights of the Ku Klux Klan, "The Heart of a Klansman," accessed April 23, 2014, https://www.originalknightriders.net/.
34. Ibid., "Welcome," accessed April 23, 2014, https://www.originalknightriders.net/.
35. Ibid., "Dragon's Lair," accessed April 23, 2014, https://www.originalknightriders.net/.
36. Ibid.
37. Ibid., "I Am a Soldier," accessed April 23, 2014, https://www.originalknightriders.net/.
38. Aryan Nation, Knights of the Ku Klux Klan, "The 7 Sacred Symbols of the Aryan Nations Knights of the Ku Klux Klan," accessed April 10, 2014, http://www.aryannationsknightskkk.org/why_light_the_cross.html.
39. Aryan Nation, Knights of the Ku Klux Klan, "America's Task," accessed April 10, 2014, http://www.aryannationsknightskkk.org/why_light_the_cross.html.
40. Church of the National Knights of the Ku Klux Klan, "Ideals a Klansman Stands For," http://www.cnkkkk.com.
41. Invisible Knights of the Fiery Cross, "White Rights," accessed April 10, 2014, http://www.kukluxklan.us/Imperial_Wizard_Notes.html.
42. Invisible Knights of the Fiery Cross, "Race Equality," accessed April 10, 2014, http://www.kukluxklan.us/Imperial_Wizard_Notes.html.
43. Invisible Knights of the Fiery Cross, "Double Standard," accessed April 10, 2014, http://www.kukluxklan.us/Imperial_Wizard_Notes.html.
44. Invisible Knights of the Fiery Cross, "The Ku Klux Kreed," accessed April 10, 2014, http://www.kukluxklan.us/Imperial_Wizard_Notes.html.
45. The Traditionalist American Knights of the Ku Klux Klan, "Here are the Fundamental Ideals of the Traditionalist American Knights of the Ku Klux Klan," accessed April 11, 2014, http://www.traditionalistamericanknights.com/Who_We_Are.html.
46. White Kamelia Knights of the Ku Klux Klan, "Equality," accessed March 21, 2014, http://www.wckkkk.org/eql.html.

## Chapter 8

1. "The Firm Foundation," *Kourier Magazine*, April 1932, 9.
2. Ibid.
3. Ibid.
4. "Just Kluxing," *Kourier Magazine*, December 1933, 29.
5. "Shall We Quit or Shall We Fight?" *Kourier Magazine*, February 1934, 11.
6. Ibid.
7. "Good-Bye Valedictorian," *Kourier Magazine*, November 1936, 22.
8. Ibid., 21.
9. *Fiery Cross*, July 1939. The newspaper was published monthly with its first edition dated July 1939.
10. Ku Klux Klan, *America for Americans* (Atlanta, GA: Knights of the Ku Klux Klan, 1922), 6.
11. Louis R. Beam, Jr., *The Klansman's Handbook: Being a Compendium of Ku Klux Klan Ideology, Organizational Methods, History, Tactics, and Opinions* (n. p.: First Printing 1979, Revised and republished by Aryan Nations, 1982), 33.
12. "Klan in Las Vegas," *Klansman*, July 1983, 6.
13. "Faith," *Klansman*, April/May 1985, 8.
14. Ibid.
15. "Anti-Christ Take Over," *Klansman*, June/July 1985, 8.
16. Louis R. Beam, Jr., *Essays of a Klansman* (Hayden Lake, ID: A.K.I.A. Publications, 1983), 8–9.
17. Frazier Glenn Miller, *A White Man Speaks Out* (n. p.: Aryan Nations, 1999), i. This work was accessed April 23, 2014, at http://whty.org/book/ and contains no pagination. As the pages cited come from the Introduction, liberty was taken to assign pagination as is typically assigned to published material.
18. Ibid., iii.
19. Ibid.
20. Ibid.
21. Ibid., v.
22. Ibid., ix.
23. Ibid.
24. Church of the National Knights Realm of Kentucky, "Who Are the Jews?" accessed June 20, 2014, http://cnkkkkkentucky.webs.com/whoarethejews.htm.
25. Original Knight Riders, Knights of the Ku Klux Klan, "Imperial Proclamation," accessed April 23, 2014, https://www.originalknightriders.net/.

26. Ibid.
27. Aryan Nation, Knights of the Ku Klux Klan, "Why We Light the Cross," accessed April 10, 2014, http://www.aryannations knightskkk.org/why_light_the_cross.html. Also see Loyal White Knights of the Ku Klux Klan, "Why We Light the Cross," accessed April 24, 2014, http://kkkknights.com/why-we-light-the-cross.html. The same statements regarding the "lighting" of the cross also appears on their webpage.
28. Ibid.
29. The Knights Party, "The Christian Lighting Ceremony," accessed May 15, 2014, http://kkk.bz/main/?page_id=200.
30. American Knights of the Ku Klux Klan, "Jesus Christ Is the Light of the World," accessed March 27, 2014, http://www.kuklux klan.info/presents/americanknights/jesus_christ.htm.
31. Church of the National Knights Realm of Kentucky, "Why We Light the Cross," accessed June 20, 2014, http://cnkkkkkentucky. webs.com/whywelightthecross.htm.

# Chapter 9

1. "Paul's Message to Klansmen," *Kourier Magazine*, October 1931, 4.
2. Ibid., 5.
3. What the Symbols of the Ku Klux Klan Mean to Me," *Kourier Magazine*, December 1933, 16.
4. "Just Kluxing," *Kourier Magazine*, December 1933, 29.
5. "To the Ministers of the Gospel in Ohio County," *Kourier Magazine*, February 1934, 45.
6. "Ideals and Principles of the Ku Klux Klan," *Kourier Magazine*, October, 1936, 14.
7. Ibid., 15.
8. Ibid., 16.
9. Dr. Gene Neil, "The Equality of Man?" *Klansman*, June 1981, 3.
10. "Klan in La Vegas," *Klansman*, July 1983, 6.
11. "Bible Does Not Support Mixing of Races," *Klansman*, October 1985, 6.
12. J. A. Colescott, "Imperial Wizard's Message," *Fiery Cross*, April–May 1940, 1–2.
13. "Our God Is a Consuming Fire," *Klansman*, February 1984, 8.
14. United Klans of America, *The Principle of the United Klans of America Knights of the Ku Klux Klan*, (Tuscaloosa, AL: United Klans of America, 1960s), 4–5.
15. Ibid., 5.
16. Ibid., 1.
17. Ibid., 3.
18. "Interracial Marriage Is a Sin," *Klansman*, November/December 1987, 8.

19. Rev. Gene Neill, "The War Is On!" *Klansman*, April 1981, 3.
20. Rev. Gene Neill, "Guest Editorial," *Klansman*, May 1981, 2.
21. "Faith," *Klansman*, December-January 1984–85, 5.
22. "Caucasian Roots," *Klansman*, August–September 1985, 3.
23. "White Christian Roots," *Klansman*, July/August 1986, 4.
24. Ibid.
25. "Anti-Christ Take Over," *Klansman*, June-July 1985, 8.
26. Gregory Beckett, "Klansmen Defends Christ and the Gospel of the Kingdom," *Klansman*, January/February 1987, 9.
27. Ibid.
28. Original Knight Riders, Knights of the Ku Klux Klan, "The Heart of a Klansman," accessed April 23, 2014, https://www.original knightriders.net/.
29. Ibid.
30. Aryan Nation, Knights of the Ku Klux Klan, "The 7 Sacred Symbols of the Aryan Nations Knights of the Ku Klux Klan," accessed April 10, 2014, http://www.aryan nationsknightskkk.org/why_light_the_cross. html.
31. Ibid.
32. The entire proclamation deserves a close reading by those interested in deconstructing the beliefs of these groups based on their biblical interpretations. See Appendix A, "Our Beliefs."
33. See Appendix A, "Our Beliefs."
34. Phillip Lamy, "Christian Identity: A White Supremacist Religion," In *White Supremacists*, edited by Regine I. Heberlein (San Diego, CA: Greenhaven Press, 2002), 13–15.
35. Mate Hale, as told to Bill Bickel, "Inside the Mind of a White Supremacist," In *White Supremacists*, edited by Regine I. Heberlein (San Diego, CA: Greenhaven Press, 2002), 78–83.
36. http://www.ethicsdaily.com/news. php?viewStory=16564, Downloaded July 3, 2014.
37. http://www.ethicsdaily.com/sbc-leader-compares-judaism-to-deadly-tumor-cms-2707, Downloaded July 6, 2014.

# Summary

1. Hiram W. Evans, "The Klan's Fight for Americanism," *American Review*, March-April-May 1926, 25.
2. Ibid., 2.
3. Ibid. 10.

# Bibliography

Alexander, Charles C. *The Ku Klux Klan in the Southwest.* Norman: University of Oklahoma Press, 1995.
Baker, Kelly J. *Gospel According to the Klan: The KKK's Appeal to Protestant America, 1915–1930.* Lawrence: University Press of Kansas, 2011.
Beam, Louis R. *Essays of a Klansman.* Hayden Lake, ID: A.K.I.A. Publications, 1983.
\_\_\_\_\_. *The Klansman's Handbook: Being a Compendium of Ku Klux Klan Ideology, Organizational Methods, History, Tactics, and Opinions.* N.p.: First Printing 1979, Revised and republished by Aryan Nations, 1982.
Brown, Norman D. *Hood, Bonnet, and Little Brown Jug: Texas Politics, 1921–1928.* College Station: Texas A&M University Press, 1984.
Bushart, Howard L., John R. Craig and Myra Barnes. *Soldiers of God: White Supremacists and Their Holy War for America.* New York: Kensington Publishing, 1998.
Chalmers, David M. *Hooded Americanism: The First Century of the Ku Klux Klan, 1865–1965.* New York: Franklin Watts, 1965.
Cook, Ezra A. *Ku Klux Klan Secrets Exposed: Attitudes toward Jews, Catholics, Foreigners and Masons. Fraudulent Methods Used. Atrocities Committed in Name of Order.* Chicago: Ezra A. Cook, 1922.
Cook, Fred J. *The Ku Klux Klan, America's Recurring Nightmare.* New York: Messner, 1980.
Curry, Leroy A. *The Ku Klux Klan under the Searchlight: An Authoritative, Dignified and Enlightened Discussion of the American Klan.* Kansas City, MO: Western Baptist Publishing Company, 1925.
Curry, Meaghan. "Communicating Whiteness: The Changing Rhetoric of the Ku Klux Klan." Masters thesis, University of Missouri–Columbia, 2004.
Dalrymple, A.V. *Liberty Dethroned: An Indictment of the Ku Klux Klan Based Solely Upon Its Own Pronouncements, Philosophy, and Acts of Mob Violence.* Philadelphia: The Times Publishing Company, 1923.
Dever, Lem A. *Confessions of an Imperial Klansman: Hot Tar and Feathers.* Portland, OR: Lem A. Dever, 1924.
Evans, Hiram Wesley. *Attitude of the Knights of the Ku Klux Klan toward Immigration.* Atlanta, GA: Knights of the Ku Klux Klan, 1923.
\_\_\_\_\_. *The Attitude of the Knights of the Ku Klux Klan toward the Jew.* Atlanta, GA: Knights of the Ku Klux Klan, 1923.
\_\_\_\_\_. *The Attitude of the Knights of the Ku Klux Klan toward the Roman Catholic Hierarchy.* Atlanta, GA: Knights of the Ku Klux Klan, 1923.
\_\_\_\_\_. *The Klan: Defender of Americanism.* New York: [Billboard Publications], 1925.
\_\_\_\_\_. *The Klan Answers.* Atlanta, GA: American Print and Mfg. Co., 1929.
\_\_\_\_\_. *The Klan of Tomorrow.* [Atlanta, GA]: Knights of the Ku Klux Klan, 1924.

———. *The Klan Spiritual: An Address Delivered at the Second Imperial Klonvokation Held in Kansas City, Missouri, September 23, 24, 25, and 26, 1924.* [Kansas City, MO]: Knights of the Ku Klux Klan, 1924.
———. *The Klan's Fight for Americanism.* [New York]: North American Review, 1926.
———. *The Menace of Modern Immigration.* Atlanta, GA: Knights of the Ku Klux Klan, 1923.
———. *Negro Suffrage: Its False Theory.* Atlanta, GA: American Print and Mfg. Co., 1920s.
———. *The Pope Clutches at World Supremacy.* Atlanta, GA: American Print and Mfg. Co., 1929.
———. *The Rising Storm; an Analysis of the Growing Conflict over the Political Dilemma of Roman Catholics in America.* Atlanta, GA: Buckhead Pub. Co., 1930.
Ezekiel, Raphael S. *The Racist Mind: Portraits of American Neo-Nazi and Klansmen.* New York: Viking Press, 1995.
Fleming, John S. *What Is Ku Kluxism? Let Americans Answer—Aliens Only Muddy the Waters.* Birmingham, AL: Masonic Weekly Recorder, 1923.
Gitlin, Martin. *The Ku Klux Klan: A Guide to an American Subculture.* Santa Barbara, CA: Greenwood, 2009.
Heberlein, Regine I., ed. *White Supremacists.* San Diego, CA: Greenhaven Press, 2002.
Horowitz, David A. *Inside the Klavern: The Secret History of a Ku Klux Klan of the 1920s.* Carbondale, IL: Southern Illinois University Press, 1999.
Jackson, Dallas. *Whom Has God Joined Together? A Biblical Examination of Miscegenation.* Royal Oak, MI: Jackson Pub., 1990.
Jackson, Kenneth T. *The Ku Klux Klan in the City, 1915–1930.* New York: Oxford University Press, 1967.
Kaufman, Herbert. *Scum o' the Melting-pot.* [Atlanta, GA]: Knights of the Ku Klux Klan, 1920s.
Ku Klux Klan. *America for Americans.* Atlanta, GA: Knights of the Ku Klux Klan, 1922.
———. *Constitution and Laws of the Knights of the Ku Klux Klan (Incorporated).* Atlanta, GA: Knights of the Ku Klux Klan, 1921.
———. *The Fourteen Point Program.* Detroit, MI: Ku Klux Klan, Realm of Michigan, 1950s.
———. *A Fundamental Klan Doctrine.* [N. p.: Knights of the Ku Klux Klan], 1924.
———. *Funeral Services: Knights of the Ku Klux Klan.* [Atlanta, GA]: Knights of the Ku Klux Klan, 1925.
———. *Ideals of the Ku Klux Klan.* Atlanta, GA: Knights of the Ku Klux Klan, 1923.
———. *An Introduction to the Knights of the Ku Klux Klan.* Denham Springs, LA: Knights of the Ku Klux Klan, 1960s.
———. *An Introduction to the Knights of the Ku Klux Klan.* Tuscumbia, AL: National Office, 1966.
———. *Isms Compared.* Atlanta, GA: Knights of the Ku Klux Klan, [1920–1939].
———. *The Klan in Action: Leadership, Responsibility, Organization, Methods. A Manual of Leadership for Officers of Local Klans.* Atlanta, GA: American Print and Mfg. Co., 1922.
———. *The Klan Kreed.* Macon, GA: U.S. Klans, 1950.
———. *Klansman's Manual.* [Atlanta, GA]: Ku Klux Klan, 1924.
———. *Kloran. Klan in Action. Constitution.* [Tuscaloosa, AL]: Imperial Press, 1968.
———. *Kloran: Knights of the Ku Klux Klan.* 7th ed. Atlanta, GA: Knights of the Ku Klux Klan, 1934.
———. *Ku Klux Klan Song Book: Ten Stirring Songs for Real Americans.* Hammond, IN: The Hoosier, 1923.
———. *Nightmare! What Could Happen to White America in the Late 1970's.* Denham Springs, LA: Knights of the Ku Klux Klan, 1970.
———. *Papers Read at the Meeting of Grand Dragons Knights of the Ku Klux Klan at Their First Annual Meeting Held at Asheville, North Carolina, July 1923.* Atlanta, GA: Ku Klux Klan, 1923.

\_\_\_\_\_. *The Practice of Klanishness.* Atlanta, GA: Knights of the Ku Klux Klan, 1924.
\_\_\_\_\_. *The Principle of the Knights of the Ku Klux Klan.* Tuscaloosa, AL: U.S. Klans, 1958.
\_\_\_\_\_. *The Principle of the U.S. Klans, Knights of the Ku Klux Klan, Inc.* College Park, GA: [Knights of the Ku Klux], 1953.
\_\_\_\_\_. *Proceedings of Eighth Imperial Klonvokation, Knights of the Ku Klux Klan, Held in Philadelphia, Pa., Sept., 25–26–27, 1936.* N.p.: Knights of Ku Klux Klan, 1936.
\_\_\_\_\_. *Proceedings of the Fourth Imperial Klonvokation Held in Chicago, Illinois July 17, 18 and 19, 1928.* N.p.: Ku Klux Klan, 1928.
\_\_\_\_\_. *Proceedings of the Second Imperial Klonvokation Held in Kansas City, Missouri Sept, 23, 24, 25 and 26, 1924.* [Atlanta, GA]: Ku Klux Klan, 1924.
\_\_\_\_\_. *The Seven Symbols of the Klan.* Tuscaloosa, AL: Office of Imperial Wizard, 1966.
\_\_\_\_\_. *Why You Should Become a Klansman: Of Interest to White, Protestant, Native-Born Americans Who Want to Keep America American* [United States]: Knights of the Ku Klux Klan, 1924.
Lamy, Phillip. "Christian Identity: A White Supremacist Religion." In *White Supremacists*, edited by Regine I. Heberlein. San Diego, CA: Greenhaven Press, 2002.
Lay, Shawn. *War, Revolution, and the Ku Klux Klan: A Study of Intolerance in a Border City.* El Paso: Texas Western Press, 1985.
\_\_\_\_\_, ed. *The Invisible Empire in the West: Toward a New Historical Appraisal of the Ku Klux Klan of the 1920s.* Chicago: University of Illinois Press, 1992.
Likins, William M. *The Trail of the Serpent.* Uniontown, PA: William M. Likins, 1928.
Linkins, W. M. *Patriotism Capitalized or Religion Turned into Gold.* Uniontown, PA: The Watchman Publishing Company, 1925.
MacLean, Nancy. *Behind the Mask of Chivalry: The Making of the Second Ku Klux Klan.* New York: Oxford University Press, 1994.
Mecklin, John M. *The Ku Klux Klan: A Study of the American Mind.* New York: Russell & Russell, 1924.
Miller, Frazier Glenn. *A White Man Speaks Out.* N.p.: Aryan Nations, 1999.
Missouri Knights of the Ku Klux Klan. *The Missouri Knights of the Ku Klux Klan and the Missouri White Man's Association.* Gladstone, MO: The Klan, 1980s.
Moore, Leonard J. *Citizen Klansmen: The Ku Klux Klan in Indiana, 1921–1928.* Chapel Hill: University of North Carolina Press, 1991.
Moore, William Vincent. "A Sheet and a Cross: A Symbolic Analysis of the Ku Klux Klan." PhD diss., Tulane University, 1975.
Nelson, Jack. *Terror in the Night: The Klan's Campaign against the Jews.* New York: Simon & Schuster, 1993.
Newton, Michael. *The Ku Klux Klan: History, Organization, Language, Influence and Activities of America's Most Notorious Secret Society.* Jefferson, NC: McFarland, 2007.
\_\_\_\_\_. *White Robes and Burning Crosses: A History of the Ku Klux Klan from 1866.* Jefferson, NC: McFarland, 2014.
Paul, John Michael. "God, Race and Nation: The Ideology of the Modern Ku Klux Klan." Master's thesis, University of North Texas, 1999.
Quarles, Chester L. *The Ku Klux Klan and Related American Racialist and Anti-Semitic Organizations: A History and Analysis.* Jefferson, NC: McFarland, 1999.
Randel, William Peirce. *The Ku Klux Klan: A Century of Infamy.* Philadelphia: Chilton Books, 1965.
Rhomberg, Chris. *No There There: Race, Class, and Political Community in Oakland.* Los Angeles: University of California Press, 2004.
Ridgeway, James. *Blood in the Face: The Ku Klux Klan, Aryan Nations, Nazi Skinheads, and the Rise of a New White Culture.* New York: Thunder's Mouth Press, 1990.
Robb, Thomas. *This Is the Klan: Take Back America.* Harrison, AR: Thomas Robb, 1993.
Roney, C. P. *Is The Knights of the Ku Klux Klan Scriptural? A Biblical, Sane and Dignified*

*Discussion of the Principles, Ideals and Policies of the Order.* Shreveport, LA: M. W. Drake, 192?.

Roy, Jody M. *Love to Hate: America's Obsession with Hatred and Violence.* New York: Columbia University Press, 2002.

Russo, Pasquale. *Ku Klux Klan, Church and Labor.* Chicago: Pasquale Russo, 1923.

Sánchez, Juan O. "A Content Analysis of the Leadership Language of the Ku Klux Klan in the 1920s." PhD Diss., Our Lady of the Lake University, San Antonio, TX, 2009.

Shelton, Robert M. *All Men Are Not Created Equal.* Tuscaloosa, AL: Imperial Press, 196?.

\_\_\_\_\_. *The Third Color.* Tuscaloosa, AL: Imperial Press, 196?.

\_\_\_\_\_. *The White Knight of the Far Right.* Tuscaloosa, AL: United Klans of America, 196?.

\_\_\_\_\_. *Why the Negro Is Inferior.* Tuscaloosa, AL: Imperial Press, 196?.

Simmons, William Joseph. *ABC of the Invisible Empire.* Atlanta, GA: Knights of the Ku Klux Klan, 1916.

\_\_\_\_\_. *The Ku Klux Klan: Yesterday, Today and Forever.* [Atlanta: Ku Klux Klan, 1916].

Stanton, E. F. *"Christ and Other Klansmen" or Lives of Love, the Cream of the Bible Spread on Klanism.* Kansas City, MO: S. T. Harper, 1924.

Tenniswood, Erica M. *RAHOWA [Racial Holy War]: A Provocative Comparison of International and National White Supremacy Group*s. N.p.: n.p., 2000.

United Klans Knights of the Ku Klux Klan of America. *Kloran: United Klans of the Ku Klux Klan of America, Inc.* Atlanta, GA: Imperial Palace, United Klans of the Ku Klux Klan of America, 1950s.

United Klans of America. *The Principle of the United Klans of America Knights of the Ku Klux Klan.* Tuscaloosa, AL: United Klans of America, 1960s.

Venable, James R. *Choose Your Side: Or the Thinking of the Ku Klux Klan.* N.p.: n.p., 1971.

\_\_\_\_\_. *Invisible Empire: Knights of the Ku Klux Klan (1866, 1915–1974).* Stone Mountain, GA: National Knights of the Ku Klux Klan, 1974.

\_\_\_\_\_. *The Light of Right, Yesterday—Today—and Forever: The Ku Klux Klan.* [Tucker, GA]: n.p., 1951.

Wade, Wyn Graig. *The Fiery Cross: The Ku Klux Klan in America.* New York: Simon & Schuster, 1987.

Wright, Walter C. *Religious and Patriotic Ideals of the Ku Klux Klan: Being a Plain, Practical and Thorough Exposition of the Principles, Purposes and Practices of the Ku Klux Klan; a Textbook on Klankraft for the Instruction of Klansmen and the Information of Non-Klansmen.* Waco, TX: W.C. Wright, 1926.

\_\_\_\_\_. *The Twelfth Chapter of Romans as a Klansman's Law of Life.* [Little Rock, AR]: n.p., 1920s.

Women of the Ku Klux Klan. *Constitution of the Women of the Ku Klux Klan, Accepted and Adopted June 2nd, 1923, at Washington, D.C.; Incorporated June 8th at Little Rock, Ark.* Little Rock, AR: Parke-Harper Pub. Co., 1924.

\_\_\_\_\_. *Ideals of the Women of the Ku Klux Klan.* [Little Rock, AR: Women of the Ku Klux Klan], 1920s.

\_\_\_\_\_. *Out of Their Own Mouths Shall They Be Condemned.* [Little Rock, AR: Women of the Ku Klux Klan], n.d.

\_\_\_\_\_. *The Truth About the Women of the Ku Klux Klan.* Little Rock, AR: Parke-Harper, 192.

\_\_\_\_\_. *Women of America! The Past! The Present! The Future! Outline of Principles and Teachings.* Little Rock, AR: Parke-Harper, 1923.

White, Alma Bridwell. *Heroes of the Fiery Cross.* Zarephath, NJ: The Good Citizen, 1928.

\_\_\_\_\_. *The Ku Klux Klan in Prophecy.* Zarephath, NJ: The Good Citizen, 1925.

Zeller, W. W. *Countercultures: A Sociological Analysis.* New York: St. Martin's Press, 1995.

Zuber, Glen Michael. "Onward Christian Klansmen! War, Religious Conflict and the Rise of the Second Ku Klux Klan, 1912–1930." PhD diss., Indiana University, 2004.

# Index

Abihu  155
Abraham (biblical)  59, 124, 136, 177, 178, 180
Acts  68, 136, 156, 178, 179, 180
Adam (biblical)  135, 136, 156, 178; father of white race 168, 178, 181
African Americans  38, 49, 50, 91, 96, 111, 118, 141, 146, 147, 150, 154, 155, 156, 157; beasts, biblical 135; beasts, during Reconstruction 121; Mau-Mau 115, 118; U.S. government, undermining 118
Alabama  30, 46, 75
Alamo  119, 132
Alexander, Charles C.: *The Ku Klux Klan in the Southwest* 6, 28
Aliens  16, 17, 18, 19, 43, 45, 46, 62, 63, 84, 139, 140, 165, 170, 171, 172; anti–Klan 21; un–American 18, 26, 28, 39, 43–44 62, 88, 111, 129 ,143
Allah  140
Alpha and Omega  48
Amalekites  76
*America for Americans*  144
American Knights of the Ku Klux Klan  150–151
American Legion  9
American principles  156
American Revolution  84
Americanism  14, 19, 24, 32, 37, 39, 41–42, 44, 46, 49, 53, 56, 69, 78, 100, 111, 112, 118, 122, 142, 143, 171, 184, 185
Amos  136, 180, 181
Anglo-Saxon  35, 40, 65, 90, 124, 136; Ten Tribes of Israel 40
Anti-alien  18, 19, 21, 22, 26, 38, 39, 43, 44, 46, 49, 62, 139
Anti-Black  38, 50, 91, 115, 126
Anti-Catholic  5, 6, 9, 18, 22, 25, 26, 30, 32, 34–36, 39, 40–41, 46, 49, 50, 51, 62, 68, 74, 75, 76, 77, 84, 89, 91, 95, 96, 97, 101, 104, 112–113, 115, 116, 118, 131, 166, 167
Anti-Christ  53, 74, 78, 79, 136, 145, 146, 151, 152, 159, 160, 163, 180

Anti-Christian  90, 146
Anti-Communist  18, 118, 119, 129, 131, 154
Anti-government  36, 125, 126, 132, 137, 138, 173
Anti-immigrant  5, 9, 18, 19, 38, 40, 42, 91, 126, 139, 143, 154, 167
Anti-Protestant  122
Anti-Semitic  6, 39, 91, 114, 115, 116, 118, 126, 131, 146, 160, 167, 173
Anti-White  146, 147, 148, 149
Armageddon  76, 134
Armenians  9
Army of God  38, 46, 75, 76, 77, 130, 140, 145
Aryan  79, 114, 115, 116, 117, 118, 119, 133, 138, 139, 140, 147, 168
*Aryan Knight Views*  113, 130, 131
Aryan Nations Knights of the Ku Klux Klan  20 134, 140–141, 148–149, 150, 162; flag 20, 140, 141; God, created by 20, 141; Twelve Tribes of Israel 20, 141
Aryan Protection Association  118
*Aryan Views and White Folk News*  113, 119
Asians  38, 118, 150, 156
Assyria  158, 159
Atlanta, Georgia  4, 52–53
Atlantis  47
Augean stables  47

Babylon  159
Baker, Kelly J.: *Gospel According to the Klan: The KKK's Appeal to Protestant America, 1915–1930* 5–6, 7, 8, 9, 10, 22, 24, 41–42, 61, 114
Baptist  35, 157; Aryan 118
Barnes, Myra: *Soldiers of God: White Supremacist and Their Holy War for America* 7, 36
Barr, Daisy Douglas  81
Barton, Bruce: *The Man Nobody Knows*  65
Bauchle, S.E.  95
Beam, Louis R.: *Essays of a Klansman* 132, 133, 134, 144, 146

203

Beast (devil) 40
Beaumont, Texas, Kligrapp 88
Beckett, Georgy 160–161
Bell, Arthur H. 74
Bell, Edward Price 67
Bethlehem 25, 103
Bible 2, 4, 12, 15, 16, 19, 20, 23, 26, 29, 43, 50, 53, 54, 58, 61, 67, 68, 71, 72, 74, 75, 79, 100, 102, 103, 109, 111, 120, 122, 124, 125, 127, 135, 137, 139, 140, 145, 148, 153, 155, 157, 158, 159, 161, 164, 165, 166, 167, 169; Klan ideology, basis of 1, 3, 9, 14, 19, 28, 36, 67, 69, 70, 73, 76, 79, 102, 114, 123, 125, 126, 136–140, 145, 153, 154, 155, 156, 157, 159, 160, 161, 163, 165, 167, 168–170, 173, 175, 177–182; Word of God 9, 35, 136, 156, 161, 162, 163, 167, 177, 178, 180
Bigotry 4, 5, 12, 113, 115, 160, 165 168, 169, 170, 174
Black Sea 158
Blair, Jim 134
Boone, Daniel 110
Bosnia 9
Boston Tea Party 129
Brandywine 119
British Klan, Kingdom Ministries 177
Brown, Bruce 35
*Brown v. Board of Education of Topeka* (1954) 113, 114, 156, 168–169
Bryant, J.L. 36
Bund 129
Bunker Hill 119
Bushart, Howard: *Soldiers of God: White Supremacist and Their Holy War for America* 7, 36

C.A.B. 92
Caesar, Roman Emperor 37
Cain 180
California 23, 87, 97, 145, 154
Calvary 55, 57, 99, 149, 178
Calvin, John 129
Canaan 60, 157
Carlson, Lois 79
Carpetbaggers 121
Carruth, William Herbert: *Each in His Own Tongue* 84
Caspian Sea 158
Catholicism 5, 6, 9, 17, 30, 32, 36, 39, 40, 46, 49, 50, 62, 68, 74, 77, 84, 89, 95, 96, 97, 101, 104, 131, 164, 167; aligned with Jews 18, 25, 75, 76, 115, 116, 117, 118; Church 18, 22, 34, 35, 51, 63, 68, 74, 76, 113, 166; conspiracy to overthrow U.S. 40, 41, 75, 97, 112, 113, 117, 166; immigration 9, 40, 50; opposition to Klan 18, 25, 117, 118; seeking world domination 40, 74, 115; un–American 22, 26, 39, 75, 89, 91, 97, 112, 167
Caucasus Mountains 158, 159
Chalmers, David: *Hooded Americanism* 174

Chicago, Illinois 92
*Chicago Daily News* 67
Chinese 96
Christ 1, 3, 4, 5, 21, 25, 26, 27, 28, 29, 31, 36, 37, 43, 44, 46, 47, 48, 50, 58, 61, 62, 63, 66, 71, 76, 80, 81, 83, 85, 86, 87, 88, 90, 94, 99, 100, 101, 102, 107, 109, 113, 124, 125, 126, 127, 132, 133, 134, 140, 144, 145, 147, 153, 154, 157, 158, 159, 161, 163, 164, 177; comparison of Klansmen to Christ 9, 11, 17, 24, 26, 46, 51, 52, 54, 55, 56, 57, 59, 64, 65, 66, 69, 82, 143, 144, 162, 166, 169; criterion of character for Klansmen 3, 5, 11, 19, 20, 23, 52, 53, 54, 59, 60, 69, 72, 79, 83, 108, 109, 110, 120, 123, 144, 149, 151, 162, 169, 186; Eternal Emperor of Klan 148; Klannish 3, 59, 60, 61, 69, 70, 166, 169; Klansman, as 3, 48, 49, 52, 59–60, 61, 62, 69–70, 166, 169; light of the world 53, 143, 149, 150, 184; Messiah 47, 136, 164, 178, 179, 180, 182; not Jewish 61, 152, 169, 178; Protestant, as 68–69; represented by cross 19, 45, 53, 54, 55, 78, 88, 96, 120, 143, 151, 152; Savior 5, 14, 16, 48, 52, 55, 63, 84, 90, 91, 94, 110, 133, 143, 162, 163, 179, 180, 182; Son of God 53, 54, 65, 136, 159, 178, 179, 181; soul of the Ku Klux Klan 58; white robe, righteousness of 19, 54, 162, 187 ; Yahshua 136, 178, 179, 182
Christian 3, 16, 19, 22, 23, 25 26, 27, 28, 29, 31, 37, 43, 48, 51, 52, 53, 56, 60, 61, 62, 63, 64, 67, 69, 70, 71, 72, 76, 79, 80, 96, 108, 109, 113, 123, 124, 125, 128, 129, 133, 136, 137, 141, 142, 145, 146, 148, 149, 150, 151, 153, 157, 158, 159, 160, 162, 163, 164, 169, 180, 181, 182, 183, 184; Chosen by God 24, 124, 141, 158; identity (groups or ideology) 7, 24, 67, 79, 111, 123–124, 134, 137, 141, 160, 161, 163, 167, 173; Klansmen as 16, 19, 26, 35, 43, 44, 46, 48, 53, 56, 60, 61, 67, 76, 96, 109, 113, 133, 134, 135, 149, 150, 151, 157; organization, Klan as 3, 6, 14, 16, 19, 21, 26, 29, 35, 37, 42–43, 46, 51, 56, 61, 63, 64, 67, 71, 72, 73, 76, 108, 109, 113, 123, 125, 133, 134, 135, 139, 157
Christianity 3, 8, 14, 16, 23, 24, 25, 26, 27, 28, 29, 35, 42, 46, 52, 61, 71, 74, 78, 90, 104, 109, 110, 113, 114, 125, 151, 156, 157, 158, 159, 163, 167, 169, 184; basis for Klan 14, 16, 21, 29, 35, 67, 123, 164; chosen by God 24, 133; Klankraft, as 15, 27, 74, 79
Christmas 27, 113
Chronicles 158
Church of the American Knights of the Ku Klux Klan 134–135, 150–151
Church of the National Knights of the Ku Klux Klan Realm of Kentucky 125, 135, 141, 147–148, 151
Civic Messiah 17, 51
Civil Rights Movement 146, 168, 170
Civil War 6, 111, 121

## Index

Colescott, James A  112, 144, 155
Colorado  35, 130
Colossians  179
Communism  17, 42, 115, 116, 129, 130, 131, 151, 154, 156, 157; AGENCY of Satan 133; enemies of Klan 118–19, 129, 131, 154; infiltrated NAACP 156; influence on Supreme Court 114; leaders in Civil Rights movement 146; subverting us government 117, 118, 159–160
Corinthians 6:9,  137, 179, 181
1 Corinthians  137, 178, 179, 181, 182
2 Corinthians  179, 180, 181
Covenant (group or ideology)  134, 136
Craig, John R.: *Soldiers of God: White Supremacist and Their Holy War for America* 7, 36
Credo of the Ku Klux Klan  133
Cross lighting, as religious ceremony  21, 149, 150, 151, 152, 155, 169
Crusade (historical)  9, 140, 184; Klan activity 9, 11, 16, 21, 26, 39, 45, 80, 86, 90, 99, 125, 134, 165, 167, 171
Cuba  96
Curry, Leroy: *The Ku Klux Klan Under the Searchlight* 37, 53, 77, 78

Daniel (biblical figure) interpreting dream of Nebuchadnezzar 72; Klan compared to 25
Daniel  72, 179, 182
Dark Ages  46, 47
David, biblical  49
Davidians  168, 169
*Dawn*  57
Declaration of Independence (U.S.)  14, 17, 38, 73; Texas 118
Dees, Morris  174
Deuteronomy  78, 136, 155, 157, 158, 178, 179, 180, 181, 182
Dever, Lem A.: *Confessions of an Imperial Klansman: Hot Tar and Feathers* 4
Discrimination  12; against Klan 117, 123; anti-discrimination policies 173, 174
Divine origin of Klan  1, 3, 10, 11, 14, 17, 21, 30, 31, 33, 34, 35, 36, 37, 38–39, 40, 41, 42, 40, 43, 44, 45, 46, 48, 49, 50, 62 72, 73, 75, 76, 77, 79, 84, 93, 103, 104, 123, 127, 129, 130, 131, 133, 134, 137, 138, 140, 165, 166, 168, 174
Dr. Jekyll and Mr. Hyde  86
Dunning, William Archibald  120–121, 129

Early church, Klan compared to  21, 22–23, 25, 29
East (Asia)  26
East Hammond, Indiana  100
E.C.  85
Egypt  54, 76, 121
Eighth Imperial Klonvokation  113, 127
Eisenhower, Dwight D.  130

Elijah  36, 156
Elwood, Indiana  35
England  77, 159
English barons  129
English colonists  44
English language  158
Ephesians  178, 179
Ephraim and Manasseh, tribes of  159
Estes, Joe E.  114
Eugenics  79, 173
Euphrates River  158
Europe  9, 24, 47, 78, 111, 113, 129, 158, 159, 165, 167; immigration 38
Evans, Hiram Wesley (Klan Imperial Wizard)  3, 5, 14, 24, 26, 30, 34, 35, 38–39, 41–42, 46–47, 52, 57–58, 63, 67, 72, 113, 127, 170–171, 174; Alfred Smith, attacks 46; Christ, compared to 65–66; Klan, asserts divine approval of 3, 27, 33, 34, 38–39, 43–44, 47
Eve, biblical  135, 156
Exalted Cyclops  53, 69, 90, 120, 122, 131, 138; Illinois 90; Monroe, Louisiana 4, 18, 69; OKRKKKK 138; Plainview, Texas 19; Texas 19; Wisconsin 108
Exodus (reference to)  155, 157
Exodus  73, 159, 178, 181, 182
Extremists  1, 6, 15; Islamic 5, 8, 9, 140, 168, 169
Ezekiel  178, 182
Ezekiel (biblical figure)  54
Ezra  2; 9; 10, 156; 9:2; 9:10–12; 10:10–14, 181

Falfurrias, Texas  36
Fascist  129, 151
*Fiery Cross* (periodical, 1939–1944)  111, 112, 116, 128, 129, 130, 144, 151, 155
*Fiery Cross* (periodical, 1968–1972)  116, 151
Fiery Cross (symbol)  13, 16, 19, 24, 25, 31, 37, 50, 53, 55, 64, 71–72, 76, 77, 78, 81, 82, 83, 85, 87, 88, 89, 92, 97, 98, 99, 100, 101, 102, 104, 111, 112, 113, 119, 120, 121, 143, 150
First Amendment  135
Florida  157
Fontana, California  154
Fourth Imperial Klonvocation  75, 79
Franklin, Benjamin  110
Fundamentalism  5, 7, 11, 116, 164, 166, 167; Klan 7, 30, 116

Gabriel, angel  103
Galatians  178, 179, 181
Garden of Eden  156
Gebhart, H.R.  35
General Tire & Rubber Co.  130
Genesis (reference to)  67, 124, 155, 157
Genesis  136, 154, 156, 158, 159, 161, 178, 180, 181, 182
George III, King  130
Georgia  23, 52, 57, 108, 111

Germany 112, 124, 136, 147, 163
Gethsemane 57
Gibraltar 47
Gideon 76
Gill, Robbie 17
God 1, 4, 7, 9, 11, 12, 13, 14, 15, 16, 17, 18, 19, 20, 24, 26, 29, 31, 32, 33, 35, 36, 37, 39. 40, 41, 43, 44, 47, 48, 52, 53, 54, 56, 57, 58, 59, 62, 64, 65, 66, 67, 68, 70, 71, 72, 73, 74, 76, 77, 78, 79, 80, 84, 85, 87, 88, 89, 90, 91, 92, 93, 94, 96, 97, 100, 102, 103, 104, 107, 108, 109, 110, 111, 112, 113, 114, 118, 120, 124, 125, 127, 128, 130, 131, 132, 134, 135, 136, 138, 140, 145, 148, 149, 150, 152, 153, 154, 155, 156, 157, 158, 159, 160, 161, 162, 163, 164, 165, 166, 167, 177, 179, 178, 179, 180, 181, 183, 184, 186, 187; Commandments 4, 20, 49, 67, 68, 110, 130, 131, 132, 137, 138, 140, 155, 156, 160, 161, 163, 164, 167, 169, 170, 171, 174, 177, 181; covenants made by 136, 158, 159, 163, 178, 179, 180; fire, as 53–54, 155–156; Great Searchlight 37, 77, 78; kingdom of 26, 27, 73, 77, 108, 110, 133, 182; Klan, created 1, 3, 10, 11, 17, 21, 30, 31, 33, 34, 35, 36, 37, 38–39, 40, 41, 42, 40, 43, 44, 45, 46, 48, 49, 50, 62 72, 73, 75, 76, 77, 79, 87, 93, 104, 105, 113, 123, 126, 127, 128, 129, 130, 131, 133, 134, 137, 138, 140, 141,165, 166, 168, 174; ordained separation of races 20, 50, 78–79, 94, 107, 129, 130, 131, 137, 154, 155, 156, 167, 168–169, 173; Protestant Reformation, soul of 58; U.S., created 17, 26, 39, 40, 44, 166; YAHWEH 20, 137, 140, 162; YHVH 136, 137, 162, 163, 178, 180, 181
Gomorrah 155
*The Good Citizen* 149
Good Samaritan 76
Gospel as Klankraft 16, 114; according to the Klan 16
Graig, Calvin 52–53
Grand Canyon, Arizona 84
Grand Chamberlain 91
Grand Dragon 14, 16, 31, 33, 55, 72, 138, 139; Alabama 31; Arizona 84; California 145, 154; Colorado 35; Georgia 52; Indiana 128, 174; Mississippi 71; Oklahoma 14, 15; OKRKKKK 138, 139; Texas 14; Virginia 55; West Virginia 160
Grand Klokard, Kentucky 88, 143
Great Cause 27
Great Depression 92, 144
Great Klaliff, New York 96
Great Kludd, Ohio 144

Habakkuk 75
Ham 157
Hanani 62
Hatred 4, 5, 8, 12, 15, 50, 68, 85, 92, 98, 114, 121, 129, 138, 147, 150, 187

Heaven 13, 14, 15, 20, 23, 25, 26, 33, 37, 38, 48, 50, 54, 58, 64, 65, 73, 74, 77, 78, 79, 82, 95, 102, 103, 119, 120, 128, 131, 133, 134, 156, 162, 178
Hebrew (language) 159
Hebrews 136, 156, 158, 161, 178, 179, 180, 181
Heflin, Thomas 46, 75
Hellespont 26
H.E.R. 31, 85
Hercules 47
Hispanics 50, 150, 156
Holland, J.G.: *Wanted* 94
Hollywood 150
Holocaust 147
Holt, John W. 79
Holy Ghost 155, 161, 178
Holy Land 90
Holy Roman Empire 112
Holy Trinity 161
Homosexuality 126, 136, 138, 141, 150, 157, 160, 174, 181; against laws of God 137, 139, 177, 181
Hooded Order 25, 29, 31, 32, 44, 46, 48, 50, 52, 61, 70, 73, 84, 86, 93, 95, 129, 131, 137, 144, 157, 171
Hosea 158, 179, 181, 182

Illinois 45, 79
Immigration 5, 17, 37, 39, 40, 50, 116, 147, 167, 172; Catholic 9, 18; non-white 137; un–American 26, 37, 38, 42; un–Christian 42, 101
Imperial Klonsel 16
Imperial Knights of America 135–137, 163
*Imperial Night-Hawk* 3, 15, 16, 17, 19, 21, 22, 23, 24, 25, 33, 35, 37, 38, 49, 51, 55, 56, 64, 67, 68, 69, 70, 73, 183
Indiana 81, 102, 128
Internet 123, 134, 147, 161, 173, 174
Invisible Empire 6–7, 10, 13, 16, 46, 48, 55, 57, 62, 67, 72, 73, 74, 76, 77, 108, 110, 112, 119, 120, 129, 131, 138, 141, 143, 153, 157, 161, 162, 202, 143
Invisible Knights of the Fiery Cross 137, 141–142
Irish 101, 102
Isaac 136, 163, 178, 180
Isaiah 136, 158, 178, 179, 180, 181, 182
Island of Patmos 54, 72, 162, 186
Israel 20, 40, 48, 59, 60, 62, 69, 111, 124, 136, 137, 140, 141, 146, 157, 158, 159, 160, 161, 163, 167, 168, 177, 178, 179, 180, 181, 182
Italy 89

Jackson, Kenneth T.: *The Ku Klux Klan in the City, 1915–30* 6–7, 61, 62
Jacob 136, 163, 178, 180, 182
James 136, 180, 181
J.E.M. 93
Jeremiah 136, 140, 161, 179, 180, 181, 182
Jerusalem 62, 63 159

Jews 9, 17, 18, 42, 48, 59, 60, 61, 62, 68, 70, 76, 78–79, 96, 111, 114, 115, 116, 118, 124, 131, 135, 141, 150, 157, 159, 164, 167; Abrahams seed 158; anti–Christ 79, 146, 152, 160, 163; Catholics, aligned with 25, 75, 115, 117; Christ, killed 50, 180; God, not chosen by 24, 124, 148, 152, 158; Hittites, Amalekites, Canaanites 148, 157; human vultures 50, 119; Klan, opposition to 18, 25; Klannishness 49, 59, 61, 69; miscegenation, responsible for 138; non–Christian 69, 146; non–White 148; Satan, descendants of 79, 136, 163, 147–148, 152, 160, 161, 163, 169, 177, 180; supremacy 59; un–American 39, 117; White, as 151, 159; world domination, seeking 75, 115, 141, 146–147, 163; Zionist 138, 139, 146
J.N.M. 90
Joan of Arc 47, 48
John 136, 158, 179, 180, 181
1 John 180, 181
2 John 7–9, 145, 160
John the Baptist 77
Joshua 79, 181
J.P.K. 72
Judah 159
Judaism 42, 159, 164; anti–Christ religion 159; deadly tumor 164; hostile to America 42
Judges 76, 157
J.W.T. 98

Kaiser 77
Kansas 33
Kentucky 88, 143
Kenya 115
King John 129
King Nebuchadnezzar 72
King Solomon 79, 155, 156
Kingdom Identity Ministries 163; religious beliefs 177–182
Kings (Book of) 36, 158
1 Kings 77, 155, 181
2 Kings 158
Kith, Kind, Kin, Klan 118, 124
Kladd 120
Klan Fourth Imperial Klonvocation 79
Klan Kard 108
Klan Kreed 49, 94, 107, 127, 133, 142, 156
Klankraft 14, 15, 16, 19, 20, 27, 30, 38, 45, 53, 59, 60, 64, 70, 71, 74, 79, 82, 84, 108, 109, 123, 127, 130, 166, 186, 187; Bible, founded on 74, 79, 108–109; Christ, provides validity 166; Christianity, as 15, 27, 79, 123; Divinely-directed 45; Evangelist 30; love, through 64; spirituality, aim of 16, 30;
Klannish 3, 49, 59, 60, 61, 69, 70, 79, 83, 93, 98, 130, 166, 169, 186
*The Klansman* 145, 156, 157, 159
*Klansmans Manual* 16

Klanton 122
Kligrapp, Texas 88; Georgia 108; Ohio 109
*Kloran* 127
Kludd 15, 93, 122, 124, 144
Knights of the White Kamelia 36
Knights Party 150
Knox, John 129
Kol Nidre 114, 115, 117
Koran 140
Korsmo, Howard 130
*Kourier Magazine* 20, 24, 25, 28, 29, 30, 31, 32, 41, 45, 51, 53, 54, 55, 63, 65, 66, 68, 79, 92, 94, 107, 109, 143, 144, 151, 153, 154
Krusaders 91, 135

Larson, Ray 135
League of Nations 72
Lee, Robert E. 110
Leviticus 137, 138, 155, 159, 181
Liberal 125, 135, 139, 171, 172
Likins, William M.: *Patriotism Capitalized or Religion turned into Gold* 4–5
Lincoln, Abraham 65, 110
Little Red School House 100
Little Rock, Arkansas 38
Louisiana 36, 95, 145
Louisiana Knights of the White Kamelia 36
Louisville, Kentucky 164
Luke 10, 76, 136, 157, 158, 178, 179, 180, 181, 182
Luther, Martin 50, 129
Lynn Lorena, Howard D. 130

Macedonia 26
Magna Carta 129
Malachi 155, 161, 181, 182
Manifest Destiny, religious 24, 26, 164
Marginalization of Klan 1, 15, 170, 172
Mark 178, 179
Marvin, Z.E. 14
Masons 8
Matthew 21, 68, 69, 155, 159, 161, 178, 179, 180, 181, 182
Mayfield, Billie 34
Methodist 35, 150; Aryan 118
Micah 75
Middle Ages 140
Middle East 167
Midianites 76
Midwest 146
Miller, Glenn Frazier: *A White Man Speaks Out* 146–147
Miller, Sherman Horace 113, 114, 115, 116, 117, 118, 119, 130
Milton, John 4
Minorities 6, 15, 29, 34, 50, 86, 90, 112, 118, 141, 146, 147, 154, 156, 163, 170, 173; non–Christian 6, 33, 86, 90; non–White 6, 29, 33, 86; un–American 86, 90, 112
Minute Men 130
Miscegenation 18, 30, 50, 79, 110, 111, 116,

117, 130, 138, 139, 146, 151, 155–156, 157, 158, 160, 164, 168–169, 173; against God's law 79, 130, 137, 139, 155, 156, 169, 177, 181; goal of Satan 137, 181; racial suicide 137
Mohamed 140
Mohler, Albert 164
Monroe, Louisiana 4 18, 69
Montana 78
Moore, William Vincent: "A Sheet and a Cross: A Symbolic Analysis of the Ku Klux Klan" 9, 10, 11, 21, 116, 117
Moral Majority 164
Mormon fundamentalists 168, 169
Mosaic Laws 159
Moses 55, 62, 73, 76, 124
Murry, Charles 124
Muslim 145, 146

Nadab 155
National Association for the Advancement of Colored People (NAACP) 156
Native American 37, 77–78; separation from white 156
Naturalization Ceremony 131
Nazi 129, 151
Nehemiah (biblical) 62, 79, 181
Neil, Gene 157
Neo-Nazi 125
New Empire Knights of the Ku Klux Klan 124–125, 163, 177
New Jersey 20, 30, 74, 153
New Testament 76, 178, 124
New World 44, 75, 78
New York 46, 91, 96,
Non Silba Sed Anthar 15, 87, 99–100, 113
Nordic, as white 35, 39, 167; created by God 39
North America 71, 158, 182
*North American Review* 171
Numbers 157, 181

Ohio 26, 33, 93
Old Testament 124, 178
Old World 120
Original Knight Riders, Knights of the Ku Klux Klan 124, 137–140, 148–149, 161, 162

Pacific Ocean 26
Paganism 135
Palestine 158
Palm Sunday 63
Parker, John 95, 96
Patriotism 9, 13, 29, 32, 49, 53, 79, 86, 89, 92, 97, 98, 100, 102, 116; Klan, used by 14, 39, 44, 49, 53, 79, 80, 81, 120, 142, 144, 167
Paul (biblical figure) 26, 54, 68, 148, 153, 154
Paul, John Michael: *"God, race and nation"; The Ideology of the Modern Ku Klux Klan* 7, 15
Pennsylvania 88
Pepper, George 145, 154–155

1 Peter 179, 181
Pharisees 61, 68
Philippians 179
Philistines 49
Pilar of Fire 49
Pilate 52
Pilgrims 29, 39, 103, 110; Klan, compared to 29, 102
Plainview, Texas 3, 59, 69
*Plessy v. Ferguson* (1896) 168
Plymouth Rock 24
Political Romanism 77
Pope 40, 46, 72, 75, 89, 95, 98, 102, 117, 118; anti–Christ 40, 74; overthrow America 40, 89, 101, 113; world supremacy 76
Potomac River 41
Prejudice 6, 165, 170, 174; Klan 7, 12, 138, 168, 169, 170, 174
Presbyterian, Aryan 118
Prohibition 5, 8
Prometheus 119
prophecy: coming of Klan 11, 31, 40, 51, 71, 72, 73, 75, 166, 167; Whites selected by God 136, 157, 158, 163, 167, 178, 180
Protestant Reformation 9, 50, 58; Christ as soul of 58; Klan compared to 29, 57–58, 58, 75, 80
Protestants 8, 9, 15, 16, 18, 27, 30, 39, 42, 55, 75, 77, 79, 86, 97, 135, 115, 150, 162, 164, 165, 166, 167, 168, 172, 173; Klan working for 6, 7, 9, 21, 22, 24, 26, 27, 28, 29, 35, 36, 41, 42, 43, 44, 49, 50, 56, 59, 63, 68, 69, 77, 109, 111, 122, 154, 166; ministers, Klan supporters 15, 16, 22, 25, 27–28, 30, 43, 52, 67, 73, 82, 122, 166, 174
Psalm 136, 178, 179, 180, 181, 182

race 1, 6, 7, 9, 14, 15, 20, 22, 24, 28, 34, 35, 39, 42, 56, 62, 64, 76, 78, 79, 94, 101, 107, 110, 111, 116, 121, 124, 131, 132, 133, 134, 136, 138, 139, 141, 145, 147, 150, 151, 154, 155, 156, 160, 163, 166, 167, 169, 170–171, 180, 181, 185, 186; anti–Christ 145, 160; Aryan 114, 115, 116, 117, 118, 119, 138, 147; Caucasian 154, 159; equality 34, 137, 141; Holy, 20, 140, 141, 162; Klan, racism of 1, 6, 30, 114, 116, 117, 160; mixing 30, 50, 79, 130, 137, 138, 139, 145, 146, 155, 156, 157, 158, 168, 169, 181; non-white 22, 49, 147, 154, 156, 181; Nordic 39, 166, 167; privacy 130; purity 24, 58, 78, 79, 116, 130, 157; separation of 131, 154, 155, 167, 168, 173; Vulture (Jews) 119; war 157; white 35, 49, 58, 86, 110, 115, 119, 125, 129, 131, 134, 135, 136, 137, 138, 139, 140, 141, 145, 147, 154, 156, 158, 159, 163, 167, 181
Racial Nation 140
Reconstruction Klan 6, 7, 8, 111, 120–122, 129, 138–139, 168
religion, Klan as 8, 9, 24, 31–32, 35, 74, 114, 115, 116, 117, 118, 119

# Index

religious beliefs of Klan 1, 5, 7, 9, 10, 24, 31, 67, 70, 74–79, 102, 114, 122, 127, 134, 135–142, 145, 149, 150, 154, 156,-157, 161–162, 163, 167–170, 173, 174, 177–182
religious intolerance 1, 7, 25, 167
religious legitimacy of Klan 1, 2, 3, 4, 5, 6, 7, 8, 10, 11, 22, 35, 61, 67–68, 72, 79, 87, 107, 114, 126, 162, 165, 168, 169, 174–175
Renaissance 133
Republicans: modern day 172; Reconstruction 138
Revelation 40, 52, 54, 67, 71–77, 92, 134, 148, 160, 162, 179, 180, 181, 182; Klansmen as multitude in white robes 52, 71, 72, 92, 160, 162
Richmond, California 23
Roman blitzkrieg 112
Roman Empire 13, 164
Romans (reference to) 18, 28, 41, 67, 69, 70, 72, 109, 136, 137, 153, 154, 155, 158, 160, 162, 178–183
Rome 40, 41, 50, 63, 74, 75, 76, 77, 84, 89, 95, 96, 98, 100, 102, 112, 118, 154, 156; religious conquest of U.S. 41, 42, 89, 90, 97, 98, 101, 113; scarlet mistress/mother/woman, as 40, 74, 75, 77, 112, 166; seeking world domination 40, 74; seven hills 40, 74, 112
Romney, Mitt 172
Roney, C.P.: *Is The Ku Klux Klan Spiritual? A Biblical, Sane and Dignified Discussion of the Principles, Ideals, and Policies of the Order* 3
Roosevelt, Franklin D. 113
Rubicon 103

Sabbath 29
Salvationist 25
Samaritan 59
Samuel 158
2 Samuel 182
San Diego, California 87, 97
Sánchez, Juan O.: "A Content Analysis of the Political Leadership of the Ku Klux Klan in the 1920s" 116–117
Saratoga 119
Satan 4, 18, 68, 75, 78, 99, 132–133, 134, 135, 140; against Klan 128; anti–Christ 136, 160, 163, 180; Communism, as 133; Jews, descendants of 79, 136, 147–148, 152, 160, 161, 163, 169, 177, 180; Pope as 76; serpent 161, 163, 180; supports miscegenation 137, 181
Saul of Tarsus 52
Scalawags 121, 138
Scandinavia 124
Scottish tribes 111, 150
Scribes 61, 68
secular humanism 160, 161
Seed Line ideology 111, 134, 136, 137, 139, 161, 163, 167, 168, 173, 177, 178, 180, 181

segregation 34, 145, 154, 155, 169, 173, 177, 181; anti-segregation 114, 117, 130, 154, 173; God's law 20, 154, 155, 156, 165, 181; Klan, supported by 34, 114, 130, 145, 154, 156, 164, 169, 173, 181
September 11, 2001 10
Sermon on the Mount 4
Seven Symbols of the Klan 19, 20, 53, 148, 153, 183–187
Shivers, Allan (Texas governor) 117, 130
Silas 68
Simmons, William Joseph (Imperial Wizard): *God Give Us Men* 94; *The Ku Klux Klan: Yesterday, Today, and Forever* 51, 111, 174
skin heads 125, 134
slavery 40, 139, 147, 154
Smith, Alfred E. 40, 112
Smith, Bailey 164
Smith, James Hardin 57
Sodom 155
Soul of America 29, 30, 41; foreigners against 26; Klan as 29, 30, 81
Soul of Klan 119, 121
South 111, 121, 129, 138
South America 96
Southern Baptist Convention 164
Southern Baptist Theological Seminary 164
Southern Poverty Law Center 174
Soviet (Union) 115; Sovietism 42
Spirit of Adamic man 62, 136, 137, 160, 179, 181; America, of 29, 30, 37; Boston Tea Party 129; burning cross 54, 55, 87; Christ 36, 56, 60, 61; Christians 23, 37, 129, 145; Church 21, 22, 55; Democracy 26, 38; English barons 129; Enlightenment 75; God 78, 129, 140, 144, 148, 178; human independence of 46; Jews (lack of) 148; pioneers of 47, 65, 68
Spirit of the Klan 6, 11, 14, 15, 16, 18, 19, 26, 27, 29, 30, 37, 42, 43, 45, 46, 54, 56, 60, 61, 64, 69, 71, 72, 74, 81, 94, 109, 110, 120, 121, 122, 123, 129, 130, 165, 186
Stanton, E.F.: *Christ and Other Klansmen or Lives of Love, the Cream of the Bible Spread Upon Klanism* 15, 43, 48, 52, 61–62, 64, 75, 110
Statue of Liberty 73
Stephens, W.H. 82
Stephenson, David C. (Indiana Grand Dragon) 174
Stone Mountain, Georgia 23–24, 57–58, 72, 78, 91, 111, 112
Story, Jess F. 79
Supreme Court 113–114, 135, 141, 156, 158

Talmudist 115, 116, 118, 146
Tea Party 171, 172
Ten Commandants 161
Ten Tribes of Israel 40, 79, 136, 137, 141, 158, 159, 163, 177, 179, 180; Anglo-Saxon 40, 160; White Aryan Christians 79

Texas 14, 19, 34, 53, 96, 114, 117, 132; Lobby Law 118–119
Texas Knights of the Ku Klux Klan 123
Thanksgiving Day 23, 29, 58, 78, 128
Theocracy 181
1 Thessalonians 136, 180, 181, 182
2 Thessalonians 179, 182
Tiber River 41
Timbuktu 96
1 Timothy 179
2 Timothy 136, 178, 179, 182
Traditionalist American Knights of the Ku Klux Klan 142
Travis, William B. 132
Turks 9

Un-American 18, 52, 139; Aliens 18, 16, 39, 42, 86, 88, 129, 143, 165; Catholics 75
Un-American Activities Committee 52
Uncle Sam 23, 100, 104
United Klans of America 52, 122, 142, 156
United States 1, 6, 8, 13, 17, 18, 21, 26, 29, 38, 39, 40, 41, 42, 44, 45, 46, 47, 48, 52, 54, 55, 57, 61, 62, 63, 71, 72, 73, 75, 77, 81, 83, 88, 91, 92, 95, 96, 97, 98, 100, 102, 103, 107, 108, 110, 112, 113, 114, 115, 116, 118, 120, 123, 124, 129, 130, 134, 135, 139, 143, 144, 147, 150, 151, 157–158, 159, 164, 165, 166, 167, 168, 171, 172, 175; biblical prophecy 167, 177, 181; Christian nation 114, 145, 160; Congress 25, 34, 49, 115; Constitution 14, 17, 37, 53, 62, 63, 75, 76, 94, 104, 109, 114, 132, 140, 141, 142, 153, 154, 156, 160, 173; cultural history 1, 7, 10, 17, 30, 39, 114, 150, 165–166, 169–172; divine origin 17, 26, 39, 41, 44, 84, 94, 166; flag 13, 14, 16, 19, 20, 36, 37, 62, 76, 91, 96, 97, 100, 103, 104, 111, 120, 126, 141, 153, 154, 157, 175; ideals 19, 49, 76, 90, 142, 168, 171, 172; Racial Nation 132; society 6, 7, 9, 10, 11, 12, 15, 21, 24, 28, 30, 35, 37, 40, 46, 62, 63, 67, 74, 84, 137, 138, 149, 165, 167, 169, 170, 171, 172; Soul of 26, 29, 30, 81; suppression of religion 125, 141; ungodly 132, 149, 158–159
Upton, Illinois 89

Valley Forge 119
Vermont 86
Violence 12, 18, 120, 157; by aliens 139; by Klan 5, 6, 7, 9, 10, 20, 21, 30, 32, 147, 168; through cross burning 149, 151
Virgin Mary 178

Waco CIO-URW 130
Waco, Texas 113, 130

Warren, Earl 117
Washington, George 72, 110
Washington D.C. 130
W.B.W. 87
Webster Encyclopedia of Dictionaries 158
West Virginia 160
W.F.R. 83
White, Alma Bridwell, 49, 50, 57, 73, 74, 74–77; *The Ku Klux Klan in Prophecy* 51, 57
White Kamelia Knights of the Ku Klux Klan 123–124, 142
White House 112
White Liberation Movement 162
White Pride 134
White race 2, 5, 6, 9, 15, 22, 28, 29, 33, 44, 58, 110, 115, 119, 123, 125, 129, 131, 132, 133, 134, 135, 136, 137, 139, 141, 146, 147, 148, 155, 156, 159, 181; Anglo Saxon 35, 40, 90, 124, 136, 160, 163, 180; Aryan 79, 90, 114, 115, 116, 117, 118, 119, 130, 133, 138, 139, 140, 147, 168; Caucasian 22, 121, 129, 154, 158, 159, 160; Chosen by God 20, 24, 39, 78, 86, 124, 131, 133, 135, 136, 137, 140, 141, 157, 158, 159, 160, 162, 163, 167, 177, 178, 179, 180, 181; Christians 24, 79, 123, 124, 125, 134, 145, 146, 148, 158, 159, 160, 165, 167, 173; enemy of federal government 141; Gentiles 49, 59, 70, 123, 159; supremacy 6, 8, 14, 24, 30, 34, 35, 36, 39, 49, 50, 58, 59, 78, 79, 91, 92, 94, 107, 110, 111, 114, 116, 118, 129, 131, 134, 135, 137, 139, 144, 154, 156, 161, 163, 167, 168, 173, 177; trichotomous 181; True Israel 136, 137, 141, 160, 167, 168, 180
*Why You Should Become a Klansman* 58
Wichita, Kansas 14
Women of the Ku Klux Klan 17, 31, 38, 49, 50, 81
World War I 5, 9, 18, 71, 77
World War II 9, 146
Wright, Walter Carl 3, 22, 48, 59, 60, 61, 69, 70, 71

*Yankee Doodle* 80
Yom Kipper 114
Yorktown 119

Zechariah 14:21, 181; 9:10; 14:9, 182
Zionist Occupation Government (ZOG) 138, 139
Zuber, Glenn Michael: *Onward Christian Soldiers! War, Religious Conflict, and the Rise of the Second Ku Klux Klan, 1921–1928* 7, 8, 9, 28, 35, 80

www.ingramcontent.com/pod-product-compliance
Ingram Content Group UK Ltd.
Pitfield, Milton Keynes, MK11 3LW, UK
UKHW042001140426
5217IPUK00015B/915